Resounding praise for Ingrid Fetell Lee's

Joyful

THE SURPRISING POWER
OF ORDINARY THINGS
to CREATE EXTRAORDINARY
HAPPINESS

"A completely original treatment of a completely new and original idea: we all have within us the power to design joy into our lives. *Joyful* is an inexhaustible and exciting guide to what makes life good."
—Arianna Huffington, founder and CEO of
Thrive Global and founder of the *Huffington Post*

"Ingrid Fetell Lee creates a compelling case for the pursuit of joy, dispelling a lot of myths along the way." — *Goop*

"Joy is the most basic building block of happiness, and this mesmerizing book reveals where to find it—and how to create it. Ingrid Fetell Lee's blockbuster debut will open your eyes to all the places where joy is hiding in plain sight. And it just might cause you to become more joyful too." Adam Grant, author of *Think Again*

"I've never reached out to an author to request their permission to endorse their book...until now. Ingrid Fetell Lee invites us into a dimension of the human experience that was, ironically, hidden for most of us. She shows us how we can mindfully see joy in the simple aesthetics of our surroundings—and it has already changed my everyday life. If I'm feeling blue, I remember to look at the new leaves on the tree outside my window. It is simple but profound. *Joyful* is irresistibly compelling. The idea of *Joyful* fills me with joy."

—Amy Cuddy, author of *Presence*

"Joyful is a delightful book with a powerful message: joy is easy to find if you know where to look. In *Joyful,* designer Ingrid Fetell Lee explains why some experiences are laden with joy, explores how we can cultivate these experiences every day, and shows us how to identify the most joy-inspiring people, places, and objects in our lives."

—Adam Alter, author of *Irresistible* and *Drunk Tank Pink*

"Joyful overturns conventional wisdom about happiness: that it comes from within and that experiences—not things—make us happier. Ingrid Fetell Lee's delightful book evokes the same positive feelings she describes. It is full of whimsy, wonder, energy, and joy. I loved it."

—Sonja Lyubomirsky, professor of psychology,
University of California, Riverside, and author of
The How of Happiness

"Joyful reveals the powerful notion that joy can be cultivated to flourish within all of us. This idea can change the world."

—David Kelley, founder of the design
and innovation company IDEO

"*Joyful* is an invaluable field guide to discovering delight in all its forms. It's hard to look at the world—and your place in it—quite the same way again." —Bianca Bosker, author of *Cork Dork*

"A tender and moving book about one of our most important feelings—joy." —Johann Hari, author of *Lost Connections*

Joyful

THE SURPRISING POWER

OF ORDINARY THINGS

to CREATE EXTRAORDINARY

HAPPINESS

INGRID FETELL LEE

Little, Brown Spark
New York Boston London

Little, Brown Spark
Hachette Book Group
1290 Avenue of the Americas
New York, NY 10104
littlebrownspark.com

Originally published in hardcover by Little, Brown Spark, September 2018
First Little, Brown Spark trade paperback edition, May 2021

Little, Brown Spark is an imprint of Little, Brown and Company, a division of Hachette Book Group, Inc. The Little, Brown Spark name and logo are trademarks of Hachette Book Group, Inc.

The publisher is not responsible for websites (or their content) that are not owned by the publisher.

The Hachette Speakers Bureau provides a wide range of authors for speaking events. To find out more, go to hachettespeakersbureau.com or call (866) 376-6591.

Excerpt from "The Dream That Must Be Interpreted" by Rumi on p. 274 reprinted with permission. © Coleman Barks

ISBN 978-0-316-39926-5 (HC) / 978-0-316-42209-3 (B&N signed) / 978-0-316-42210-9 (B&N Black Friday signed) / 978-0-316-39927-2 (pb)
LCCN 2018939517

Printing 1, 2021

LSC-C

Printed in the United States of America

For Albert

Without emotion, there is no beauty.

DIANA VREELAND

JOYFUL

INTRODUCTION

I stood in front of a panel of professors, a full swarm of butterflies in my stomach. As they eyed the small collection of objects on display behind me — a starfish-shaped lamp, a set of round-bottomed teacups, and a trio of stools fashioned from layers of colored foam — their faces were stern, and I couldn't help but wonder if I'd made a mistake in leaving a promising career in branding to go back to graduate school in design. Then, after a long silence, one professor broke the ice. "Your work gives me a feeling of joy," he said. The others nodded.

Suddenly, they were all smiling. I felt a wave of relief. I had passed my first review in the industrial design program at Pratt Institute. But my relief soon gave way to confusion. Joy was a feeling, ephemeral and elusive. It wasn't something we could see or touch. How, then, could such simple objects — a cup, a lamp, a stool — elicit joy? I tried to get the professors to explain, but they hemmed and hawed as they gestured with their hands. "They just do," they said. I thanked them, but as I packed up my things for the summer, I couldn't stop thinking about this question.

How do tangible things create an intangible feeling of joy?

At first, the answer seemed unequivocal: They don't. Sure, there's a certain pleasure in material things, but I'd always been led to believe that this is superficial and short-lived, not a meaningful source of joy. In all the books on happiness that I'd consulted over the years, no one had ever suggested that joy might be hiding inside my closet or kitchen cabinets. Instead, countless experts agree that the kind of joy that matters is not *around* us but *in* us. This perspective has roots in ancient philosophical traditions. The teachings of Buddha, for example, advise that happiness comes only from letting go of our attachments to worldly things, while in ancient Greece the Stoic philosophers offered a similar prescription, rooted in self-denial and rigorous control over one's thoughts. Modern psychology likewise embraces this inward lens, suggesting that the way to a happy life is to change how we look at the world and our place in it. From mantras and meditation to therapy and habit change, true joy is an exercise of mind over matter, not matter over mind.

Yet in the weeks and months that followed my review, I noticed many moments when people seemed to find real joy in the material world. Gazing at a favorite painting in an art museum or making a sandcastle at the beach, people smiled and laughed, lost in the moment. They smiled, too, at the peachy light of the sunset and at the shaggy dog with the yellow galoshes. And not only did people seem to find joy in the world around them, but many also put a lot of effort into making their immediate environment more delightful. They tended rose gardens, put candles on birthday cakes, and hung lights for the holidays. Why would people do these things if they had no real effect on their happiness?

A body of research is emerging that demonstrates a clear link between our surroundings and our mental health. For example, studies show that people with sunny workspaces sleep better and laugh more than their peers in dimly lit offices, and that flowers improve not only people's moods but their memory as well. As I delved deeper into these findings, joy started to become less amorphous and abstract to me and more tangible and real. It no longer seemed difficult to attain, the result of years of introspection or disciplined practice. Instead, I began to see the world as a reservoir of positivity that I could turn to at any time. I found that certain places have a kind of buoyancy—a bright corner café, a local yarn shop, a block of brownstones whose window boxes overflow with blooms—and I started changing my routines to visit them more often. On bad days, rather than feeling overwhelmed and helpless, I discovered small things that could reliably lift my spirits. I started incorporating what I learned into my home and began to feel a sense of excitement as I put my key into the lock each evening. Over time, it became clear to me that the conventional wisdom about joy was wrong.

Joy isn't hard to find at all. In fact, it's all around us.

The liberating awareness of this simple truth changed my life. As I started to share it with others, I found that many people felt the impulse to seek joy in their surroundings but had been made to feel as if their efforts were misguided. One woman told me that buying cut flowers lifted her spirits for days, but she felt like it was a frivolous indulgence, so she only did it on special occasions. It had never occurred to her that for the price of one of her weekly therapy sessions, she could buy a bunch of flowers every other week for a year. Another described how she had walked into her living room after repainting it and felt an "ahhh" feeling—a sense of relief and lightness that made her wonder why she had waited so long to do it. I realized that we all have an inclination to seek joy in our surroundings, yet we have been taught to ignore it. What might happen if we were to reawaken this instinct for finding joy?

I needed to know exactly how the physical world influences our emotions and why certain things spark a feeling of joy. I began asking everyone I knew, as well as quite a few strangers on the street, to tell me about the objects or places they associated with joy. Some things were specific and personal: "my grandmother's kitchen," "a signed Grateful Dead poster," "the canoe at the house we used to go to on Lake Michigan." Some were shaped by cultural heritage or upbringing, like favorite foods or sports teams. But others were neither personal nor cultural in origin. A friend of mine told me about a summer afternoon when she got caught in a sudden downpour on her way home from work. She took refuge under an awning with a motley crew of others who had been caught without umbrellas, making guesses as to how long the storm would last. It passed after a few minutes, and people began to venture out onto the sidewalk, when suddenly a man shouted, "Look!" A brilliant rainbow was arcing across the sky, right over the Empire State Building. People stopped and stared, their wet clothes clinging to them, big grins on their faces.

I heard countless variations on this story. The day was frigid or steamy, the people were friends or strangers, the rainbow was over a concert or a mountaintop or a sailboat. Everywhere, it seems, rainbows are joyful. I began to make a list of things like this, ones that I heard over and over again: beach balls and fireworks, swimming pools and treehouses, hot-air balloons and googly eyes and ice-cream sundaes with colorful sprinkles. These pleasures cut across lines of age, gender, and ethnicity. They weren't joyful for just a few people. They were joyful for nearly everyone. I gathered pictures of these things and pinned them up on my studio wall. Each day I spent a few minutes adding new images, sorting them into categories and looking for patterns.

One day as I was studying the images, something clicked. I saw lollipops, pom-poms, and polka dots, and it dawned on me: they were all round in shape. Vibrant quilts kept company with Matisse paintings and rainbow candies: all bursting with saturated color. A picture of a cathedral's rose window puzzled me at first, but when I placed it next to a snowflake and a sunflower, it made sense: all had radiating symmetries. And the common thread among bubbles, balloons, and hummingbirds also became clear: they were all things that floated gently in the air. Seeing it all laid out, I realized that though the feeling of joy is mysterious and ephemeral, we can access it through tangible, physical attributes. Specifically, it is what designers call *aesthetics*—the properties that define the way an object looks and feels—that give rise to the feeling of joy.

Up until this point, I had always thought of aesthetics as decorative, even a bit frivolous. I had come to design school because I wanted to make things that changed people's lives for the better. I was obsessed with finding ways to make my products ergonomic, functional, and eco-friendly. And while I enjoyed the classes on how to work with color and texture, shape and movement, I treated these elements as extras, not essentials. This attitude is common in our culture. Though we pay a fair amount of attention to aesthetics, we're not supposed to care *too* much about them or put too much effort into appearances. If we do, we risk seeming shallow or insubstantial. How many times have you complimented a fashionable friend, only to hear her say, "Oh, this old thing? It's just something I threw together!" Yet when I looked at the aesthetics on my studio wall, I realized they were far more than just decorative. They elicited a deep, emotional response.

In all, I identified ten *aesthetics of joy*, each of which reveals a distinct connection between the feeling of joy and the tangible qualities of the world around us:

Energy: vibrant color and light

Abundance: lushness, multiplicity, and variety

Freedom: nature, wildness, and open space

Harmony: balance, symmetry, and flow

Play: circles, spheres, and bubbly forms

Surprise: contrast and whimsy

Transcendence: elevation and lightness

Magic: invisible forces and illusions

Celebration: synchrony, sparkle, and bursting shapes

Renewal: blossoming, expansion, and curves

What is the relationship between these aesthetics and our emotions? And why do these particular aesthetics stimulate feelings of joy?

These questions sparked a journey that led me to some of the most joyful places in the world. In these pages, we'll visit a treehouse bed-and-breakfast and a city transformed by color, an apartment designed to prevent aging and a seaside mansion made entirely of spheres. We'll look at natural wonders, like the opening of the cherry blossoms in Japan, and man-made ones, like the rising of hundreds of hot-air balloons over the Albuquerque desert. Along the way, I'll share insights from new research in the fields of psychology and neuroscience that helps explain why these places and experiences have such power to unlock joy within us.

But ultimately, *Joyful* isn't about seeking joy in the far-flung corners of the world. It's about finding more joy right where you are. In the following pages, you'll meet celebrated artists and designers—architects, interior designers, color specialists, gardeners, quilters, DIYers, florists, and even an artist who works with balloons—and learn their secrets for finding and creating joy in every aspect of the physical world. And you'll get to know real people who are making joy in their homes and communities—cottages and camper vans, living rooms and office cubicles, sidewalks and rec centers—to see how small changes can infuse ordinary objects and places with extraordinary joy.

You have a whole world of joy right at your fingertips. There's no method you need to learn, no discipline you need to impose on yourself. The only requirement is what you already have: an openness to discovering the joy that surrounds you.

* * *

In my years as design director at the renowned innovation company IDEO and in my own practice, as well as through curating the design blog *The Aesthetics of Joy*, I've seen firsthand how aesthetics change people's attitudes and behavior from the outside in. They reveal why some stores and restaurants bustle with activity, while others stand quiet and empty. And they help us understand why one environment makes people anxious and competitive, while another brims with sociability and tolerance. Think about the way people act in the sterile cabin of an airplane, breaking into fights over three degrees of seat recline and jostling elbows for control of an armrest. Now contrast this with how people behave in the convivial atmosphere of a music festival. Surrounded by vibrant decorations and music, people share food and drink, make space on the crowded lawn for newcomers, and dance with strangers. The power of the aesthetics of joy is that they speak directly to our unconscious minds, bringing out the best in us without our even being aware of it.

How can you tell if your surroundings are joyful or not? There's no exact standard, but think about these questions:

How often do you laugh?

When was the last time you felt a true, unfettered moment of joy?

What emotions do you feel when you walk into your home at the end of the day? How about when you enter each room?

How highly does your significant other or family value joy?

Who are the most joyful people in your life? How often do you see them?

How often do you find joy in your work?

Do you work for a company that is pro-joy, joy-neutral, or anti-joy? How appropriate is it to laugh out loud at your workplace?

What activities bring you the most joy? How often do you engage in them? Can you do them at or near your home?

How much joy do you find in the town or city where you live? In your specific neighborhood?

What are your "happy places"? Are any within ten miles of your home? When was the last time you visited one?

Every human being is born with the capacity for joy, and like the pilot light in your stove, it still burns within you even if you haven't switched on the burners in a while. What you hold in your hands is the key to reigniting those joyful flames, one that promises to radically change the way you look at the world around you. At the heart of this book lies the idea that joy isn't just something we find. It's also something we can make, for ourselves and for those around us.

You can use this book as a field guide to spotting and savoring more joy in your surroundings, to help you gain a better understanding of why certain things and places light you up inside. And you can also use it as a palette, to design and craft more joy into your world. The chapters build on one another, so the book will probably make the most sense if you read them in order. But don't let that stop you from jumping to an aesthetic that is calling your name. You may just want to flip back later to see what you missed.

You will probably find that some aesthetics speak to you more than others. If you're a nature lover, you might find yourself especially drawn to freedom, for example. If you happen to be afraid of heights, then some aspects of the transcendence aesthetic may not be for you. You may also find that the aesthetics that feel best change depending on where you are and what's going on in your life. A drab office may benefit from an infusion of energy, while the harmony aesthetic can bring joy to a hectic family home. When the kids leave the nest, however, that same home might need some of the play aesthetic to make it feel lively again.

Feel free to mix, match, and layer aesthetics to create an experience that brings *you* joy. There are no specific rules, but to help you feel your way through, I've tried to note where aesthetics are particularly complementary and where they may be in tension. Though some chapters describe particular products that can help bring the aesthetics to life, you don't need to buy anything expensive to transform a space in a joyful way. In the last chapter, you'll find a Joyful Toolkit, full of guides and worksheets designed to help you apply the ideas in this book to your own space and your own life.

Too often, we move through the physical world as if it were a stage set, a mute backdrop for our daily activities. Yet in reality it is alive with opportunities for inspiration, wonder, and joy. I hope this book empowers you to see more of these opportunities in the world around you and to seize them. Joy's power is that small moments can spark big changes. A whimsical outfit might prompt a smile, which inspires a chance kindness toward a stranger, which helps someone who is struggling to get through her day. Even the tiniest joyful gestures add up over time, and before we know it, we have not just a few happier people but a truly joyful world.

1.

ENERGY

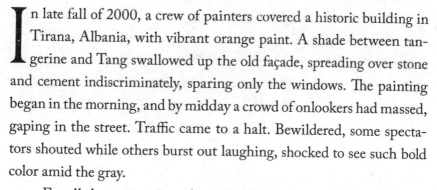

I n late fall of 2000, a crew of painters covered a historic building in
Tirana, Albania, with vibrant orange paint. A shade between tan-
gerine and Tang swallowed up the old façade, spreading over stone
and cement indiscriminately, sparing only the windows. The painting
began in the morning, and by midday a crowd of onlookers had massed,
gaping in the street. Traffic came to a halt. Bewildered, some spectators shouted while others burst out laughing, shocked to see such bold
color amid the gray.

For all the commotion, the painting might have seemed a prank
by a particularly brazen mischief-maker. But this wasn't an act of graffiti, and the commissioning artist was no ordinary street vandal. He
was the mayor.

Edi Rama won the World Mayor award in 2004 for his stunning
success at restoring the capital city of Albania, just four years after he
was elected. Visit Tirana today, and you will see few traces of the filthy,
dangerous city that Rama inherited when he took office. Broken by
decades of repressive dictatorship, and starved of resources by ten years

of chaos after the fall of Communist rule, by the late 1990s Tirana had become a haven for corruption and organized crime. Pickpockets and prostitutes loitered on corners. Garbage piled uncollected in the streets. As Rama has described it, "The city was dead. It looked like a transit station where one could stay only if waiting for something."

The painted buildings were an act of desperation by a mayor faced with an empty treasury and a demoralized populace. An artist by training, Rama sketched the first designs himself, choosing vibrant hues and gaudy patterns that disrupted the bleakness of the urban landscape. The orange building was joined by others as Rama's project quickly spread throughout the city, enveloping public and private buildings alike.

At first, the reactions were mixed: some citizens were horrified, others curious, a few delighted. But soon after, strange things began to happen. People stopped littering in the streets. They started to pay their taxes. Shopkeepers removed the metal grates from their windows. They claimed the streets felt safer, even though there were no more police than before. People began to gather in cafés again and talk of raising their children in a new kind of city.

Nothing had changed, except on the surface. A few patches of red and yellow, turquoise and violet. And yet everything had changed. The city was alive, ebullient. Joyful.

* * *

When I first heard the story of Tirana, it struck me as nothing short of miraculous. There were no massive infusions of capital, no large-scale public works projects. It was as if the city had been revitalized by the sheer power of joy. But how could joy bring an entire city back to life?

It was around this time that I was beginning to research joy, and

I found myself asking an even more basic question: What is joy? At first, this was tricky to figure out, as many people have different ideas about joy, and even scientists don't always agree on a definition. But broadly speaking, when psychologists use the word "joy," they mean an *intense, momentary experience of positive emotion*, one that can be recognized by certain telltale signs: smiling, laughing, and a feeling of wanting to jump up and down. While contentment is curled up on the sofa, and bliss is lost in tranquil meditation, joy is skipping, jiving, twirling, giggling. It is a uniquely exuberant emotion, a high-energy form of happiness.

So it's not surprising that we equate a feeling of energy with one of liveliness, vitality, and joy. Energy animates matter. It is the currency of life, transforming inert material into breathing, beating organisms. Simply to be alive is to vibrate with an essential dynamism. The more energy we have, the more we are able to play, create, love, lead, explore, rejoice, and engage with the world around us. If Tirana had been revived by joy, then perhaps this energetic quality had something to do with it. But where does this joyful energy come from? And how do we get more of it?

We tend to think of energy as something that comes from what we ingest, like the buzz of a cappuccino or a sugary lick of buttercream frosting. But as I thought about it, I realized that energy is all around us, all the time. Most days it flows through our homes unnoticed, but we are constantly awash in its invisible pools and ripples: the lambent particles that emanate from our light bulbs, the sound waves of music from the stereo, the breezes through our windows, and the currents of heat from our radiators. It's so inconspicuous that we often forget about it until dry winter days, when we touch a metallic doorknob and it startles us with a zingy pop.

Of course, unlike plants, we can't just absorb it from our sur-roundings. Yet sometimes, the energy around us *does* affect the energy within us. How many times have you gone to a party exhausted after a tough week of work, insisting you'll stay for just one drink, only to perk up once you hear the beat of the music? Or have you ever noticed that it's easier to get out of bed on sunny days than on gray ones? I began to wonder why some environments have this stimulating effect, and how we might be able to bring more joyful energy into our lives.

THE POWER OF COLOR

From the moment I first started studying joy, it was clear that the live-liest places and objects all have one thing in common: bright, vivid color. Whether it's a row of houses painted in bold swaths of candy hues or a display of colored markers in a stationery shop, vibrant color invariably sparks a feeling of delight. Bright color adorns festivals around the world, and it almost seems as if the more intense the colors, the more intense the joy. In China, bright dancing dragons usher in the new year, while Brazil's Carnival dazzles with brilliant feathered cos-tumes. During India's Holi festival, people dispense with decorations and instead throw handfuls of pure colored powder, creating a stun-ning spectacle of polychromatic smoke that stains grinning revelers from top to toe.

Though we don't often think consciously about the connection, it is nearly impossible to separate color and feeling. Our language con-fuses the two with regularity. Our moods brighten and darken. On a sad day, we might have a black cloud over us or merely feel a bit blue. And when things are going well, we say life is golden. We can see things in a dark light or look on the bright side. While the symbolic meanings of different colors vary across cultures, it seems that brightness is a dimension universally understood to be joyful. Children feel this connection intuitively. In a study of preschool children's drawings, bright colors were associated with happiness and excitement, while dark colors like brown and black were often used to signify negative emotions. Adults follow suit. Graphic designer Orlagh O'Brien conducted a study asking people in the UK and Ireland to match colors to their emotions. The strip showing the colors picked for joy is full of bright, lively hues, with sunny yellows and oranges making up nearly half the area of the graph.

If bright color buoys our spirits, it's not surprising that people expend a great deal of energy to obtain the brightest hues. The Dieri tribe of Australian aborigines was known to make an annual pilgrimage on foot each year to gather golden-red ochre pigment from a mine in Bookartoo, a round-trip journey of more than six hundred miles. There were plenty of nearby ochre mines, but the Dieri wanted only the brightest, shiniest ochre for their ritual body paintings. The ancient Romans coveted a purple dye eked, in a stinking process, from the anal glands of a mollusk. During the colonial period, the brightest pigments often became heavily guarded state secrets, such that at least one French botanist risked his life to smuggle a box of red-pigment-producing cochineal beetles out of Mexico. Even today, color continues to inspire great journeys. People make pilgrimages to hike in red-rock canyons and lie on pink-sand beaches, and each autumn the populations of New England and Canada swell as so-called leaf peepers fill B and Bs in search of the most brilliant fall colors.

In an account of his experiences taking the drug mescaline, the writer Aldous Huxley once posited that the ability to see color is superfluous for human beings. "Man's highly developed color sense is a biological luxury," he wrote, "inestimably precious to him as an intellectual and spiritual being, but unnecessary to his survival as an animal." Yet our eyes are adept at distinguishing between subtly different colors, with scientists estimating that we can see as many as seven million distinct shades. Though not as broad a rainbow as that seen by many birds, whose eyes detect colors well into the ultraviolet spectrum, it's still a staggering range. Doesn't it seem implausible that we should have such a chromatic bounty for no purpose other than to be tickled pink?

In fact, our color vision is not an extravagance but an integral sense that relates directly to our survival — in particular, our need to find sources of energy. Our distant ancestors were nocturnal animals and, like most mammals, had little use for color vision. Soft-skinned and warm-blooded, they foraged under cover of darkness, relying more on smell than on sight. But twenty-five million years ago, a band of brazen night monkeys ventured out into the daylight, adopting the diurnal schedule we still follow today. In this new ecological niche, the ability to see color suddenly became a useful advantage. While the eyes of their nocturnal cousins had only two types of color-sensing cone cells, our ancestors evolved a third cone, sensitive to light in the middle of the spectrum, that radically multiplied the number of colors they were able to see. This extra cone offered up a tantalizing array of new shades, including the ability to distinguish red from green. Eventually this capability would come in handy in helping us tell the difference between "stop" and "go" on a traffic light, but its immediate benefit to our primate ancestors was far more significant. That's because scientists believe it allowed them to identify sugar-rich ripe fruits and nutritious young leaves in the dense foliage of the treetops they inhabited. (Young leaves are often tinted red because they contain anthocyanin pigments that have not yet been masked by chlorophyll.) Research suggests that color vision provided such an advantage that our ancestors' brains evolved a reduced capacity for processing smells in order to allow for an increase in the handling of visual information. Far from being a luxury, as Huxley believed, color vision is so vital to our survival that we sacrificed other senses to have more of it.

The central concern of any organism, whether a single-celled paramecium or a two-hundred-ton blue whale, is to find energy to power its activities: gathering food, seeking shelter, fighting off predators, having sex, raising children, playing tennis, dancing the rumba. And this is particularly true for large, warm-blooded animals like ourselves. At a microscopic level, just staying alive is a frenetic endeavor. Our cells hum around the clock: zipping and unzipping their chromosomes, spinning threadlike RNA telegrams, stacking amino acids into proteins, repairing and copying themselves. To keep this metabolic furnace running, we have evolved mechanisms that promote an almost constant search for food: hunger, which sends us in search of it; and joy, which rewards us for finding it. Over millions of generations of evolution, bright color so reliably predicted nourishment that it became intertwined with joy.

Color is energy made visible. It activates an ancient circuit that lights up with pleasure at the idea of finding something sweet to eat. Now, in a world that contains rainbows of artificial colors, we still feel the same joy, even if a colorful object contains no physical nourishment. More broadly, color is an indication of the richness of our surroundings. It is an unconscious signal not only of immediate sustenance but of an environment that is capable of sustaining us over time. In the words of German painter Johannes Itten: "Color is life; for a world without colors appears to us as dead." At the core of the energy aesthetic is this: a vibrancy that lets us know our surroundings are alive and can help us thrive.

Knowing this shed new light on the magical transformation of Tirana, Albania. Mayor Edi Rama's colors took a place that looked dead and infused it with life, signaling to citizens that their home was no longer "a trash city," as one resident described it, but a living locus with its own brisk vitality. Once I understood that our relationship to color evolved not as an incidental pleasure but as an integral signifier of life and of the conditions that support life, I realized that the colors prompted an unconscious change in people's relationship to their environment: from fight or flight to stay and grow. In five years, the number of businesses in Tirana tripled, and tax revenue increased by a factor of six. The increased tax revenue paid for public development projects, like tearing down five thousand buildings that had been illegally erected in public spaces and planting four thousand trees. Journalists visiting the city in the year or so after the first paintings observed that the desolate streets that had once been havens for crime were bustling with activity, people sitting in cafés and strolling in parks. The Albanian artist Anri Sala described how the change began to take on its own momentum. "In the beginning it was the colors which were the change, and now you see the city changing around the colors," he said. The murals were like a fire lit within the heart of the city. They were catalytic, sparking a transformation that eventually dwarfed their initial impact. As one resident wrote, "Even a blind person can bear witness to the utter change of Tirana."

It is hard to believe that color could have this kind of power. Even Rama, who has witnessed the metamorphosis firsthand, at times appears a bit bewildered by the scale of it, and many similar mural projects have been dismissed as mere "beautification efforts" that squander public funds. I think we underestimate the impact of color because we view it as an instrument of decoration, not utility. In the man-made world, color sits on the surface—a thin veneer, a finishing touch. This is reflected in the root of the word "color," which comes from the Latin *celare*, "to conceal." But in nature, color extends through the full thickness of an object. The persimmon is orange equally in skin and flesh; the brown elk is red inside. Color in nature *means* something: a stage of growth, a concentration of minerals. We think of color as something that hides what's underneath it, but we respond to color as something that reveals. Edi Rama acknowledges this when he says that a "normal city" might wear colors like a dress or like lipstick, but that in Tirana, where the basics of civic life had been so badly neglected, the colors function more like "organs." They might look cosmetic, but they go straight to the heart of things.

* * *

Not long after I learned about Tirana, I met someone closer to home who also believed in the power of color to enliven dreary places and the people in them. In the early 1990s, Ruth Lande Shuman was visiting middle schools in East Harlem when she suddenly became aware that they resembled a different kind of institution. "Every single school looked and felt like a prison," she said, reflecting on the moment that sparked her decision to launch the nonprofit Publicolor, which transforms underserved New York City public schools by painting them with vibrant colors. I thought about the public schools I've known: the concrete façades, the windowless corridors lined with banks of taupe lockers, the sand-colored linoleum floors. "They're so hostile looking," Shuman said, shaking her head. "No wonder kids are dropping out like flies. No wonder teachers are becoming burned out. And no wonder parents won't enter these buildings." (Roughly 24 percent of New York City students don't finish high school in four years, though when Shuman first started to paint schools, the number was higher than 50 percent. Among black and Hispanic students, a third still don't graduate.)

Shuman had worked for the Big Apple Circus and had seen the joy that comes from entering a colorful space. She had also studied color theory, and like Edi Rama, she believed that color could have a profound effect on behavior. The first school she painted was in East New York, a Brooklyn neighborhood where nearly half the residents live in poverty. She faced resistance initially from school administrators who scoffed at the bright colors she had chosen. But twenty years later, Publicolor has painted more than four hundred schools and community centers, has received awards from the White House and the city, and counts many school principals among its fans.

Schools are complex systems, making it challenging to isolate the impact of color on academic outcomes. Nevertheless, anecdotal evidence reveals that significant changes follow in the wake of a Publicolor intervention. Graffiti almost completely disappears, and principals report that both student and teacher attendance improves. Some principals say they have noticed a difference in test scores as well. Perhaps the most surprising finding is that teachers and students consistently say they feel safer in a school that has been painted by Publicolor. Just like the shop owners in Tirana who removed the metal grates from their windows, students and teachers find that the brightly colored walls ease their perception of danger in the space. Perhaps feeling safe frees up more mindshare for teaching and learning, which translates to more-focused students and better-performing schools.

I also suspect there may be another effect at play. Bright color operates like a stimulant, a shot of caffeine for the eyes. It stirs us out of complacency. The artist Fernand Léger related the story of a newly renovated factory in Rotterdam. "The old factory was dark and sad," he noted. "The new one was bright and colored: transparent. Then something happened. Without any remark to the personnel, the clothes of the workers became neat and tidy.... They felt that an important event had just happened around them, within them." Comprehensive research on color and the workplace suggests that Léger's observations play out at scale. In a study of nearly a thousand people in Sweden, Argentina, Saudi Arabia, and the UK, people working in bright, colorful offices were more alert than those working in duller spaces. They were also more joyful, interested, friendly, and confident. The drab tones of most school buildings and offices are understimulating, leading to restlessness and difficulty concentrating. The liveliness of color helps us marshal the energy we need to learn, be productive, and grow.

Publicolor involves students and administrators in the process of choosing the colors for their schools, but over the years the organization has developed a signature palette that features citrusy yellows, greens, and oranges, with accents of turquoise and salmon pink. Bright and saturated, it's a joyful palette, but I wondered what it would be like on a larger scale. Would such vivid colors feel overwhelming on a large building?

My curiosity landed me with a roller in hand one July afternoon, smoothing Aruba Blue paint onto a door at the Help homeless shelter in Brownsville, Brooklyn. During the summer, Publicolor runs a program that teaches high-school kids math and literacy in the mornings, and in the afternoons the kids paint community spaces in underserved areas. We arrived in the early afternoon, and Shuman buzzed around in paint-spattered clothes, checking on colors and supplies, asking the kids about their summers and how the project was going. She knew them all by name. When the whole group had arrived, we went outside to the courtyard between the shelter's five buildings, and Shuman introduced me to my guide for the day: Kiyana, a sixteen-year-old living in the Sunset Park area of Brooklyn. We got to work on the door to one of the units facing the courtyard. Kiyana was a Publicolor veteran, with five painting projects under her belt, so I let her take the tricky spots around the doorframe while I focused on trying to roll the paint evenly on the surface of the door without leaving it too thick or gummy. I asked Kiyana which of the painting projects she'd done was her favorite, and she smiled reflectively. "Definitely my school. It actually made the school feel a lot better," she said, the word "actually" betraying her surprise. "The colors just make me feel a lot happier to be there."

I didn't have to look far to imagine the feeling Kiyana was describing, because right then the shelter was split down the middle into a perfect before and after. The buildings on the facility's western side had been painted with a sunset palette of yellows and oranges. The bottom floor was the lightest, a soft golden color, while the top floor was the hue of a ripe apricot. The teal doors we were painting added a tropical vibe. The buildings on the eastern side, which the kids were going to start painting next week, wore a brown putty color from top to bottom. Standing in the middle, I found the difference striking. I turned to my right, and I was in a wasteland, a dismal place of last resort. Yet when I looked to my left, I felt like I was in a residential neighborhood in Miami, headed over to a friend's place for a party. The warm colors seemed to radiate sunshine and, maybe it's just me, a bit of optimism as well.

COLOR COURAGE

Few people would name their favorite color as gray or beige, yet our homes are often cloaked in bland neutral tones. I wondered, Why is there such a gap between the colors that enliven us and the colors that surround us?

"Chromophobia" was the immediate answer I received when I posed this question to Peter Stamberg and Paul Afcriat, architects of the colorful Saguaro Hotel in Palm Springs, which credits its electric hues with making it the third-most-Instagrammed hotel in the world in 2016. "People are afraid of color," Stamberg told me. He was clearly referring to people other than himself and Aferiat, who live in a veritable temple to vibrancy: an open loft divided not with walls but with colors, panels of yellow, green, blue, and orange. Across from me, the two sat perched on a violet sofa, next to a pair of vermilion chairs, a pink rug underfoot. A large collection of glassware and ceramics in a gradient of warm hues adorned a table by the window, casting shards of amber light onto the floor.

"It's the fear of making a choice," Aferiat said, "of making a mistake and having to live with it." I could relate. I didn't know the term at the time, but I used to be a certified chromophobe, so afraid of color that the entire spectrum of my apartment fell between white and cream. My sofa was ivory, my bookshelves off-white. My bed linens, towels, and curtains were all crisp, clean white. I had a big inspiration board covered in a raw linen fabric, and in the corner of my bedroom I piled my clothes on a director's chair covered with—you guessed it—white canvas. Whenever I needed a new piece of furniture I perused colorful catalogs, ogling mustard velvet sofas and pink striped slipper chairs. But in the end, I always came home with trusty old white.

Then one day I moved into my dream apartment: a railroad layout on the top floor of a brownstone, with immaculate wood floors, windows overlooking a green yard, and even a small skylight in the bathroom. The only problem was that the walls were painted a buttery

Chromophobia

yellow. From the moment I first saw the apartment, I fantasized about repainting it. But then something funny happened. Each time I came home to that apartment, it felt like the sun was shining, even in the dead of winter. When I returned from a trip, I felt overjoyed—every time. I ended up living there for six years, and after the first week I never again thought about repainting.

I wish I could say that was the end of my chromophobia, but in fact it was design school that really changed my relationship to color. I spent many hours clipping and arranging swatches of colored paper, mixing paints, and studying the interactions between different hues. I realized that the world is full of colors I hadn't actually been taught to see. I had spent my life thinking of shadows as gray, but I now saw they were tinged purple. I thought of an apple as red without realizing how dramatically different that red is if the apple is on the windowsill rather than the counter. The joy of this new way of seeing was indescribable to me.

We think of color as something only artists study, but that's a relatively recent view. Historian John Stilgoe writes that until the turn of the last century, educated people were apt to study chromatics, the interplay of light and color across a scene. People learned to see just as they learned to read and to count. It's not surprising that without this education, we feel a little lost when it comes to color.

The difference between energetic, joyful colors and more somber hues has to do with how pure and how bright the pigments are. Designers use the terms "saturation" and "lightness" to describe these properties. When I first learned them, I felt the whole world of color open up to me, in the same way that learning addition and subtraction once demystified the world of math. A saturated color is its purest version, the kind you might find on a children's building-block set. The truest blue and the sunniest yellow: these colors are strong and intense. To *desaturate* colors, you add gray to them, making them duller versions of themselves. Spring green becomes olive; cerulean becomes slate. Beige is a desaturated yellow—a yellow with all the joy sucked out of it! Gray is the ultimate desaturated color, containing only white and black. Desaturated colors can be useful as part of a color scheme, but if you look around and all you see are grays and khakis and beiges, then your surroundings are pretty drab. The lightness of a color has to do with how much white or black is mixed into it. White reflects light, while black absorbs it. So adding white makes a color lighter and more reflective, while adding black makes it darker and more muted. Light pink and sky blue are more energizing than burgundy and navy because they reflect more light, imbuing a space with life. Dark, desaturated colors absorb light, bringing down the energy in a space.

It can take a little practice to become confident with color. Fortunately, there are shortcuts for finding joyful color combinations and training our eyes to see and use color in all its delightful depth. Once, when Stamberg and Aferiat were stuck on choosing a color for a house they were designing, they turned to a good friend of theirs, the painter David Hockney, who said, "Do what I do whenever I have a color problem. Look at Matisse." Not only did the vibrant paintings of Henri Matisse inspire them to choose the right blue, but they also began to use this approach with clients. When people see such bold colors coexisting amiably on a canvas, it gives them confidence that the colors will also work in their homes. Matisse's light, bright palette makes an ideal choice for color inspiration, but other artists I often look at include Helen Frankenthaler, Sonia Delaunay, Pierre Bonnard, and, of course, David Hockney.

And if you still don't feel confident, take heart in the wisdom of legendary interior designer David Hicks, who believed that the idea of colors clashing with one another was a fiction cooked up by "genteel women" in the 1930s. "Colors do not clash," he said. "They vibrate."

* * *

Another person who definitely does not have chromophobia is Ellen Bennett, the thirty-year-old founder of LA-based apron manufacturer Hedley & Bennett. "I love color," she said when I met her one rainy September afternoon, drawing out the *o* in "love" to express the depth of her affection. "In my house, everything is Roy G. Biv," the acronym for the colors of the rainbow. She ran through the highlights: color-coded bookshelves, a blue bedroom, a kelly-green front door, and a bright yellow stove that Bennett bought her boyfriend after only three months of dating. For Bennett, an exuberant spirit and self-described "hugger" who gave me a tight squeeze and a kiss on the cheek within seconds of meeting me, it's clear there's an equation between color and warmth. "I want to make spaces feel very welcoming," she has been quoted as saying, "as if you were getting a big hug from the room."

Bennett credits her heritage with kindling her love of vivid color. Half Mexican by birth, she grew up bouncing back and forth between Mexico and California. "It was a Technicolor life in Mexico. My grandma's house is bright turquoise blue. Everything is colorful there, from the corn on the side of the road to the mangoes at the grocery store. But when I was living in the United States, everything was a lot more brown. Brown sand, brown schools…it was just brown. Then I'd go back to Mexico and it was yellow and green and red and every single house was a different color. And things just felt alive. From the eyes of a little kid, I felt that energy in me, and I thought, I want that energy. I like this."

Listening to Bennett's childhood impressions of her two worlds, I felt a pang of something I can only describe as color envy. Like Bennett, I'd spent time in parts of the world where vibrancy was natural and effortless: Southeast Asia, Latin America, the Caribbean. These colorful places exude a warmth and vitality that's absent from most modern American cities, where the greatest source of color seems to be signs and advertisements. "There's just a higher wavelength of life," Bennett said. Color pulls joy to the surface. Why do some cultures reserve color only for celebratory moments, while others make it a part of the everyday?

It would be easy to conclude that it's a simple matter of preference: certain cultures have developed an appetite for color, while others prefer a grayscale life. But I think the real answer lies in a cultural bias deep in Western society that runs toward sophistication, away from joy. This bias was forcefully expressed by Johann Wolfgang von Goethe when he wrote in 1810 that "savage nations, uneducated people, and children have a great predilection for vivid colors," but that "people of refinement avoid vivid colors in their dress and the objects that are about them, and seem inclined to banish them altogether from their presence." We may not realize it, but in most of Europe and America, Goethe's philosophy permeates our lives. We dismiss color and joy as childish and frivolous, prizing neutral hues as a mark of coolness and mature taste. The color spectrum of the modern home is dictated by a moral compass where self-restraint is true north, and exuberance is an indulgence. The message is clear: to be worthy of society's approbation, we must outgrow our natural inclinations toward joy or learn to suppress them.

This cultural bias has left us in a place where many of us feel almost ashamed to have color in our lives. I recently met a woman who told me that she loves color, but she only feels comfortable using it in her child's room, not in the rest of the house. Women are told to wear muted colors as they age, lest they appear as if they're trying too hard to look young. This is a far-more-insidious kind of chromophobia, driven not by lack of confidence but the tyranny of public opinion. Could it be that our world would be much more colorful if only people weren't afraid of looking foolish?

I am inspired by people like Ellen Bennett, who are finding ways to marry joyful color and serious business. Bennett moved to Mexico City full-time when she was eighteen, paying her way through culinary school with odd jobs, including one as a lottery announcer on Mexican TV, calling out the numbers from the weekly drawings. But a few years later she moved back, determined to retain the vibrancy of her Mexican life back in the United States. She found a job working as a line cook at a restaurant. She loved the work, but there was one part of the job that she hated: the apron. As she started complaining about the garment, she discovered her coworkers shared her sentiments. One day her boss was about to place an order for new aprons for the whole staff, and Bennett begged him to give her the order instead. She had no pattern, no fabric, not even a sewing machine, but in that moment, her apron company, Hedley & Bennett, was born.

The first apron was made of yellow linen, and other colors soon followed. Bennett knew the aprons also had to work well, not just look good, and she was relentless about performance. "It's a serious garment that looks really happy and playful," she says, "but it makes you feel secure and proud and having a sense of dignity. It's colorful, but it's functional, it's very well made." The practicality gives people permission to choose a piece of work wear that looks lighthearted and fun. This combination has evidently been successful, as Hedley & Bennett now outfits more than four thousand restaurants.

Ultimately, Bennett's ambitions run beyond aprons. What her business is really about is transforming the concept of the uniform from an ugly, cheap garment laborers are forced to wear into a piece of gear that brings pride and, yes, joy to work. She described an apron in a way I'd never heard before: "It's like your little cape," she said, evoking superhero associations. I raised an eyebrow when I first heard this, but the more I think about the metaphor, the more sense it makes. When Clark Kent changes into Superman's sleek blue-and-red Kryptonian skinsuit, he becomes someone different, endowed with energy and strength unimaginable when he's wearing a dull tweed jacket. What Bennett is doing for April Bloomfield, David Chang, and countless line cooks, service workers, and craftspeople is "outfitting" them, preparing them not just physically but emotionally for the work they're about to do.

My conversation with Bennett started me thinking about other kinds of clothing. We've all been told we should dress for the job we want. But what about dressing for the *joy* we want? When I first started exploring the aesthetics of joy, I began experimenting with wearing bright colors in situations that brought me down. I bought a pair of rubber rain boots in taxicab yellow. When the forecast called for a downpour, I put them on gleefully, grabbed my umbrella (also yellow), and dashed outside to splash around on my way to work. When I was single and going on a seemingly endless spree of awkward blind dates, I started buying dresses in bright prints to give myself energy for the small talk ahead. More recently, I received a lime-green workout top as a gift. Seeing that neon color first thing in the morning kindles my desire to get up and do yoga. Now as my old workout clothes wear out, I try to replace them with ones in bold hues.

dress for the joy you want

My friend Beth, the most colorful dresser I know, thinks not just about the effect of wearing color on herself but also about its effect on other people. At five foot ten, Beth is tall. She's also whip-smart and not afraid to speak her mind. "My whole life," she says, "I've been told I was intimidating or scary." Wearing bright color became a way to make herself more accessible to people, short-circuiting their tendency to judge her too quickly. Beth owns no dark coats, only ones in vivid shades like yellow and green. On a miserable winter day she notices that people walk by and smile. It's almost as if a colorful garment is a tiny gift, a brilliant spot of joy in a bleak landscape.

When Beth and I worked together, one of our coworkers planned a Dress Like Beth Day. People showed up in pink polka-dot pants, yellow sweaters, and turquoise dresses, making the office so bright we all nearly needed sunglasses. It was one of the best days I can remember. The whole office came to life.

THE DELIGHT OF LIGHT

Can the world be joyful without color? I wasn't sure until I came across a story related by Dr. Oliver Sacks about a trip he took in 1994 to Pingelap, an island where many natives have a persistent genetic defect that leaves them completely unable to see color. Sacks brings along with him on the trip a Norwegian scientist named Knut Nordby, who also suffers from the severe color blindness, or *achromatopsia*, that afflicts many of the islanders. At one point, the travel party encounters a soaking storm, leaving behind a stunning rainbow. Sacks describes Nordby's impression of the rainbow as "a luminous arc in the sky" and goes on to share Nordby's joyful tales of other rainbows he has seen: double rainbows and even a complete rainbow circle. In the end, Sacks concludes that the visual world of the color blind is "if impoverished in some ways, in others quite as rich as our own."

We might be able to find joy without color, but it would be much harder without light. Every sight we find joyful, from a sunrise to a baby's face, we owe to light reflected from the environment into our eyes. Light is color's power supply. But more than that, it's a pure form of energy that creates joy in its own right. We rely on sunlight to regulate our circadian rhythm, the twenty-four-hour clock that determines our energy levels. Sunlight also stimulates the production of vitamin D by the skin, modulates our immune system, and influences levels of serotonin, a neurotransmitter that helps balance emotions. Many people living at high latitudes suffer from wintertime depression known as seasonal affective disorder (fittingly abbreviated SAD) due to the lack of daylight. Light and mood often travel a conjoined orbit: dim the light, and we dim our joy.

People around the world eschew dark corners and seek out light-filled places, coveting apartments with good natural light and vacationing in sunny, tropical locales. In *A Pattern Language*, a landmark collection of observations on the ways that people use space, architect Christopher Alexander and his colleagues note that the single most important fact about a building is this: "People use open space if it is sunny, and do not use it if it isn't, in all but desert climates." In a study of a residential street in Berkeley, Alexander found that residents on the north side of the street didn't use their backyards. Instead, they sat in the small front yards next to the sidewalk while the backyards collected junk. Shaded yards and plazas create dead zones, while those that face south ensure "the building and its gardens will be happy places full of activity and laughter." The same is true indoors. Because the sun travels from east to west across the southern half of the sky, houses where the most important rooms face south tend to be cheerful and convivial. Meanwhile, houses where the main rooms face north are often dark and gloomy, causing people to retreat from the common areas toward the lighter rooms at the edges of the house. (In the Southern Hemisphere, the sun passes through the northern part of the sky, so these directions should be reversed.)

'Ihe joy we find in a sunlit room is matched by tangible measures of well-being. Research consistently shows that increasing exposure to daylight reduces blood pressure and improves mood, alertness, and productivity. Employees who sit near windows report higher energy levels and tend to be more physically active both in and out of the office. In a study of elementary schools, students in classrooms with the most daylight advanced as much as 26 percent faster in reading and 20 percent faster in math over the course of a year. Hospital patients assigned to sunnier rooms were discharged sooner and required less pain medication than those in rooms with less light.

Sunlight is best, but when it isn't available, broad-spectrum artificial light can provide similar benefits. Scientists have known for years that seasonal depression can be alleviated by spending up to an hour a day in front of a glowing box that radiates twenty-five hundred lux, but newer research shows that light therapy can be effective for nonseasonal depression as well. In a meta-analysis of twenty studies, researchers reached the startling conclusion that light therapy can be as effective at treating depression as antidepressants. And among Alzheimer's patients in long-term-care facilities, bright light reduced both depression and cognitive decline. Yet because light is not as lucrative a remedy as pharmaceuticals, there has been much less research into these treatments.

The irony is that the salutary effects of light have been understood for centuries. "Put the pale withering plant and human being into the sun," wrote the famous English nurse Florence Nightingale, "and, if not too far gone, each will recover health and spirit." In 1860, Nightingale reported that her patients naturally turned toward the light, even as they would complain about the pain of lying on an injured side. "Then why do you lie on that side?" she would ask the patient. "He does not know—but we do. It is because it is the side towards the window."

Stories like this make me think that while technology has moved our health and well-being immeasurably forward, it has also robbed us of a wisdom that existed when our relationship to our environment wasn't mediated by so many dials and controls. Instead of starting a fire or opening a window, we tweak the knob on the thermostat. Instead of eating a medicinal plant, we swallow a pill. We have gained convenience and efficacy, but at the cost of abstraction: the changes within our bodies no longer seem connected to the world around us, giving us the illusion that we are independent of our environment and unaffected by it. Thus we have built environments that lack elements, such as color and light, that are essential to our well-being.

While brightness is important, creating joyful, energizing light is more than just a matter of lumens. When I posed the question "What is joyful light?" to lighting designer Rick Shaver, he started by calling my attention to what it's not. Describing an office he'd recently been to, he noted that the even rows of fluorescent lights made it feel like the place was covered by an "overcast sky." Offices are designed for uniform lighting, so that there's enough light to read wherever you sit. But that flat, even light creates a dull energy. According to Shaver, who has designed lighting schemata for the Getty Museum and countless private homes, "it's those streaks of sunlight coming through" that create "a joyous environment."

Studies affirm that people generally prefer lighting that is variable, rather than uniform. These hills and valleys of light attract our eyes to points of interest within a space, but even more important, they draw us together. As Alexander emphasizes in *A Pattern Language*, because people are unconsciously attracted to light, the brightest spots will be the ones where people congregate, making these the most lively and joyful hubs of activity in a space. If a space feels dead, a powerful remedy is to create focal points of light where you want people to be. A sofa by the fireplace, a window seat, a dining table bathed in the warm light of a pendant lamp: these places are always alive because we, like moths, cannot resist the light.

PAINTING LIGHT

When I met with the color-loving architects Stamberg and Aferiat, they showed me pictures of a beach house they had designed on Long Island for a couple that had suddenly decided, after years of living in mostly monochrome apartments, that they wanted color in their home. The architects started with crisp white walls and lots of big black-and-white patterns that they knew would feel natural to the couple. Then they added a front door in bright yellow, picked to match the beach goldenrod that grew near the house. From the outside, the door is a cheery beacon, making the house seem to smile at passersby. But from the inside, the effect is totally different. The door acts like its own light source. The white walls pull the yellow color into the center of the home. It literally glows.

We think of color as an attribute, but really it's a happening: a constantly occurring dance between light and matter. When a beam of light strikes an object—let's say a multicolor glass vase—it is effectively pelting the surface with tiny energetic particles known as photons. The energy of some of those photons is absorbed, heating the glass imperceptibly. But other photons are repelled, sent ricocheting back out into the atmosphere. It's these photons, landing on our retinas, that create the sensation of color. The specific hue we see has to do with the energy of the photons: the high-energy short wavelengths look blue to us, while the low-energy long ones appear red. The brightest pigments, those found in flower petals and leaves as well as many commercial pigments, tend to have a more "excitable" molecular structure. Their electrons can be disturbed with very little light, making the colors appear intense to our eyes.

Ultimately, the goal of the energy aesthetic is to increase the activity of these vibrating little particles in a space. It's not just about light, and it's not just about color; it's about the alchemy between the two. Bright colors animate the light that shines on them, reflecting it around a space and magnifying its effect. This is why the yellow door in the house designed by Stamberg and Aferiat is so powerful. It takes the invisible light and turns it golden. Yellow is especially effective as a brightening agent. Because it is the lightest of all the hues in its pure state, it has an inherent brightness and warmth. Publicolor uses paints with a yellowish undertone for this exact reason. The bright, warm paints bring light into a space, combatting the dreariness of inner-city settings. "We paint light," says founder Ruth Lande Shuman, making me curious as to what might happen if we applied some bright paint to the dark alleys, underpasses, and other shadowy corners of our cities.

If you want a brighter, more energized space, whether your home or office or anywhere else, the experts agree that the best first step is to lighten the largest surfaces: walls, floors, cabinets, and counters. Dark walls may look sophisticated, but because they absorb light, they're going to reduce the overall amount of light bouncing around the room. Many designers I talked to prefer to start with a canvas of white walls, bringing color into the space through furniture and decorative objects. But even if that's not possible, small pops of pure color can reflect enough light to energize a dingy space. This approach of using bursts of bright color can be an appealing strategy for chromophobes—I speak from experience here—and is surprisingly effective. Hilary Dalke, a designer and color expert who works with the National Health Service in Britain, told me she uses this strategy regularly. When she was asked by a hospital in the south of England to redesign the patient rooms without moving any of the patients, she swapped the neutral blankets on the beds for ones in a vivid fuchsia color and took before-and-after pictures of the room. The reflected light from the bedding was so vibrant that the whole room seemed suddenly much warmer, and for very low cost.

The very best pigments for creating light are fluorescent colors, because they absorb photons at higher-energy wavelengths that lie in the invisible ultraviolet range and reflect them back at visible wavelengths. This makes them look brighter than normal colors, almost as if they're glowing. These so-called Day-Glo colors, the kind you find on traffic cones and tennis balls, imbue surfaces with an intensely upbeat vibe, but use caution: a little goes a long way!

We may be aware of the way that color affects light in space, but we rarely notice the reverse: the way light affects color. There's a good reason for this, according to lighting designer Rick Shaver: old incandescent light bulbs all used to give off the same color of light. "When you would screw in a light bulb that you bought at the supermarket," says Shaver, "you knew that it was always going to burn at a color temperature of twenty-seven hundred degrees Kelvin, which is warm and very flattering to the skin." As lighting manufacturers developed new, more energy-efficient technologies, such as LEDs and fluorescents, suddenly a light bulb was not just a light bulb anymore. But no one told us light-bulb buyers. "People don't know they should be looking for three thousand degrees Kelvin, or what we call warm light, so instead they come home with four thousand or five thousand degrees Kelvin, which is cool light." This information is printed on packages, but most people don't know to look for it. As a result, Shaver often sees people living unhappily under a patchwork of different light colors.

The color of light varies because, unlike the sun, which carries wavelengths across the full visible spectrum, artificial lights can only reproduce a part of that spectrum. We've all had the experience of being in a badly lit dressing room or catching our reflection in an airport bathroom and thinking, Ugh, do I really look this tired? This happens because the light is missing wavelengths needed for our eyes to see color accurately. It's hard to feel upbeat and energized when you and all the people around you look sallow and run down and bright colors turn sickly shades. So Shaver's advice is to look at the color rendering index (CRI) of a bulb. Incandescent bulbs have a rating of 100, a fact that fuels demand for them even though they have been banned by many countries. But newer LED bulbs have recently been developed that give off light as warm and vibrant as those old Edison bulbs. Choosing bulbs with a CRI close to 100 will keep you and your spaces looking bright and colorful.

* * *

For most of my life, I thought about my color choices through the lens of what they said about me. Did I have the guts to rock red shoes? Would a pink dress make people take me less seriously in a client meeting? Perhaps that's why I so often ended up with white furniture and black clothes. My research on this aesthetic liberated me to choose colors based not on what others think but on how the colors make me feel.

Noticing color and light has changed the world around me. Bright hues in the cityscape, found on street signs and in bike lanes, window boxes and graffiti, have become little gifts for me—small infusions of warmth and life. Energy gives you the power to make your own hearth, your own sun.

2.

ABUNDANCE

The bearded man shook his head, but he was smiling as he watched the two boys whiz by him clutching their cellophane bags, a blur in their green Little League shirts. "Zack, your mom is going to kill me," he called out after the older of the two. It seemed an attempt to encourage moderation, but Zack was oblivious to his father's plea as he zigzagged between the clear acrylic bins of Swedish fish, malt balls, and gummy chicken feet. He knew this was like Halloween without the itchy costume and small talk with the neighbors, and he wasn't wasting the opportunity. His younger brother followed his path loosely, like the tail of a kite. Not a lot of candy made it into his bag, but he grinned as he tried to keep up. He came to a stop in front of a display of giant swirly lollipops, his eyes wide.

"Like a kid in a candy store" is one of the most iconic images of joy in our culture, expressing the wild, almost delirious pleasure we take in being let loose in a bountiful world. When I first started hearing about the places that give people joy, I realized that many of them evoke this giddy feeling of abundance: carnivals and circuses, dollar stores and flea markets, and giant old hotels like the Grand Budapest of director Wes Anderson's imagining. The same feeling also exists on a smaller scale. An ice-cream cone covered in rainbow sprinkles is like a candy store held in your hand. A shower of confetti, a multicolored quilt, a simple game of pick-up sticks, have this irresistible allure. Even the language of joy is rife with excess. We say we're overjoyed or that we're brimming with happiness. We say, "My cup runneth over." And this is very much how it feels to be in a moment of joy, when our delight is so abundant it feels like it can't be contained by the boundaries of our bodies.

But why, I wondered, do we get such a burst of joy from abundance? Why are we so enthralled by the feeling of having more than we could ever possibly need? It was this question that had brought me to the flagship store of Dylan's Candy Bar, which boasts more than seven thousand different types of candy, a decision I was now questioning as I realized I'd chosen just the moment that school was beginning to let out. Candy flew through the air as kids raced around in pursuit of a sugar high.

I took a step back out of the frenzy and felt a crunch under my foot. The crisp scent of a crushed peppermint wheel mingled with the chocolaty background aroma. Watching the kids as they scrambled among the rainbow of offerings—crouching, grabbing, reaching—made for a surprisingly primal scene. It reminded me of a day earlier in the summer. I had been walking along a country road in upstate New York when I caught sight of a cluster of dark purple berries in a tangle of brush. I tasted one: blackberries, perfectly ripe. I started picking, quickly gathering them into a cupped hand. Some were deep in the brambles, others surrounded by vines that looked suspiciously like poison ivy. But I couldn't stop myself. I felt elated and at the same time overcome by a savage hunger. I kept picking until the berries were falling out of my hands. I saw this same gleeful rapacity on the faces of the kids at Dylan's Candy Bar. They weren't shopping. They were foraging.

Candy stores (and supermarkets and shopping malls) are so common in contemporary society it's easy to forget that until recently such abundance was a rarity. For the thousands of generations of early humans who foraged and hunted for subsistence, even a gas station mini-mart would be a wealth of riches. Their lives cycled through unpredictable periods of sufficiency and devastating scarcity. In this seesaw of daily existence, it seems only natural that humans developed a predilection for abundance. This ensured that people would take advantage of a windfall when it came, shoring up resources for the lean times that would inevitably follow. Those who reveled in abundance were more likely to survive than those who were indifferent to it, encoding this preference deep in our genes. Though we inhabit a very different world from our hunter-gatherer ancestors, we carry the legacy of their fragile subsistence when we pig out at buffets and buy too much at clearance sales. Just like our taste for sugar and fat, our love of abundance is a remnant of a biological drive designed to help us navigate a scarce and uncertain world.

If the candy store has a natural antecedent, it would be somewhere lush and verdant, with fertile soil, ample water, and a rich array of edible plant and animal life. And as it turns out, according to research by psychologist John Balling and ecologist John Falk, this is the kind of environment people prefer to live in, even today. Balling and Falk studied landscape preferences among people aged eight to over seventy, in the United States and in Nigeria, and discovered that people consistently choose lush biomes like grasslands and forests over dry, sparse habitats like deserts. Children's preferences run most strongly in this direction, which suggests that while the proclivity for lushness can modulate with age, it is likely our default setting. More support for this hypothesis comes from a study showing that people who spent time in parks with a higher density and diversity of plant and bird life experienced a greater sense of restoration and psychological well-being than those who hung out in less biodiverse parks. We no longer rely on those plants and birds for sustenance, of course. But somehow, we sense the abundance in our surroundings, and it creates an unconscious ease.

The idea that the joy of abundance might have a deeper resonance was compelling to me, but I was also becoming aware that this joy had limits. On one side of the line lived quirky collections, potluck dinners, and boxes of assorted chocolates. On the other loomed overstuffed landfills, obesity, and hoarders. While it is hard to overdose on the energy aesthetic (I don't think anyone has died from too much color!), abundance, by its very nature, could take people overboard. Our impulses toward abundance evolved in a world of scarcity. In a world overflowing with things, I wondered if the abundance aesthetic had become maladaptive. Maybe we just don't need abundance anymore.

Around the time I was weighing the pros and cons of abundance, a friend sent me a picture of a local house that had been featured in the newspaper. It looked like a child's drawing of a house, built in real life. Every surface was covered in bright construction-paper colors: big rectangles of pink and purple, orange and blue, and at least three shades of yellow. One door was green, another red. The inside was equally colorful, with a bright green ceiling and walls painted every shade in the crayon box. There was no traditional furniture, just a peculiar sloping floor and a series of poles painted in primary hues around the space. There were so many colors, shapes, and angles—it was like I was looking at the abundance aesthetic in house form.

It was called Bioscleave House, and it had a strange subtitle: "Lifespan Extending Villa." I discovered that its creators were an artist and a poet couple, Shusaku Arakawa and Madeline Gins, who claimed not just that the house was a delightful place to live but that it could actually prolong the lives of its inhabitants. I was intrigued. Maybe this house could help me figure out how to get the benefits of abundance, without the downsides.

It turned out the house was in transition between owners, and I wasn't able to visit. But a few months later I discovered that Arakawa and Gins had designed an apartment building outside of Tokyo. And not only could I see it, I could stay in one of the apartments for the night!

ARCHITECTURE AS MEDICINE

When I arrived in Mitaka, the suburb on the outskirts of Tokyo where Arakawa and Gins built their lofts, I was worn out from jet lag and sodden after two trains, a bus ride, and a walk in the rain without an umbrella. The April sky was a flat panel of gray, and I was in a grumpy mood made worse by the feeling of my clammy feet squishing in my shoes. But as I rounded a bend and caught a glimpse of my destination, a smile rose up unbidden. It looked just like the pictures: an assemblage of brightly colored cubes and cylinders stacked on top of one another, with a patchwork of different-sized windows. My bad mood eased before I even crossed the street.

I unlatched the wooden gate and noticed that it was inlaid with colorful marbles that caught the light like stained glass. Down a hallway lined with more colors than I could count, I found the office, where I met Takeyoshi Matsuda-san, the slightly harried but affable general manager. He was about my age, shaggy hair threaded with grays, a scruff of beard at the tip of his chin. He offered me tea and presented me with a standard-looking rental agreement and a folder containing some background on the facility, a map of local restaurants, and brochures about other properties. Then before turning to lead me up the stairs to my loft, he handed me a mysterious gray packet. "These are the instructions for the apartment," he said. I looked at it quizzically, prompting him to explain: "Arakawa and Gins believed that architecture has an effect on the body like medicine," he said. "So, like medicine, they made instructions." I took the packet from him, preparing myself for an interesting night.

Matsuda unlocked the frosted-glass door to unit 302 and dashed around showing me the locations of the light switches and the thermostat, the English directions for the range and the fridge. He was gone in a flash, and suddenly I was alone. There was a lot to take in. At the center of the loft was a small kitchenette, its surfaces mint green and royal blue, arranged around a column painted a bright spring green. There were no closets anywhere in the apartment. Instead, the ceiling, which was pink, was inset with metal rings from which to hang things. A swing dangled from a ring in one corner, the only thing in the space resembling traditional furniture. There were distinct "rooms" off of the central core, a word I put in quotes because only one of them looked like what you or I might recognize as a room. The simplest was a bedroom, a basic cube furnished in muted tones of brown with a taupe shag carpet. The second room was a yellow cylinder placed on its side. It was a kind of doorless bathroom with a cylindrical shower that looked like a teleporter and a curved floor you had to scramble over to get to the toilet. The third room was just a hollow sphere, red on the outside and lacquered on the inside with a glossy sunflower yellow. No surface in the apartment was left uncolored, no wall or column without a slick of orange or purple paint. I later learned that Arakawa wanted a minimum of six colors to be visible from every angle. It was the visual equivalent of being in an orchestra where every instrument is playing at the same time.

And then there was the floor. Picture a sand dune blown by gusty winds so that it banks this way and that, and then imagine hard little lumps all over the surface, like goose bumps on the skin of a giant. It wasn't a floor you walked on so much as one that you clambered over, finding and refinding your balance with each movement. As I scuttled around the apartment, stubbing my toes here and there, I realized how much I take flatness for granted. But feeling a little off-balance and overwhelmed was par for the course, the brochures told me, and in service of a higher purpose. Because I wasn't just staying overnight in an apartment. I was trying to teach my body how not to die.

If the phrasing is outlandish, the theory behind it is more grounded. Arakawa and Gins believed that the dull comfort of modern buildings lulls our bodies into a stupor that hastens our demise. In their view, our flat floors and white walls numb our senses and our muscles, leading them to atrophy. To combat this problem, they advanced a provocative theory they called reversible destiny, which states that people can prevent aging and thwart death by living in a stimulating environment that challenges their bodies on a regular basis. I started to think about how little I'm aware of my body in my daily life. Sometimes I can navigate through the entire New York subway system with my nose buried in a book. It's like we've designed a world that's so easy on us, we move through it on autopilot. Ease and comfort are the twin North Stars for the design of nearly everything in modern life, from coffee shops to iPhone apps. I used to think that was a good thing, but suddenly I wasn't so sure.

If I was going to take full advantage of my night in the loft, I decided, I better open the instructions. There were thirty-two numbered cards. I picked one at random. Card number 9 said, "At least once a day, amble through the apartment in total darkness." I burst out laughing. I was just barely managing to get through the place in full daylight. I pictured myself trying to explain the resulting injuries to Japanese emergency services and decided I'd skip this one. I drew another card. "Every month, move through your loft as a different animal (snake, deer, tortoise, elephant, giraffe, penguin, etc.)." This seemed safer, but since I had only one night, I hopped, waddled, slithered, and skipped around in rapid sequence. I suddenly felt self-conscious. But the windows were all frosted, and my animal improv session had total

privacy. Some of the instructions read like riddles. Take card number 12: "Interact with the floor so as to produce sunlight." I had no idea what to do there, but I had better luck with number 8, which declared: "The floor is a keyboard that is in the process of being invented. Try to help figure out what type of keyboard this is." I danced around, imagining the loft as a giant musical instrument. I hummed, and I sang.

I had to shed my adult reserve to follow these instructions, which I soon learned was by design. When I talked to Momoyo Homma, the director of the foundation that carries on Arakawa and Gins's work, she told me that Arakawa used to say, "You have to remember when you were a baby. You knew the world through your body." I imagined a baby scooting over the floor of my reversible destiny apartment, exploring the colorful surfaces with sticky fingers. Babies have an intimacy with the world. They put everything in their mouths. Arakawa felt that acquiring language created a barrier that inhibits our ability as adults to feel our way through the world. Part of reversible destiny, it seems, is an attempt to resuscitate the childlike wonder we feel in a world full of novel sensations. Along these lines, Homma told me that Arakawa believed our concept of the senses is too narrow. "That's nonsense that we only have five senses," he was known to say. "We have thousands of senses, we just don't have names for them." A little research shows that Arakawa's estimate of "thousands" might be excessive, but scientists do count somewhere between twelve and twenty-one. We have senses of time, equilibrium, and direction. We have internal senses, like stretch sensors that tell us when our bellies are full and proprioception, which tells us where our bodies are in space. The sense that we call touch actually comes from four distinct receptors—pain, temperature, pressure, and tactility—which combine to give us a remarkably robust sense of the world.

All of these senses felt alive as I maneuvered around the apartment. My sense of balance was constantly working. I felt muscles in my feet I didn't know were there. Even brushing my teeth didn't afford me an opportunity to tune out: the floor curved away from the sink, and I had to hold on to the wall because my sock-clad feet kept sliding backward. It was work, but it was also a lot more fun than an ordinary apartment. A man named Shingo Tsuji, who has lived in one of the lofts for four years, says a friend describes it as "a place where you can never be real sad or angry." I thought of the people whose moods were boosted by sitting in the biodiverse parks, and I wondered if there's something about abundant environments that jostles our minds so that melancholy can't linger. What this quirky loft and its even-quirkier designers were making me realize is that the kind of abundance that really matters is not material accumulation but sensorial richness. The circus and the flea market are so joyful because of the collection of rich, delightful sensations they offer. The abundance aesthetic is defined by a layering of color, texture, and pattern, and you don't need a lot of stuff to achieve it.

SENSE AND SENSIBILITY

While the reversible destiny loft might be an extreme example, there is clear evidence that exposure to an abundance of sensations is not only pleasurable; it's vital to healthy neural development. Monkeys and cats reared without visual stimulation fail to develop normally in the part of the brain that processes visual information, leaving them with permanent vision defects as adults. Mice will spend more time in sensorially enriched environments than in sterile ones when given the choice, and those raised in enriched environments perform far better on tests of learning and memory than their peers in ordinary cages. Research with humans has shown that babies are drawn toward sounds and patterns at various stages of development in order to fuel the growth of new neural connections. According to neurobiologist Gene Wallenstein, this behavior is the result of a "pleasure instinct" that motivates the infant to seek out sensory input. This input helps fine-tune the connections between neurons, in a process called synaptic pruning. Think of our brain like a scale that needs to be calibrated before it can accurately measure weight. Because sensory stimulation inside the womb is limited, much of our perceptual capacity must be developed after birth. Our brain can't develop in isolation; it requires a constant dialogue with the environment, particularly one with an abundance of textures, colors, and shapes.

Perhaps this is why children embrace the abundance aesthetic so easily, whether in their insistence on wearing polka dots with stripes to school in the morning or in their choice of toys that tend to clash with many style-conscious parents' living rooms. A few years ago I saw a

magazine feature on spare, modernist dollhouses and felt a wave of pity for any child who received one under the Christmas tree. Fortunately small children make terrible modernists, and they'd be apt to add found objects and handmade trimmings until the place is more in line with their exuberant sense of décor.

While children's developing brains are the most sensation seeking, we never lose our craving for sensorial stimulation, as the popularity of everything from massages to tasting menus to skydiving will attest. But research suggests these aren't just idle pleasures: adult brains also benefit from exposure to a diverse array of sensations. In studies, adults exhibit significant activation in the emotional regions of the brain when stimulated by touch, taste, or smell. Studies of touch in particular show that it can lead to reduced stress, improved mood, and enhanced attentiveness. Though sensory deprivation tanks are currently in vogue, offering brief escapes to a quiet, device-free space, most of the time we need a fundamental level of sensory stimulation to maintain normal cognitive functioning. Research has shown that as few as fifteen minutes of sensory deprivation can cause hallucinations, paranoid thoughts, and negative moods. In one study, participants left alone in an unadorned room for fifteen minutes opted to give themselves electric shocks rather than sit alone with nothing to do or look at. Sensation is a big part of how the world makes sense to us. Without information coming into the brain, we slowly go insane.

The potential therapeutic value of sensory stimulation is well known in Europe, particularly in the Netherlands, where a therapy called Snoezelen is used to treat developmental disabilities, brain injury, and dementia. Snoezelen, a portmanteau of two charmingly onomatopoeic Dutch words, *snuffelen* (to sniff) and *doezelen* (to doze), is a practice of creating multisensory environments and letting patients gravitate to sensations that feel good to them. Snoezelen rooms look a little bit like psychedelic lounges from the 1970s, complete with cushy furniture, swirly holograms, moving light displays, and colorful bubbling tubes of water that resemble Lava lamps. Many include aromas, like orange or strawberry, and music as well. Trippy as they seem, the intensely pleasurable sensations they offer can have a real influence on mood and behavior, without the side effects that come with medication. Caregivers report that the sensations bring dementia patients out of a withdrawn state. Their eyes snap open; they reach for things; they laugh. Research on Snoezelen therapy is still in its early stages, but studies show that adding sessions of Snoezelen therapy to standard psychiatric care reduces apathy and agitation among elderly dementia patients, and it alters neurological activity of brain-injured patients in ways similar to meditation. In Canada, some long-term-care facilities have found Snoezelen helpful in reducing their need to control problem behaviors with antipsychotic drugs.

When you look at a typical nursing home, is it any wonder that most patients withdraw? Senses and memory, the anchors that keep us tethered to the world, both decline with age. Just as elderly people's hold on their lives is slipping away, we place them in facilities with a drab hospital aesthetic that neither energizes them nor invites their engagement. Hilary Dalke, the British color specialist, notes that limited mobility can make this situation even more acute. "A person in a nursing home only has a very simple journey," Dalke told me. "They go from a bedroom down a corridor to a lounge, and those may be the only spaces they ever get to see." To combat this problem, she uses a variety of different paints and wallpapers when designing nursing homes to differentiate spaces and immerse elderly residents in a richness of sensations. Residents in one facility were so hungry for stimulation, they asked for the brightest colors to be placed in their bedrooms, where they spent the most time. Dalke pointed out to me that sensorial impoverishment should be a concern for anyone confined to a small or monotonous environment, from prison inmates to inpatients at mental health facilities to astronauts on the International Space Station.

We normally think of our surroundings as inert, lifeless containers. But all the research on sensation makes me start to see why Arakawa and Gins viewed the home and the inhabitant as a single living entity, one they called the architectural body.

Instruction card 6 reads, "As you step into this unit, fully believe you are walking into your own immune system." It sounds preposterous on the surface. But we now know that our immune system is very much integrated with our surroundings: the allergens we're exposed to, the microbes that constantly test and build our immunity. Light regulates our immune response. Perhaps our emotional well-being is similarly conditioned by the sensations in our midst. A sparse environment acts as an anesthetic, numbing our senses and emotions. The abundance aesthetic does the opposite. It wakes the senses up. It brings us to life.

*   *   *

With this in mind, I was a little bit apprehensive as I packed my bag the next morning to leave the reversible destiny loft and head back to my dull business hotel in downtown Tokyo. Would the brown doors and beige carpets suck me down into a depressing slump? But when I put my key in the lock and opened the door, it was like walking into a completely different room from the one I had left the day before. My eyes caught every sliver of light and shade, my fingertips every tiny ridge and furrow. In the corner of the room by the window sat a burgundy velour chair. The sunlight streamed over it, lighting it as if it were on fire. I sat down in it, running my fingers over the velvety pleats, and it felt like I was experiencing softness for the first time. Even the muted tones and banal textures seemed to thrum with vibrancy. I imagine it was not unlike being under the influence of drugs.

The effect of the Mitaka loft lasted a few days—though, like a high, it eventually wore off. But I take heart in the fact that Momoyo Homma and her colleagues are working on a reversible destiny hotel, a kind of architectural medicinal retreat where people can come for short stays. I think of it as being like a spa, but instead of mellowing out your senses, it fires them all up to eleven.

SENSE HUNGER

Newly aware of my need for sensation, I began to see it as a nutrient. Was I getting enough vitamin C? Enough calcium? Enough color, texture, and pattern to keep myself truly alive? Some days I looked around and unfortunately the answer was no. Much of our built environment bears a stripped-down, minimalist aesthetic that looks far more like cold desert than lush woodland. Office parks and shopping centers blanket the suburbs with gray boxes, leaving swaths of land in a sensory vacuum. Most airports, train stations, and municipal buildings are featureless monoliths, vast echoing caverns that agitate rather than engage the senses. For this we can thank modernism, a movement that arose in Europe early in the twentieth century, determined to shed flourishes and traditions and build a new kind of architecture grounded in simple materials and geometric forms. Modernists embraced machine-made structures and hard materials like glass, steel, and concrete. At their best, the resulting buildings can be starkly beautiful. Yet on some level, I believe they leave us uneasy. Maybe this is why so many movie villains live in modernist houses. Designer Benjamin Critton examined a range of films, from Bond movies like *Diamonds Are Forever* to Ridley Scott's *Blade Runner* to *The Big Lebowski*, and found that evil characters consistently inhabit severe-looking lairs. Stripped of all ornamentation, the matte surfaces have an inhospitable quality, the emotional equivalent of bald rock and fallow fields.

Minimalist homes promise a Zen-like serenity, but to live permanently in that kind of environment seems to go against the grain of human nature. Even the supposed minimalist Philip Johnson didn't live full-time in his famous Glass House. After only a few years, he remodeled the adjacent Brick House into a cushy haven for sleeping and reading, complete with plush carpet, vaulted ceilings, and patterned fabric on the walls. It's almost as if the craving for sensations is inexorable and can be held at bay only for so long. The architect Oscar Niemeyer learned a similar lesson through the planned city of Brasília. Intended as a symbol of Brazil's orderly and egalitarian future, the new capital city featured massive, identical apartment blocks in neat geometric rows. Gone were the slums and the traffic, and in their place was a clean, spacious, modern city. But when residents moved in, they found the big apartment blocks sterile and disorienting. As urbanist Charles Montgomery writes, "They missed their old, cramped market streets, places where disorder and complexity led to serendipitous encounters with sights, scents, and other people." Over time, the city sprawled out, and new barrios were created that resembled the old, abundant way of living.

Left unsatisfied, the craving for sensations can become an actual hunger. A few years ago on a trip to Kauai, I noticed something funny. Five days in, I hadn't had a single snack between meals. This was strange because, at home, I'm an inveterate grazer. There's nearly always a packet of trail mix or a bowl of popcorn on my desk. But on this vacation, not a nibble. I realized that in Hawaii I was surrounded all day by the lush textures of the jungle, the whoosh of the ocean, and the smell of salt water. I had my feet in volcanic sand and a lei of plumeria flowers around my neck. I was satiated, head to toe. Sure enough, by 11:00 a.m. on that first day back in the office, I had my head in the snack cabinet, hunting for almonds. People are quick to blame habits, and to dismiss this as mindless eating, but I believe that ignores the root cause. In our humdrum environments, we live with a sensorial hunger, and without any other means to satisfy it, we feed it.

That experience has changed the way I think about nourishment. Food offers sensory satiation, not just physical nutrients, and it doesn't take much effort to create food that is as beautiful as it is filling. One of my inspirations on this front has been Kimberley Hasselbrink, a photographer and the author of a cookbook called *Vibrant Food*. Hasselbrink describes a purple cauliflower from a friend's garden that she says gave her "new eyes" when it comes to food. The surprising intensity of the colors she found in seasonal produce became a focus of her work, and she started composing dishes with vivid color schemes, like hummus tinted orange with carrots, pink deviled eggs pickled in beet juice, and an all-white winter salad. Playing with color doesn't require fancy equipment or plating, just an attention to a side of food we often overlook. Hasselbrink also talks about the importance of texture. Something as simple as how you slice your food can dramatically change the experience. For example, shaving a carrot into long ribbons not only looks beautiful, but it creates a lighter, crisper sensation than just cutting the vegetable into rounds.

When I do have a snack craving, I try to pause and ask myself if what I'm feeling is a *food hunger* or a *sense hunger* and, if the latter, if there's anything else I can do about it. I try to make my office a haven of abundance, with a string of bright pom-poms, some colorful nautical flags, and a collection of postcards from favorite art exhibits on the walls. I have pens in a dozen different colors, and I keep scented hand cream, lip balm, and a bottle of essential oils on my desk, as well as a stack of magazines underneath it. I also think about vacations differently now. I used to view a trip as a way to take a break from my overly hectic life, seeking out quiet spaces where I could just unwind and relax. Now I recognize that burnout often has as much boredom in it as exhaustion. So I look at vacations as a way to soak in sensations that are different from those at home and to sponge them up so I can call on them later. My vacations are more colorful than they used to be, and so are the souvenirs.

Minimalism is enjoying a resurgence in popularity as people seek respite from stuffed closets and the overstimulation of constantly connected lives. I was skeptical at first of this latest craze, particularly the decluttering fervor kicked off by Marie Kondo's book *The Life-Changing Magic of Tidying Up*. Kondo preaches a five-step method to achieving a joyful home, and all five steps involve removing things from it. But being newly married, Albert and I had twice as many things as we needed, and we were edging dangerously close to *Hoarders* territory. So we dutifully handled each item in our combined home and asked ourselves Kondo's question: Did the item "spark joy"? The joyless items were loaded into the car by the bag- and boxful. We emptied our closets by half and gave away practically an entire starter kitchen to a couple who were moving into their first apartment together.

I'm not going to lie. It felt good. But what I realized is that Kondo's philosophy isn't really minimalism. It's sanity. After all, we still have plenty of stuff. And now that we can see the things we have, our place actually feels *more* abundant, not less. That's because abundance isn't about just accumulating things. It's about surrounding yourself with a rich palette of textures that enliven your senses. If true minimalism is like clear-cutting a field, Kondo's method is like weeding a garden. It's a process of removing the background noise to create a canvas on which to build a joyful home. Yet it's also worth remembering that just weeding alone doesn't create a beautiful garden. You have to plant flowers, too.

CONFETTI AND RAINBOWS

This begs the question: What flowers should you plant? If you look around and find your surroundings feel more spartan than you'd like, where do you start? To answer this question, I began to assemble a pantheon of muses, women (and a few men) who embody the uninhibited joy of the abundance aesthetic. There was Iris Apfel, the white-haired style icon whose personal motto is "More is more and less is a bore." Apfel often layers three different patterns in an outfit, loves embroidery and fringe, and stacks colorful bangles up to seven deep on each arm. Well into her nineties, she is a spokesperson for more brands than I can count, from Kate Spade to Happy Socks to Macy's. But more important, she always seems to be having a ball. Sir Paul Smith, the British designer whose signature colorful stripes cover everything from bathrobes to bicycle seats, was another muse. An avid collector, Smith is so fond of the curiosities he gathers in his travels that he has turned his basement into a space he calls the Department of Silly. In Tokyo, I found Emmanuelle Moureaux, a French architect who creates tasteful yet exuberant spaces with as many as a hundred different colors. And in Brooklyn, there was Tina Roth Eisenberg, founder of the whimsical temporary tattoo company Tattly, who could tell me with a completely straight face that she believes deeply in the power of confetti.

Tina and I were friends for several years before I discovered that her office actually has an entire drawer that is always full of confetti. Naturally, I insisted on seeing it, and so one morning I stopped by Tina's office, where she greeted me with croissants and gave me a peek inside the world's most joyful storage cabinet. Since the beginning of Tattly, Tina has always wanted the company's packages to elicit the same joy as a piece of mail sent by a good friend. Rather than use an impersonal bar code from a postage meter, Tina and her team stood in line at the post office to purchase thousands of stamps in a range of denominations, sometimes using a dozen stamps on one package if that's what it took. Eventually, the need to be able to track packages meant they had to switch to a more practical form of postage. So they designed a fun-looking mailer and started offering the option to include confetti with the packages. "Confetti just makes everything better," she said.

When Tina opened the confetti drawer, I could not resist the urge to reach in and swish my hands around. As I did, I found a roll of red stickers that read: WARNING! CONFETTI INSIDE! Tina explained, laughing, "We realized we have to be respectful. If you're going to send confetti, you better put a warning sticker on the package so that people know it's coming." One day, when the confetti ran out unexpectedly due to a lost shipment, Tina's team ran interference to try to keep her from noticing. Fortunately she keeps an emergency confetti jar on her desk, in case of impromptu celebrations. Tattly also welcomes new employees with a pile of confetti arranged in the shape of a heart on their desks. It may sound silly, but the sprinkling of confetti carries a deeper significance. "I think businesses are way too serious," said Tina. "People need to have more fun at work, man."

What Tina's confetti drawer made me realize is that the

abundance aesthetic can have a huge impact, even in small doses. A woman can be wearing all black, but a polka-dot scarf makes her look like an ambassador of joy. A striped awning over a restaurant can cheer up an entire street. You can use the abundance aesthetic wherever you want to add a burst of joy but might not be in charge of the lighting and the wall colors, like your office. A striped desk lamp or a multicolor throw draped over a chair can have a disproportionate influence on the feel of a space. This also works for small spaces that you want to make feel unexpectedly delightful: a half bathroom, a care package, the inside of a lunch box.

It took me a little while to understand why confetti, polka dots, and stripes have such an outsize effect. The reason is deceptively simple: small things repeated many times create a burst of joy much bigger than each individual piece could. Think about it this way: Each confetto (yes, that's the singular of "confetti") is just a speck of paper. If you saw one on your shoe, you'd probably pick it off without another thought. But multiply that confetto a thousand times and you have a handful of one of the most potent joymakers in the world, a pocket-sized jubilee. Glitter, sprinkles, a strand of Christmas lights: all derive their joyful power from this simple act of repetition. Even functional objects when brought together can have a delightful resonance. One of the most joyful stores in New York is the diminutive CW Pencil Enterprise, whose walls are lined with hundreds of different kinds of pencils from all over the world. Designer Paul Smith also uses this technique in his stores and shows. For a recent exhibit, Smith created a touchable wall of seventy thousand colorful buttons!

Adding a bit of variety amps the sense of abundance even further. Recall the candy store: M&M's, Skittles, Mike and Ikes, and jelly beans are all made more delightful by their diverse flavors and colors.

Variety in shape or proportion can be joyful: think of a strand of hand-made beads, each one slightly different. But maximum impact comes from having an abundance of different hues, preferably all of them at once. Rainbows are so intensely joyful, just a faint, thin band of one can transform the sky, stopping a crowd of people in their tracks. A rainbow is the perfect fusion of energy and abundance aesthetics, a plethora of photons zinging around together. It's hard to think of anything that can't be made more joyful by a rush of rainbow color. I color-code my books by rainbow because it makes them feel like one big joyful art installation. Rainbows have recently been making their way into all kinds of foods, from bagels to pancakes. But perhaps the best polychromatic food trend is the rainbow bowl, which arranges a spectrum of veggies like carrots, beets, radishes, squash, and cabbage in a kind of color wheel, creating a healthy dish that looks as joyful as a box of candy.

I love rainbow color for its ability to bring joy just about anywhere, even places we don't expect to be joyful. On an unassuming corner in the northwest of Tokyo sits a building that looks like a modern, multi-colored layer cake, with the layers stacked just off-kilter, so that you can see the sherbet-hued surfaces underneath. When I saw it in a picture, I thought it was the most joyful building I'd ever seen. I wondered if it might be the headquarters for a paint company or perhaps a toy manu-facturer. But no, this colorful confection is home to a bank.

Even the bank's customers were surprised by it at first. I stopped in and struck up a conversation with a gray-haired man seated in a raspberry-colored chair. He told me that when the branch first opened, he and his neighbors were confused. "What is it? It doesn't look like a bank," he said. But he smiled and said it made him feel cheerful, a word echoed by the loan officers and bank administrators I met. What

I found most interesting was the way that everyone seemed so relaxed. There was no toe-tapping, crossed-arms impatience here. Four or five people were perched in chairs of different colors, reading quietly. The ambience was more like that of an independent bookshop than a financial institution.

The bank, one of four colorful branches of the Sugamo Shinkin Bank, is the brainchild of Emmanuelle Moureaux, the French architect living in Tokyo who is completely enamored with color. Over tea in her multihued office, Moureaux told me that she was charged with making the bank a place people wanted to linger in a moment longer. I was struck by this, because given the assignment, most people would have immediately thought of practical amenities: free coffee, Wi-Fi, a TV blaring cable news. What Moureaux sees, that so few other architects do, is that rainbow color has a seemingly magnetic power that draws people in. In this sense, the abundance aesthetic seems almost generous, like a form of hospitality. Most bank branches I've visited are so crammed with branding that they feel like walk-in billboards. But the Sugamo Shinkin bank branches don't even have a sign out front. They use the colors as their calling card.

Rainbows bring a sense of exuberant fullness to any situation, even (perhaps especially) difficult ones. The rainbow flag that symbolizes the Gay Pride movement unites diverse crusaders under a banner of joyful activism. In photos, LGBTQ rallies always look like festivals rather than protests. The expansive nature of the rainbow both welcomes outsiders and dispels bigotry, fostering the growth of the movement.

Filmy and weightless, rainbows sometimes seem trivial, but I've seen them touch people in deep ways. A few years ago I received an email from another muse, a reader who had recently lost her infant son in a tragic incident, with a story of just such a rainbow. When she was planning the baby's funeral, she requested a plain white coffin be delivered to her home so she could decorate it. She and her children spent the day before the funeral painting the coffin in rainbow colors, and that night she stayed up late painting a rainbow chrysanthemum design over the top. Something about the colors inspired her to keep going, she said, despite the grief and loss that had engulfed her family.

While many cultures typically view black as the color of mourning, some prefer to celebrate the lives of deceased loved ones with color. In Guatemalan towns such as Chichicastenango, family members paint graves with their loved ones' favorite colors, refreshing them each year as a way to honor the departed. The result is a rainbow cemetery that feels like a vibrant city and a place to celebrate life, rather than a monument to death.

Rainbows are indefatigable soldiers for the cause of joy, ones that can puncture deep despair. They swell into the empty spaces in our lives—blighted downtowns, oppressed communities, or hearts ravaged by loss—and send up a signal flag of hope.

MAXIMALIST MAXIMS

The muses I had studied showed me the power of the abundance aesthetic: how pops of pattern, texture, and rainbow color could have enormous emotional impact. But I was still left with a question: What happens when abundance goes big?

To answer that, I turned to one final muse: America's first interior decorator, Dorothy Draper. Draper was an unbridled maximalist, and she quickly established a signature style defined by bold gestures, graphic patterns, and fields of bright color—usually all at the same time. Her style has been described as modern baroque, which is amusing if you think about the fact that there's little that modernists opposed so deeply as baroque. Draper died in 1969, but her most famous project, the Greenbrier resort in West Virginia, is still maintained in her blissfully over-the-top fashion. The Greenbrier was founded more than two hundred years ago as a place for people to "take the waters" from the nearby White Sulphur Springs, though now it feels like a grown-up summer camp, with activities ranging from golf to croquet to archery. During World War II it was pressed into service as a military hospital, leaving it in shambles by 1946, when Draper was hired to redo the interior. She spent sixteen months designing everything from the lighting fixtures to the china to the housekeepers' uniforms.

It takes eleven hours to get to White Sulphur Springs from New York by train, and I was a little bleary eyed when I saw the small green van waiting in front of the station. I got on, not realizing that the hotel was just across the street, and I felt a bit ridiculous when we pulled up not a minute later. I stepped out from under the portico. The van looked like a toy in front of the Greenbrier's massive Federal-style building. The façade was clean and white as chalk. I pulled open the French doors into the lobby, and *pow!* I was in another world. It was like opening the lid of a cool grandma's jewelry box, each compartment holding a piece more colorful and intricate than the last. In the center room, the walls were forest green and aqua, with enormous arches cut in all directions. To the sides, the arches perfectly framed a pair of circular windows set into rose-colored walls. The carpet was a green tiger-stripe print, and the chandelier, which resembled an oversize birdcage, cast a starburst of light on the ceiling. Green awning stripes lined the stair-cases, following the curved ceilings up and over. The theme of Draper's redesign was "Romance and Rhododendrons," but it has more aptly been described as "Scarlett O'Hara–drops–acid." I got a second wind, as if by osmosis, and I was ready for cocktail hour.

I took my glass and wandered the high-ceilinged rooms that fanned out from the upper lobby. The Trellis Room had walls the color of mint-chip ice cream and a carpet full of pink clusters of flowers. I counted at least seven different patterns: florals of varying sizes, sea-shells, and a soft plaid. In the Victorian Writing Room, I fell in love with a wingback chair upholstered in one of Draper's favorite fabrics, Fudge Apron. It brimmed with red roses and yellow lilies. Sitting in it felt a little like riding a float in a flower parade. The same copious blooms were strewn across an array of other chairs and ottomans and the billowing drapes. It was lovely but dizzying, and I felt breathless trying to take it all in. But when I slowed down, the giddy fizz sub-sided, and the depth of the design revealed itself. Draper was essen-tially a master of layering. Instead of starting with a neutral canvas, she laid a high-contrast foundation: checkerboard floors, wide stripes, and rowdy color combinations, like flamingo pink with kelly green or cherry red with powder blue. Then she layered on patterns—cabbage roses and tropical leaves—at least two or three per room. On top of those were countless small details: trims and trellises, sconces and clocks, mantels and moldings that make the eye dance and skitter around the room. Everything in Draper's world had layers of texture. She used printed mats around pictures instead of plain ones. She dis-played magazines under the glass surface of a coffee table. Curtains were tied back with tassels. Lampshades had fringes and pleats. All together it felt opulent, whimsical, unrestrained: the grown-up version of the candy store.

Draper could not be more different from Arakawa and Gins, but I sensed a shared belief in the power of abundance to buoy the spirits and rejuvenate the body. In the Delnor Hospital she designed in Saint Charles, Illinois, Draper used her trademark flowered chintz paired with a washable pine-patterned wallpaper to create a facility that felt anything but clinical. "What is being done to create for the patient surroundings that make him want to live, that restore to him the old fight to regain his health?" she asked, echoing Florence Nightingale. In Naples, Florida, she designed another hospital, painted cerulean blue

with pink oleander planted around the outside. The rooms featured sky-blue ceilings and green-striped floors, and Draper managed to get the standard-issue hospital furniture to be produced in coral instead of regulation beige.

That Draper's designs feel joyful is no accident. She went through a bout of depression when her husband left her for a younger woman, the same week as the Wall Street crash of 1929. A therapist sent her to a lecture by Norman Vincent Peale, the minister who would go on to write *The Power of Positive Thinking*. She came away convinced of the connection between décor and emotions, proclaiming, "The Drab Age is over.... Now we know that lovely, clear colors have a vital effect on our mental happiness. Modern doctors and psychiatrists are convinced of this!"

But though her designs look lavish, she never viewed money as a prerequisite. In her *Good Housekeeping* column and her book *Decorating Is Fun! How to Be Your Own Decorator*, Draper offered accessible tips for creating sumptuous interiors on budgets pinched by the Great Depression. For those who couldn't afford fancy rugs, Draper suggested painting floors with a plaid pattern or big polka dots that "look like merry balloons." She consoled women stuck with mismatched, hand-me-down furniture, suggesting it was gauche to be too matchy-matchy and advising they cover the disparate pieces with white paint or printed chintz. If flowers were too expensive, a big vase full of foliage—laurel or pine—could substitute nicely. Or for those who wanted new curtains, why not make a patchwork fabric out of old clothes around the house? Draper's interiors always had a palace vibe, even in the most humble settings. Her advice consistently served to increase the sense of texture in the home while also reminding homemakers that the goal was joy, not perfection.

Draper urged women to think of their homes as places of delight and fantasy. She advocated for ignoring popular opinion and for feeling, rather than thinking, your way through the process of creating a home. When I look at the Greenbrier, I wonder how many of us keep the reins a little short on our desires, how much we second-guess and censor ourselves. I think about a ruffled dress that I tried on a few weeks ago and put back, hearing an anonymous voice in my head jeer, "It's so gaudy." I wonder how much joy that voice has sucked out of my life over the years.

Minimalism often tries to claim a moral high ground, dismissing aesthetics of abundance as wanton excess. "Freedom from ornament is a sign of spiritual strength," declared Austrian architect Adolf Loos in a 1910 lecture whose title, "Ornament and Crime," speaks for itself. Just like the modernist rejection of color, this drive for purity was billed as a route to a more enlightened civilization, but underneath it lay a barely concealed ethnic and racial prejudice. Loos heaped disdain on peoples he considered unsophisticated—"the Kaffir, the Persian, the Slovak peasant woman"—who couldn't help but indulge in decoration in their homes and dress. Traditional crafts like embroidery, crochet, and weaving, rich with intricate patterns (and often, though not always, practiced by women), were dismissed as inferior arts. Dorothy Draper found herself the subject of similar criticism: the architect Frank Lloyd Wright called her an "inferior desecrator," which, while punny, betrays the almost religious disdain modernists had for abundance, as if it connoted impurity. This tangle between aesthetics and values recurs again and again throughout history, creating situations where our aesthetic choices purport to be a window into our inner virtues. It persists today. In a world overwhelmed by cheap and available stuff, choosing simple, unadorned goods has become a badge of righteousness, like being thin or having good hygiene. Many of us carry the baggage of this equation, unconsciously fearing that our love of pattern, texture, and lushness will reveal us to be self-indulgent hedonists.

But in the longer arc of evolutionary history, displays of abundance often signify health and vitality. The fan of glittering medallions that the peacock wears on its backside is completely unnecessary to its owner's survival, but it tells the peahen with vibrant clarity that she's found a flourishing mate. Male bowerbirds create elaborate dens lined with flowers, leaves, shells, and even discarded pieces of plastic in order to demonstrate their fitness to prospective partners. Minimalists tout the idea that nature builds with perfect thrift, when in fact the evidence of her extravagance is everywhere. In what economical world does a fruit fly perform dances or a moose carry a coat rack on its head? Spectacles that require a substantial investment of energy—colorful patterns or exuberant movements—demonstrate that an organism is vigorous enough to afford such a lavish expenditure. Evolutionary theorist Denis Dutton believed that a similar logic applies to all human art forms, from painting to music to the folk patterning so despised by Adolf Loos. Labor-intensive artwork, produced beautifully and abundantly, is like a handmade peacock's tail. It says that you possess such copious energy and verve that you have plenty left over to devote to the joy of pure embellishment.

It turns out that the word "gaudy" has roots in the Latin *gaudere,* "to rejoice" or "delight" in something, which happens to be the same root that gave us the word "joy." Choosing abundance is not a moral failing. It's an expression of deep, human delight. It's an acknowledgment that we are here to do more than eke out an existence between birth and death and chores. We are here, as Diane Ackerman writes, to live not just the length of our lives, but the width of them as well. We are here to see rainbows and paint them, to be tickled and enthralled, to eat a second cupcake if we choose. And, occasionally, to feel the truth of Mae West's famous aphorism, that "too much of a good thing can be wonderful."

3.

FREEDOM

I was eight years old when one summer morning I packed a backpack with my windbreaker, some snacks from the pantry, and a guidebook to North American trees and told my father not to set a place for me at dinner: I was running away to live in the woods. My adventure was inspired by the classic coming-of-age story *My Side of the Mountain*, in which a boy named Sam Gribley eschews the comforts of home to make a life in a hollowed-out hemlock tree in the forest. Sam's boreal lifestyle isn't easy: he grinds acorns to make flour for pancakes, traps deer and tans the hides to make his clothing, and catches a falcon that he names Frightful and trains to hunt for food. But what he sacrifices in ease, he gets back in delight. He takes baths in a cold spring surrounded by frogs and wood thrushes. He befriends a hiker who teaches him to carve willow whistles. At night, holed up in his cozy tree home, he writes on birch bark by the light of a candle he's poured into a turtle shell.

Unlike Sam, I couldn't hack it in the woods, and I was home by dinnertime. But though my attempt to live off the land lasted only a few hours, that brief adventure was thrilling. I mucked around in a triangle of boggy ground at the end of the road, peering into jack-in-the-pulpits and digging up cattail roots with a stick. I ate wild strawberries plucked from the edge of the yard. I picked an armful of daylilies and chicory to decorate the lean-to I never quite got around to building. And when I bounded through the back door just before sunset, it was with a thick coat of mud on my Tretorns and a smile on my face.

Since then, I've often wondered: What was it about that romp through the suburban wilderness that made it so delightful?

In a moment of joy, we say we are carefree, freewheeling, footloose and fancy-free. Some of the most joyful moments in life are the ones in which we gain a kind of freedom. Think of the ecstatic opening of the school doors on the last day before summer break or the buzz in the office when the clock strikes five on a Friday. Joy thrives on the alleviation of constraints. The delicious stretch you feel in your legs on stepping out of the car at a rest stop after many hours of driving is a joyful freedom. So is sleeping under the stars, riding in a convertible, and skinny-dipping, feeling cool water against bare skin.

A love of freedom begins to assert itself early. Toddlers are unflagging campaigners for their own liberty and don't hesitate to launch a category 5 tantrum against an oppressive car seat or the tyranny of mittens. Joy has a dynamism that doesn't like to be squished in or pent up. We fight so hard for freedom because it enables us to pursue joy—as well as everything else that matters in life. For our ancestors, having room to roam meant a greater likelihood of discovering sources of sustenance, favorable habitats, and potential mates. This is why incarceration is a punishment second only in severity to death and, in more prosaic terms, why the middle seat on an airplane inspires such universal dread.

We have a visceral awareness of how free we feel as we move through the world, even though freedom, like energy, is not something we can see, taste, or touch. How do our senses know when we're free? It seems to run along a continuum, one that we define in relative terms. The playground is freer than the classroom, the picnic freer than the formal banquet. But at each end of the spectrum there are absolutes. On one end lie places we all agree are restrictive, like the tunnel of an MRI machine or a solitary-confinement cell. On the other are places that feel entirely unconstrained—fields and lakes, parks and beaches. As I thought about it, I realized that the most liberating places are, with few exceptions, found in nature.

I was reminded of this last summer, when Albert and I visited friends who live adjacent to a nature preserve along the seashore in New England. One day before sunset we all started down the mowed path, between bayberry bushes and tall grasses, into the meadow. The four adults strolled, breathing in the green aroma mixed with faint traces of salt from the nearby beach. The boys—Henry, six, and Charlie, almost three—ran ahead shouting and giggling. They hid their small bodies around a bend or behind a dense shrub, jumping out to surprise us. They ran forward and back, waving sticks they found, coaxing us into races that we could not resist. I had been working long hours in the weeks leading up to that trip, squinting into my laptop early and late. But in that meadow I felt my body expand and my mind release, like a clenched fist unfurling.

Of course, the fact that nature sets us free isn't by itself much of a revelation. Far more interesting, though, is what I learned when I began to try to understand exactly why natural settings have such power to liberate our bodies and minds.

THE IDEAL LANDSCAPE

In 1993, a pair of dissident Russian artists named Vitaly Komar and Alexander Melamid began an unusual project. Curious about the diverse artistic tastes of people around the world, they commissioned a ten-country survey about the kind of art people liked to look at, delving into specific details like favorite colors, styles, and subject matter. When it was all done, they created a *Most Wanted* painting for each country, a visual summary of the responses. The resulting paintings are not very good, and the art world mostly treated the project as a kind of high-concept joke. But they are striking in a way that has nothing to do with their quality as artworks. From China to Turkey to Iceland to Kenya, they all depict landscapes. In fact, they all depict *the same landscape*. With few exceptions, the *Most Wanted* paintings show pleasant outdoor scenes centered on grassy areas with scattered copses of trees and plenty of blue sky. There are moderate hills and bodies of water, along with a few animals and people.

Some critics attribute Komar and Melamid's peculiar results to a broad familiarity with such grassy landscapes. They point to the fact that the same scenery visible in the *Most Wanted* artworks is common in American and European landscape paintings, from the Hudson River School to the Dutch Golden Age, and that such imagery is reproduced on cheap posters and wall calendars that hang in homes the world over. Perhaps the universal affection for the meadow-like landscape in the *Most Wanted* paintings is the result of a kind of aesthetic imperialism,

wherein a preference for landscapes native to the West has taken ov
the world, much like a taste for Big Macs or Coca-Cola.

But for a group of evolutionary theorists, the startling consistency
of the *Most Wanted* paintings has a different significance. Not only is
this type of landscape common in artwork, they point out, but it also
appears in real-life contexts, from the celebrated English gardens created by Lancelot "Capability" Brown to the urban parks designed by
Frederick Law Olmsted, such as Central Park and Prospect Park in
New York City. People often go to great lengths to transform a piece of
terrain into one of these landscapes. For example, to create their
beloved parks, Brown and Olmsted cleared trees, planted grasses, dug
ponds, and sculpted earth. In Central Park alone, Olmsted oversaw the
movement of 2.5 million cubic yards of rock, soil, and clay. These landscapes aren't exactly native. Instead, they bear a striking resemblance
to another part of the world, one that most of the designers and artists
creating them had never visited: the African savanna.

Much of East Africa is covered in savanna, an ecosystem consisting of rolling grasslands punctuated by clusters of trees. While there's
some debate among paleontologists about just how much of hominid
evolution took place on the savanna, there's little doubt that it was a
significant habitat for early humans. The savanna had distinct advantages for our hunter-gatherer ancestors, with more food sources close
to the ground than in the forests, where food is primarily found high in
the tree canopy, as well as more protein per square mile than any other
habitat on earth. It also had appealing structural features. The open
grasslands and rolling hills provided long-distance views of both predators and prey, while the well-spaced trees and shrubs offered protec-
tion from the sun and a quick escape from danger. British geographer
Jay Appleton first noticed this appealing combination of features,

"prospect and refuge" to describe our attraction to ... both broad vistas (prospect) and accessible shelter ... vironments we find an ideal balance between safety and freedom.

Some evolutionary theorists suspect that over time a predilection for these features became etched in our DNA, creating a kind of internal Eden that we unconsciously seek out and even re-create wherever we go. In support of this hypothesis, research shows that people across cultures have an affinity for savanna-like landscape characteristics, such as deep sight lines, a view of the horizon, and a lack of understory vegetation that blocks movement and visibility. Studies by biologist Gordon Orians and environmental psychologist Judith Heerwagen also reveal a cross-cultural preference for trees that look like the acacias that flourish on a healthy savanna, with spreading, umbrellalike canopies and trunks that fork near the ground. Some cultures even prune their native trees into this shape.

Prospect-refuge theory originated to describe the way we relate to nature, but it can also be applied to the built environment. For example, picture windows that overlook beautiful scenery can make even a shoebox apartment feel like a castle, and most people will pay more for the luxury of a house or a hotel room with a great view. This is particularly true of water views, which we covet even if we have no intention of swimming or setting sail. Courtyards and balconies also open up a space, blurring the boundaries between inside and outside.

These views are more than just decorative. In a well-known study from the 1980s, patients recovering from gall bladder surgery left the hospital sooner and needed less pain medication when the windows in their rooms looked out on a group of trees than when they faced a brick wall. And while teachers sometimes worry that windows in a classroom will be distracting to schoolchildren, it turns out that nature views actually improve students' attention while also decreasing stress. Views of natural settings let the eyes rest and refocus between periods of staring at screens or work materials and have what researchers call a "micro-restorative effect" on our minds, relieving fatigue and refreshing our ability to concentrate. Not surprisingly, studies show that employees who sit near a window report better overall health and job satisfaction. Perhaps this is why companies like Apple, Kickstarter, and Amazon are prioritizing green views in the design of their new workspaces. Though at many offices, windows are a perk reserved for senior management, these companies recognize the importance of making expansive views accessible to all.

But if the view outside your window is less than liberating, prospect and refuge can also be achieved by opening up the interior of a space. In a home, taking down nonstructural walls can expand the sight lines and create an airy feel. Or, if that's not possible, you can create more openness by decreasing the volume of furniture in a room, either by trading in an overstuffed sofa or a giant chest of drawers for a smaller version, or getting rid of unnecessary pieces entirely. Scaling down furniture can create more *negative space*, a term used by designers to describe the space in a room that isn't filled up with objects.

A side effect of having more open space is that it allows greater freedom of movement, something biomechanist Katy Bowman discovered a few years ago when she was moving to a new home. As she and her husband waited for their furniture to be delivered, they had to sit on the floor. Bowman noticed that this prompted them to move around more, and they decided to get rid of their couch entirely. A couple of years later, they had a toddler and noticed how difficult it was to get him to sit at the table, requiring a booster seat and a set of restraints to keep him there. They ditched the chairs and lowered the table so they could all sit together on the floor.

Responding to critics who have called her furniture-free home "freaky," Bowman writes, "It's pretty straightforward, actually. I have a small house. I have two small children. I study the health benefits of movement. If I put furniture there, not only will they sit on it, they can't move in the space occupied by my couch (or TV or coffee table or whatever)." Getting rid of furniture allowed Bowman to install a set of monkey bars inside her house, which enables a range of joyful family activities. "It's not rare to see us practicing some exercise while the kids are doing jump-rolls and somersaults, all in the living room at the same time," she says. If indoor monkey bars seem a bit too wild, perhaps a swing might be a better choice of furniture to import from the playground. It probably won't surprise you to learn that Tina Roth Eisenberg, the founder of Tattly and unabashed lover of confetti, has a swing hanging in the middle of her office. The swing gives employees a fun way to change perspective during the workday and opens up the space in a delightful way.

BIOPHILIA

Toward the end of the movie *Pretty Woman*, there's a brief, joyous scene in which corporate raider Edward Lewis (played by Richard Gere) escapes a business meeting to roll up his pant legs and walk around barefoot in the small square of grass across the street. He smiles softly to himself as he stomps around, as if remembering a long-buried impulse. While wide-open spaces give us room to run free, small patches of nature can sometimes be just as liberating. Scattered throughout the man-made environment are countless backyards, community gardens, medians, and so called pocket parks. Some are barely big enough to turn around in, yet they provide a joyful sense of release.

Curious about the power of these modest green spaces, I turned to James Corner, the lead designer of the High Line, a thin ribbon of verdure planted atop an old elevated rail line on Manhattan's west side. He has been described as a modern-day successor to Frederick Law Olmsted and a rock star in the booming field of landscape architecture. If anyone knew how nature could create joy in tight quarters, it would be him.

I met Corner at his office late on a Monday afternoon. He had a serious demeanor and a deep furrow in his brow, but his face lightened when we began talking about joy. For him, the delight of a landscape is less about what we see and more about what we feel. "It's a whole host of things that will never show up in a photograph," he said, and then began to describe them in a meditative stream almost like a piece of verse. "Plants. Scent. Color. The effects of light and shadow. Water. The sounds of water. Ambient humidity. Texture. Temperature. The effects of mist. The concentration of weather effects and atmospheres...." He trailed off. "These things are not obvious, but they're very powerful. And they bring joy."

As he spoke, my mind drifted back an hour, to my stroll along the High Line on the way to his office. The memory swelled with the sensations he described. It was a sweltering summer day, and I had stopped for a while with my notebook in a grove of three-leafed maples. It was a few degrees cooler in the shade, and the breeze was fuller.

Children splashed in a shallow puddle, a water feature that bubbled up over the pavement. Tussocks of grasses swished back and forth, never still even in the midafternoon heat. Their vegetal scent came in waves, interspersed with the urban aroma of sunlight on cement. On the lawn farther north, people sat in clusters, bare shouldered and barefoot. I stepped off the pavement and walked in the damp grass. As I stepped back onto the concrete walkway, a wall of heat closed around me.

I hadn't been conscious of these sensations at the time, but listening to Corner speak, I realized how deeply I had felt them. It reminded me of Arakawa and his claim that we have thousands of unnamed senses. Corner had just identified a few new ones for me, and in so doing, he'd revealed a far-more-intimate lens on freedom, one that was not about distant horizons but about minute sensations. Suddenly I understood why we feel free even in a tiny garden or greenhouse. Indoors, the thick, insulated walls and HVAC systems remove the gentle fluctuations of temperature, scent, air, and humidity that make being outdoors such a delight. Being in nature liberates our senses.

A love of wild sensations like these is a critical part of what biologist E. O. Wilson calls *biophilia*, the innate attraction humans have toward other living things. Wilson contends that it was adaptive for early humans to take an interest in other organisms, which were more likely than inanimate objects to present opportunities for or threats to their survival. Over time, this evolved from a practical interest into a pleasurable one. In 2015, 305 million people visited US national parks, and Wilson points out that more people visit zoos each year than professional sporting events. Sixty-eight percent of American households have one or more pets. According to Wilson, these experiences with plants and animals are an essential part of our well-being.

A growing body of research supports his claim. Access to nature has been shown to improve sleep quality, decrease blood pressure, and even lengthen lifespan. Large-scale studies conducted in the United States, Britain, and the Netherlands show that people living in greener areas have a lower incidence of anxiety and depression and display an ability to recover more quickly from stressful life events than those in less green areas. One possible reason is that spending time in nature decreases blood flow to a part of the brain called the subgenual prefrontal cortex, which is associated with the tendency to brood over problems. Natural settings literally make us more carefree.

I thought back to my walk on the High Line and all of those sensations I hadn't noticed until James Corner pointed them out to me. My first thought had been to judge myself: Am I so mindless and distracted that I'm missing out on the richness of my surroundings? But while mindfulness doesn't hurt, nature reaches us even when we're focused on something else. "It's a bit like music in that way," Corner said. "Even when you're not really paying attention to it, there's still a powerful aesthetic reception." Corner and his collaborators worked to dissolve the boundaries between the natural and man-made elements of the High Line so that contact with nature would be inevitable. This can be seen in one of its most basic design features: the concrete pavers that make up the walkway. Corner's team designed the pavers so that they taper at the ends like the teeth of a comb, creating spaces where the plantings mingle with the paths. This simple design allows for immersive encounters that happen almost in the background: while passing through on your commute, reading a book under a tree, or having a picnic with friends.

If nature makes us feel so healthy and free, in such an effortless way, why don't we have more of it in our lives? I found some insight in the essays of the landscape theorist J. B. Jackson, who observes that we have long been uneasy about our membership in the animal kingdom, preferring to focus on the traits that distinguish us from other species. The built environment mirrors this anxiety, carving out ample space for our cultural aspirations while ignoring our biological needs. In Jackson's view, our cities are designed to make us feel separate from nature, when in fact we are a part of nature. For most of human evolution—eighty thousand generations—nature was not a place we went but a place we lived. A mere six hundred generations have passed since the beginning of agriculture gave rise to permanent shelters and communities, and only about twelve generations since the birth of the modern city, with its hard surfaces and mechanized sounds. From an evolutionary perspective, our current habitat is still an early stage experiment.

Now that more than half of the world's population lives in cities, the need to restore access to nature feels increasingly urgent, and nowhere is this clearer than in the design of low-income housing. While it would be naïve to think that environment by itself can remedy the massive, systemic challenges facing poor urban communities, an emerging field of research suggests that small patches of nature could have outsize effects on quality of life. Frances Kuo and William Sullivan, the founders of the Landscape and Human Health Lab at the University of Illinois, have found significant correlations between a lack of green space and violence among residents in large housing projects in Chicago. In a notable study, they examined police crime reports for ninety-eight buildings in the Ida B. Wells housing project, finding that buildings with more surrounding vegetation had 50 percent fewer crimes than those with minimal greenery.

A similar effect has been observed in prisons, where inmates displayed fewer aggressive tendencies after watching nature videos, resulting in a 26 percent reduction in violent incidents. And in another study, exposure to gardens mitigated the frequency of hostile outbursts among Alzheimer's patients that often take place as the disease progresses. One reason that natural stimuli are effective at reducing violence is that they evoke a response that is simultaneously joyful and calming ("emotionally positive" and "low arousing" in psychologists' terms). But it also strikes me that there may be another effect at play, one that hasn't yet been explored through research. Poverty, imprisonment, and residence in a nursing home are confining conditions, each with its own set of visible and invisible boundaries. In nature, we find a temporary freedom from these constraints. In nature, anyone can have a full and free experience of the world.

URBAN JUNGLE

Summer Rayne Oakes came to the door in overalls with a rust-feathered chicken perched on her shoulder. "I'm fostering her," she said in an offhand way, before leading me up the stairs to her Williamsburg loft, a verdant hideaway containing more than six hundred plants.

On that hot summer afternoon, the apartment was a relief, cool and fresh. Light streamed in through big windows and bounced off the kitchen walls, which were painted the bright sap green of new leaves. I could see why plants would be happy here, and so they seemed: climbing up trellises and columns, spilling out of pots hung from the ceiling, and sprouting out of old tea tins. There were herbs on the kitchen counters and succulents along the windowsills. In the study, a fiddle-leaf fig tree that had been just a few feet high when Oakes acquired it now reached the ceiling, its branching canopy spreading over most of the room.

"I was always that kid with dirt under her fingernails," she said when we sat down. The chicken sat in her lap making a soft chirping noise. Oakes fell in love with environmental science in college, and though her career has wandered through various fields, her passion for the environment has remained a constant thread. When she became a model, she focused on raising the profile of eco-friendly fashion and beauty, authoring a book on the subject. One of her ventures, a business-to-business marketplace called Le Souk, connects suppliers of sustainable textiles directly with designers. Oakes believes that the most impactful way to live sustainably is to look at the small things we do every day. "Change those things and you have a different life."

Hence, her green apartment. At first, she was just looking for a way to make her place feel homey after a long-term roommate moved out. She started by opening up the space, getting rid of the TV and coffee table. (Katy Bowman, the biomechanist, would approve.) Instead of a sofa, she has a hammock on one side of the living room. Then she began to bring in plants. She had always dreamed of a green wall, so her first major project was a vertical garden that she built along one side of her bedroom, filled with lush ferns, calatheas, and trailing philodendrons. The environmental scientist in her found joy in discovering new species and propagating her plants, and as her collection began to outgrow the green wall, it gave her an excuse to work on DIY projects with her dad. Together they've built several installations, including a rack of Mason-jar planters mounted on planks of reclaimed wood above the dining table and a swing garden in the kitchen consisting of shelves that hang on ropes from the ceiling. "They are like art pieces that are fully integrated into the home," Oakes said. "But unlike a regular art piece, they actually live and grow."

Oakes said that her plant-filled home feels like an oasis in her

"The plants seriously do root me."

hectic life. "I wake up and I don't feel stressed or anxious. My apartment makes me feel comfortable and stimulated at the same time," she said. "I love sleeping under the trees. Feeling like you're under the canopy is quite calming." She has noticed a sense of uprootedness in the city that comes from people moving around frequently, and she thinks that plants help to counteract this feeling. "When you have a lot of plants in your life, you begin to understand your surroundings in a different way," she said. "You become a little bit more attuned to the sun shining, or the sunset, or the way the light comes through the leaves. The plants seriously do root me. I feel rooted here, even though I don't own this apartment."

While rootedness sounds like the opposite of freedom, after hearing Oakes talk, I realized the two are intimately related. Feeling stable at home has made her feel free to take risks in her professional life she might not otherwise have embraced. By creating a subtle sense of security, the plants have fueled her liberation.

At last count, Oakes had 670 plants in her apartment, and her collection is still growing. Caring for the plants takes her about a half hour each morning and most of the day on Sunday, and while this sounds like a lot of work, for Oakes it resembles a mindfulness practice. She hosts regular group meditations in her apartment, as well as workshops on plant care, and she said that she believes a tide of biophilia is rising in popular culture that is prompting people to get more curious about houseplants. She hopes that giving people exposure to her unique apartment will help to normalize having a home rich in plant life. "See," she imagines people saying, "I'm not the crazy plant lady. She is!"

* * *

After my visit to Oakes's urban jungle, the small collection of plants in my apartment seemed meager by comparison. The good news, though, is that even small doses of nature can have significant effects. Just adding a few plants to a windowless room has been shown to decrease research subjects' blood pressure, improve their attention and productivity, and prompt more generous behavior toward others. Studies have also found that exposure to indoor plants and even just the color green can help free the mind, increasing creativity.

Though I had read the research, up until recently I had no plants in my apartment at all. I was simply too afraid I wouldn't be able to care for them. I grew up surrounded by houseplants, but the nomadic lifestyle I led in my twenties wasn't conducive to a flourishing indoor garden. (After all, the only thing worse than no plants is dead ones.) But now I was married and a homeowner. I no longer had an excuse. The first plants Albert and I chose were easy-to-grow ferns and succulents. I was shocked by the dramatic influence the plants had on the feel of the space. In the summer, their colors and textures seemed to pull in the greenery from the park outside the windows. In the winter, they substituted for the lack of color outside, making the apartment feel like a vibrant retreat. For people new to plants, Oakes offers a piece of advice I wish I'd known when I was starting out: Get to know your space first. Rather than walking into a store and choosing any plant that catches your eye, figure out which direction your windows face and whether you have mostly direct or indirect sunlight. Then pick a plant that will be happy in those conditions.

If the challenge of keeping houseplants feels daunting, you may be able to gain some of the same benefits by incorporating the shapes and textures of nature into your surroundings. Large landscape photographs, leafy wallpapers or fabrics, or paintings of plants and animals can bring the visual qualities of nature into a room. I recently stayed in a hotel that had sprigs of dried lavender in the hallways and videos of jellyfish in the elevators, making these windowless spaces feel far less confining. Oakes complements her plant collection with leaf-printed throw pillows and framed botanical drawings. For a more tactile approach, biomechanist Katy Bowman has a tray of river rocks inset into her entryway so that, when she steps inside, she can feel their textures underfoot.

Another way to bring nature into the home is through sound. Oakes told me that she sometimes plays the sounds of crickets in the background in her apartment, and this reminded me that nature often has a surprisingly boisterous soundtrack. But unlike man-made noise, which can raise levels of stress hormones in our bodies and potentially increase our risk for cardiovascular disease, natural soundscapes have a joyful, relaxing effect. Recordings of natural sounds have been used to calm patients at a children's hospital, ease the stresses of travel at an airport lounge, and relieve pain. Birdsong has even been piped into gas-station restrooms, a move that purportedly raised customer-satisfaction ratings. One possible explanation is that we evolved to rely on ambient sounds, particularly birdsong, as indicators of the safety of our environment. Before a big storm, or in other dangerous moments, birds flee, and the world goes eerily quiet. The noise of business as usual among the animals lets us know we're free to play and explore.

Scent, too, offers a way to connect with nature that is often over-looked. In Japan, an activity called *shinrin-yoku*—literally, "forest bathing"—has been promoted as a public-health initiative by the forestry ministry since 1982. The practice, which involves simply relaxing in the presence of trees (no actual "bathing" required), has been shown in several studies to increase the activity of natural killer (NK) cells, a type of white blood cell critical to immune system functioning, particularly in the body's defense against cancerous and virally infected cells. The researchers attribute part of the forest's immune-boosting influence to a series of chemicals known as *phytoncides,* which are secreted by plants to protect themselves from pests and diseases and are present in some essential oils. In a related test, researchers used a humidifier to infuse hotel rooms with essential oils from the hinoki cypress, a tree common in Japan's forests. Just the presence of phytoncides in the air was enough to decrease stress hormones and raise NK cell activity.

CALL OF THE WILD

Learning about those forest-bathing studies made me wonder: Is there a difference between the feeling we get in the placid world of gardens and houseplants and the one we find in wild nature? Research suggests there is. In a 2005 study, researchers found that while all forms of nature are considered more liberating than the city, wilder places with minimal human influence are most strongly associated with freedom.

Untamed and untempered by civilization, the wilderness gives us a reprieve not only from the hard boundaries and enclosed spaces of the built environment but also from the intangible constraints of modern life. For as much as our cities hem us in, our social and economic realities can be even more restrictive. In 1930, the economist John Maynard Keynes predicted that advances in technology and productivity would allow people in developed nations to work as few as fifteen hours a week. Yet in the United States today, a third of the workforce works on weekends and public holidays, and more than half of us don't even take all our paid vacation time. Children's freedom is similarly circumscribed, by a test-based education system that leaves little time for exploration and a culture of fear that prevents kids from being able to play outside unsupervised. Meanwhile, devices keep us preoccupied with an irresistible stream of pings and flashes, distracting us from meaningful activities and relationships. (A startling measure of our online addiction: one in ten Americans admit to checking their phones even during sex!)

The wilderness frees us from bosses, exams, and emails, connecting us to a more primal, carefree part of our nature often eclipsed by day-to-day concerns. I think of how Thoreau once described his delight at seeing his neighbor's cow break out of her pasture to swim in the nearby river as it surged with the early spring snowmelt. "The seeds of instinct are preserved under the thick hides of cattle and horses," he wrote, "like seeds in the bowels of the earth, an indefinite period." Maybe you have felt this, too, standing where the line of sand meets the foamy surf on a deserted beach, or while on a hike when you suddenly realize you've ventured beyond the noise of automobiles. No matter how domesticated we have become, we all have a wild soul that beats and breathes under layers of clothing and responsibility. The question is, how do we let it out?

This brought to mind an old friend who had recently passed away: the naturalist Jean Craighead George. Jean was the author of more than a hundred books about nature for children, including *My Side of the Mountain*, the book that had inspired my fleeting fantasy of living in the woods. As a child I lived across the street from her, and I often wandered across the dirt road that separated her house from mine to pepper her with questions about pinecones and toads and other things I'd found while poking around in the forest. She was never too busy to identify a nut that had fallen from a tree or admire a bird's nest. "Oh, Ingy, isn't it beautiful?" she'd exclaim, tossing back her head full of close-cropped curls and laughing her big laugh that rang out into the treetops.

Jean's wild stories were inspired by her own wild life. The child of an entomologist, she grew up fishing and camping along the banks of the Potomac, trying to keep up with two older brothers who taught themselves falconry and wrote about it for *National Geographic* while still in high school. Her first pet wasn't a dog or a fish but a turkey vulture named Nod. As a newlywed, she lived in an army-surplus tent in a beech-maple forest near Ypsilanti, Michigan, helping her ornithologist husband track birds for his PhD studies. She rose each morning and put on lipstick and mascara in a mirror nailed to a sugar maple tree and cooked three-course meals in a handmade rock oven to entertain guests. When the wind blew red and orange leaves off the trees onto the table, she set the plates and cups upon them, using them as "a wild autumn tablecloth." She had a mischievous pet raccoon who peeled all the labels off her canned goods and a great horned owl whose portrait she would paint by the fire. She kept this up even while pregnant, until the day she gave birth to her first child.

But when she eventually settled into a wood-shingled house in sleepy Chappaqua, New York, she didn't leave wildness behind. Her house served as a transient home for many wild pets—crows, owls, even a skunk—which often stayed for a season before the urge to migrate or mate set in. "The animals came in and out the back door just like the kids did," said her daughter Twig recently, with a laugh reminiscent of her mother's. Jean's house was layered with wild artifacts culled from her travels to the far ends of the earth. Inuit masks hung on the walls, and a shark jaw sat on top of the television. A giant whale vertebra, like a stone propeller, sat on the floor in the living room. Over the doorway to the dining room, instead of a piece of artwork, Jean had hung a blade of baleen, frayed at the edge like a giant feather. Closing my eyes, I can still conjure up the smell: the warm smoky air of the always-burning woodstove mingled with transported scents from faraway lands.

Visiting Jean was like going on an adventure without even leaving my neighborhood. But her wild home wasn't exactly something I could replicate in my city abode. For one thing, my apartment would make a poor habitat for a pet owl or raccoon, even if it were possible to acquire one. (Laws have changed since Jean's time, and wild animals are now protected by much stricter regulations.) And while I admired Jean's ability to gather wildness around her, I knew that this skill was born from instincts honed over many years spent in rare proximity to nature. How, then, could someone like me bring a bit more wildness into daily life?

One Friday in June, I brought this question to Sarah Ryhanen, the founder of the Brooklyn floral studio Saipua, who is often credited with popularizing the wild style that has swept through the floral industry over the past few years. When I first encountered Ryhanen's work, I was overcome with joy. Her arrangements looked nothing like the tight, overly stylized balls of blooms that were popular at the time. They were soft and fluid, full of tendrils and vines, branches and ferns, tumbling loosely out of mossy vessels. I took a couple of classes with her, and a few years later, she did the flowers for my wedding. Afterward, we stayed in touch.

At the new Saipua studio, a long, high-ceilinged space with whitewashed brick walls and large paned windows, Sarah made me a cup of strong tea and began to describe the genesis of her wild aesthetic. A self-taught florist, she had a background in the arts, not horticulture, and her first arrangements were the products of experimentation. "When I started going to the flower market, I was that annoying girl constantly asking, 'What is this called?'" she said. "At the time, I could identify maybe ten flowers. I was really starting from ground zero." But because she wasn't bound by formal principles or teachings, she was free to follow her intuition. This led her to plants that had often been overlooked by other florists. "At the market, I was less interested in flowers and more interested in texture," she said. That meant plants with intriguing foliage, like oak-leaf hydrangea, or sprigs of fruit or seedpods, like seeded eucalyptus. Many of the flowers she was drawn to didn't even really look like flowers. "One of the first things I fell in love with was smoke bush," she said. "It's blooming now, actually, big puffs of it." Smoke bush, or *Cotinus,* grows ten to fifteen feet tall and blossoms in a maroon haze that billows over its purple leaves.

These unconventional textures became the building blocks for her unique style. Conventional flower arrangements emphasize big blooms pressed together into geometric shapes such as domes, triangles, or ovals. Sarah uses some of these big flowers, too—roses, peonies, tulips—but rather than pack them tightly together, she intersperses them in between layers of leaves and seeds that make them look more like they've been found in a field than grown in a greenhouse. And while a typical arrangement usually has only a handful of different flowers and foliage, Sarah's arrangements often have dozens. "When I'm going about putting together an arrangement, I'm definitely looking for variation," she said. "Things that are very large down to things that are very small. And the same with texture. You want things that are very textured and very smooth. Some things that are seedy, some berries that are a bit bigger, some things that are hairier."

Seedy? Hairy? These aren't the words we usually reach for when describing a beautiful bouquet of flowers. But while cultivation takes a file to the rough edges of nature, polishing away its fuzz and bristles and wisps, wildness keeps these textures intact. This isn't true just for flowers. A gemstone with a textured surface looks wilder than one that is buffed smooth. A table made of wood that retains its bark along one edge appears wilder than one that is sanded into a perfect rectangle. Even wine can be made in a wild style. The biodynamic modes of production currently being embraced by winemakers give rise to wines that are slightly cloudy and funky and fizz gently on the tongue as if they were alive.

In 2008, the recession hit, and the delicate, weedy flowers that were the hallmark of Ryhanen's style began to disappear from the wholesale markets. Vendors couldn't risk having bunches of unsold inventory wilting on their balance sheets, so they narrowed their range to carry hardier flowers they knew they could sell. Sarah saw an opportunity. "I wanted more flowers than I could get in the market, different things, more unusual things." She began seeking out growers and ordering from them directly. Then in September 2011, she and her partner bought an old farm thirty miles west of Albany and began the process of converting it into a flower farm. It had a ramshackle barn built in 1825 and 107 acres of rocky clay soil. They called it World's End.

The work of building the farm has been frustrating at times. "There's the pain of learning to be patient," Sarah said. "At the farm, if you want something unusual, you have to find it—the seeds for it, or the plants. You have to get it there, plant it, sometimes you have to wait two years for it to flower." But the reward has been the freedom to grow flowers that might not be appreciated by the mainstream, with stems that twist, odd color patterns, and unexpected variations. They are "beautifully imperfect," in Sarah's words, just like wildness itself.

WILDER THAN WILD

In August I made my way to a small private garden in Hummelo, a couple of hours outside of Amsterdam in the Netherlands. It was an inconspicuous place, with a sign so small that I drove by it twice before finding the entrance. It seemed a perfect reflection of its owner, the seventy-three-year-old Dutch designer Piet Oudolf, who maintains a shy humility despite being one of the most celebrated figures in the world of garden design. Oudolf collaborated with James Corner on the

High Line, creating the much-loved bands of grasses and perennials that make the park's shallow beds feel like expanses of meadow. The Hummelo garden is his workshop and laboratory.

I stepped out of the car and saw Piet's wife, Anja, coming out to meet me, trailed by a small black-and-brown dog. I was a bit early, so she pointed me toward the garden, down a brick path to the left along a hedge. As I turned the corner, my breath caught in my throat. I saw an expanse of greens, golds, and purples, undulating like the surface of the sea. There were tufts of grasses long and short, stiff and floppy, some with silvery, spear-like blades, others with blond tails frayed like the end of a rope. Interspersed were flowers: tall hollyhocks, columns of blue salvia, and coneflowers rising up like rockets, along with a hundred other perennials whose names were unknown to me. Backlit by the sun, the garden glowed.

It was not a manicured garden, each labeled flower keeping to its own turf. It was a rumpus, a luxurious mesh of grasses through which constellations of flowers crept and twined. A pair of cream-colored butterflies chased each other, skimming the surface of the plantings. I followed them along the figure-eight path toward the back of the garden, where I found the way almost blocked by a grass whose arcing plumes filled the space with a luminous, seeded mist. I had a sudden urge to sit down amid the feathery grasses, right in the middle of the path. But as I looked around, I saw members of a Danish gardening club streaming into the garden, so I settled for running my hands through the soft filaments.

Soon I heard Anja's voice break through my reverie. Piet was ready to meet. I followed her into the studio, a simple, modern space with big windows on three sides. Piet stood up to greet me. Tall and ruddy, he had white-blond hair the same shade as some of his favorite grasses. We sat at a table in the center of the studio with cups of tea and cheese-and-butter sandwiches on brown bread that Anja brought in on a steel tray. A few minutes after sitting down, I found myself distracted by a peculiar, resinous aroma—almost like wood varnish but with an herbal note similar to coriander. I tried to focus, but it surrounded me like a cloud. "I know this sounds strange," I said, "but is it possible that a scent might have followed me in from the garden?"

Piet smiled as if I'd just told him I knew an old friend of his. "*Sporobolus!*" he said. "It's a grass. I can show you when we finish." His love affair with plants began at the age of twenty-five, when, tired of working in his family's restaurant, he took a job at a garden center. He started experimenting with different varieties in his mother's garden, but there wasn't enough space. So in 1982, he and Anja moved with their two sons here, to Hummelo. They began collecting seeds from botanical gardens around the world and cultivating them, specializing in varieties that had been neglected by gardeners because they didn't fit the mold of typical garden plants.

"It was a time when English garden culture was very strong," Piet said of the early days of his career. "I was trying to understand how they made gardens. But I found it too constrained. There are a lot of dogmas in gardening: what you have to do at a particular time of the year, what plants go well together, which colors match and don't match. All these rules." He spoke slowly, pausing to find the right words. "I wanted to make it feel more loose." This search for a less rigid feeling sparked an epiphany. At the time, most gardeners used shrubs pruned into stiff shapes to divide space within gardens. Piet realized he could do the same thing with grasses. Like shrubs, certain species of grasses grow in big, bushy clusters that provide structure. But grasses have soft edges that move with the breeze. Rather than being formal and solid, grasses can make a whole landscape dynamic.

In looseness, Piet found liberation. Grasses let him ease the strictures of a formal garden, akin to removing the corsetry from a dress. So much of our relationship with our environment has been a tussle between the will of nature and the will of man, trying to bend the former to the latter. Instead of fighting the willfulness of plants, Piet decided to embrace it. "I was trying to find more spontaneity in the process of gardening. Some plants disappear; some grow a little bit faster than you think. It's learning to accept that things grow and try to find their own way. You have to allow plants to do their thing." He talked like the seasoned parent of a teenager (yet another wild species). If we want more wildness in our lives, we have to be willing to let go of some control.

We left the studio and walked toward the garden. Along the way, we saw Anja saying goodbye to the Danish garden club, a neat, gray-haired group of ladies in their fifties and sixties. They visibly swooned when they saw Piet coming, and I was reminded that the gentle, soft-spoken designer was the George Clooney of the gardening world. He stopped to greet them and shake hands. The little brown-and-black dog, Duffi, had been sunning himself on a towel in the open back of a station wagon, but he jumped out when he saw Piet and followed us into the garden. Duffi disappeared into the grasses, springing joyfully in and out of the beds. Piet gazed at the scene and sighed. "It's moving, moving, moving, all the time," he said. "Even one grass can take you in completely." We walked around, and he patiently answered my questions about this plant and that one, until suddenly I smelled that pungent aroma again. As if reading my mind, Piet said, *"Sporobolus,"* and

Piet Oudolf Garden, Hummelo

pointed to the cloud of grass seeds I had been admiring a couple of hours earlier. We inhaled the strange fragrance together for a moment, and then said goodbye.

I lingered in the spot, watching Piet's figure disappear around the bend. Then, when all was quiet, I set down my notebook and camera and lay down on the bricks. I closed my eyes for a few blissful moments, feeling the grasses bowing over me, a makeshift temple of green.

* * *

A few miles down the road, as the scent of the *Sporobolus* began to dissipate, I became aware of a paradox. An Oudolf garden looks and feels wild, but in fact it is highly designed. "I never call it wild," Piet had said as we looked over his most recent drawings. "It's an unnatural world that feels like something wild, and may remind you of something, but you don't know where you've seen it. It's about intensifying and enhancing nature." Piet's gardens felt wilder to me than most meadows I'd seen. But how could a garden feel wilder than wilderness itself?

It was Sarah Ryhanen who led me to an answer to this question, via a book she recommended called *The Moth Snowstorm* by Michael McCarthy. A sort of elegy for wildness, the book laments what its author calls "the great thinning": a precipitous decline of wild species in the British countryside due to habitat loss and the extensive use of pesticides and herbicides. McCarthy points out that since 1970, the combined population of nineteen farmland bird species has diminished by more than half, and that three-quarters of the butterfly species have declined, some by as much as 79 percent. The result is a striking loss of biodiversity in wild places, not only in the UK but around the world.

Our wilderness is getting less wild. Yet because these losses have been gradual, occurring on a generational timescale, most people haven't noticed. Ecologists call this phenomenon shifting baseline syndrome; essentially it means that we adapt our definition of "wild" to the current condition of our wilderness. What we see when we visit the countryside is far less textured and diverse than what our grandparents would have seen at our age. Against this backdrop, Oudolf's gardens and Ryhanen's flower arrangements seem wilder than wild. In them we recognize a wildness that we have never seen, that we did not know we needed.

Alongside the trends toward wild food and fashion, gardens and flowers, many serious rewilding movements have emerged, promoting the restoration of native plant species, the reintroduction of locally extinct animals, and the reclaiming of disused spaces for natural habitats. And it seems that the more attracted people are to a wild aesthetic, the more invested they become in stewarding the ecosystems that produce it. In 2015, Sarah Ryhanen began saving all of the flower waste from Saipua's weddings and events and bringing it back to World's End for composting. Piet Oudolf's use of native perennials has inspired thousands of home gardeners to re-create indigenous plant communities that revitalize beneficial insect populations. In the aesthetic pleasure of wildness, these artists are cultivating a new kind of environmentalism, one that is rooted not in obligation but in joy.

4.

HARMONY

When I was a kid, one of my favorite moments of the year was just before the holidays, when my dad would take me to the *Christmas Spectacular* at Radio City Music Hall. I loved getting dressed up and going to the theater with its neon marquee and plush red seats, seeing the glittering lights and dancing bears and Santa and his elves. But the best part of every show, and the most famous, was when the thirty-six long-legged Radio City Rockettes would sashay onstage in red velvet leotards and line up shoulder to shoulder, forming the most perfect and even kick line. Their legs moved in unison, as if on invisible wires, their sparkly shoes reaching exactly up to eye level with each brisk kick. Every eye was riveted by the spectacle, and the cascade of applause that followed was always the loudest of the whole show.

Last year, I went back to Radio City to see the Rockettes kick again. I wondered if my recollection of the kick line was exaggerated, as childhood memories sometimes are. But as the Rockettes began to glide into formation, I felt the energy in the theater rise. In front of me, a woman in her seventies trembled with anticipation. At the first high kick, she began bobbing up and down in her seat, wringing her hands with emotion. I turned around briefly to look at the crowd behind me. The expressions on people's faces were beatific.

I was surprised by the collective thrill of this moment. Of all the different numbers, the kick line is easily the least evocative, having no

story line, and the most predictable, taking place at the end of every single show. The choreography isn't fancy or daring or intricate. But there is a deep, simple joy in seeing that impeccable row of dancers moving in perfect harmony.

Around that time, I stumbled on a blog called *Things Organized Neatly*. Just as the name suggests, it's a compendium of objects arranged in trim layouts, as if a fanatic house cleaner has sorted and straightened small piles of miscellany around the globe. There were fall leaves arranged in a colorful gradient, feathers lined up by size, and seashells organized by type. There were offbeat selections, like a layout of tiny utensils—forks and knives, ladles and trowels—from Barbie's various Dreamhouses, and a grid of ninety toast slices progressing from lightest in one corner to darkest in the other. Some were clever and visually stunning, like Carl Kleiner's layouts for the IKEA cookbook *Homemade Is Best*, which features neat piles of all the ingredients needed for each recipe: tidy mounds of flour, pyramids of butter, and vanilla beans lined up like soldiers. Some were poignant, like Barry Rosenthal's colorful compositions of plastic items found washed up on beaches. What was most intriguing, though, was the way that order brought delight to things that weren't particularly joyful, objects that might normally evoke even fear or disgust, like knives, surgical implements, or a pile of silvery dead fish, arrayed by size.

It didn't seem to matter what was being put into order. Simply arranging similar objects in geometric configurations was enough to transform anything into a source of delight. At first, this vexed me because, on the surface, the idea of order didn't seem particularly joyful. My impression of joy was unrestrained and energetic. Order felt rigid, static, and sedate. But I couldn't deny it. The Rockettes' kick line was joyful, attracting more than seventy-five million viewers since it began in 1932, and so were all these neat and tidy little images. Some had hundreds, even thousands, of likes and shares. So I was left with a conundrum: joy is wild and free, but sometimes it's also very organized.

As I wondered why this might be the case, I began to discover examples of order hidden within the natural world. Most plants and animals exhibit symmetry of some sort, whether the radial symmetry found in starfish and sea urchins or the bilateral symmetry of vertebrates, including humans. Tessellations composed of scales packed tightly together adorn the bodies of fish and the shells of turtles. Temporal patterns, like waves, govern the sinusoid oscillation of our heartbeat and the regular in-out of our breath.

Life is an orderly endeavor, much more so than it appears on the surface. As writer Kevin Kelly observes, "The difference between four bottles of nucleotides on a laboratory shelf and the four nucleotides arranged in your chromosomes lies in the additional structure, or ordering, these molecules get from participating in the spirals of your replicating DNA." While inorganic forms such as galaxies and atoms display striking symmetries, at the scale of the naked eye such patterns are a telltale sign of life. Most natural inanimate objects are symmetrical only by chance. Think of the uncommon delight in finding a perfectly shaped skipping stone or an evenly balanced cloud formation. Symmetrical forms and patterns that emerge from pure physical principles—crystals, tides, snowflakes—feel like miracles and are often held up as evidence of the divine. Order suggests the presence of an animate force, one that sequences molecules, assembles cell walls, circulates nutrients, and channels energy into growth and propagation. When I thought about it this way, I realized that the joy of order comes in large measure from what it opposes: chaos and disorder. Order isn't dull and staid. It is a tangible manifestation of a vibrant harmony, of disparate parts working in concert to sustain the graceful balance of life.

The influence of harmony in our surroundings is strong, and often unconscious. Hilary Dalke, the London-based color specialist we met in chapter 1, discovered this when she was asked to design the shower room in a women's prison. "Just specify the tiles," she was told, with the expectation that she would choose a basic white tile, and that would be it. But when Dalke arrived at the prison, she found the environment so harsh that she was inspired to do something a bit different. "I chose two other tile colors: a pale warm pinkish beige, and another one that was slightly darker, a bit like a light terra-cotta." She specified that simple bands of the two colors be placed along the wall, with white tiles above, and then moved on to other projects without thinking much about it.

Six months later, Dalke returned to the prison. She was eagerly greeted by the staff, who led her directly to the showers. "Look," they said. "Yeah, what?" Dalke replied. "Look!" they said again, and Dalke, not seeing anything out of the ordinary, said, "Yes? What's so special about the way it looks?" The staff told her that typically they didn't see shower rooms where all the tiles were intact, because the inmates shattered the tiles to use in self-harm or suicide attempts. With the simple addition of two bands of color, the room went from a blank expanse to a defined space that had symmetry and proportion. Not one tile had been smashed.

Harmony offers visible evidence that someone cares enough about a place to invest energy in it. Disorder has the opposite effect. Disorderly environments have been linked to feelings of powerlessness, fear, anxiety, and depression, and they exert a subtle, negative influence on people's behavior. A series of studies done in the Netherlands in 2008 showed that the presence of graffiti doubled the likelihood that passersby would litter or steal an envelope with a small sum of money in it. This is consistent with a controversial principle known as broken windows theory, which asserts that disorderly signals such as graffiti and litter tend to increase incidences of more serious crimes. The premise is that evidence of small offenses creates an impression that laws are not well enforced, making rule breaking look like the norm, rather than the exception. New York City famously used this theory as part of a strategy to reduce crime in the 1990s, showing zero tolerance for vandalism and petty offenses like subway-fare dodging. Proponents credit these efforts with contributing to a steep decrease in the city's crime rate. (Detractors contend that these crime reductions may actually be due to other factors and that the principle leads to policing strategies that disproportionately target populations based on race and economic status.) But a recent set of studies suggests a subtler effect could be at work. Researchers at the University of Chicago exposed two hundred people to images of environments that were visually disordered, having lots of asymmetrical and uneven lines but without any signs of illegal activity. Another group saw images of orderly environments. Each group had taken a math test on arriving at the lab, and now they were asked to grade themselves on this test, using the honor system, and told that they would receive a bonus for each correct answer they reported. Those who had been exposed to the disorderly environments were more likely to cheat, and to cheat by bigger amounts, than those who had viewed the more harmonious scenes.

Even Piet Oudolf, master of the wild style, believes in the value of harmony. He told me that an early movement in naturalistic gardening had failed in Europe. The resulting gardens were "too unkempt," in his view. "We need some order for our minds," he said, describing the way he creates harmony through balance, rhythm, and repetition.

Though I initially saw harmony as sitting in tension with aesthetics like freedom and energy, I began to suspect that it might ground and balance these more exuberant aesthetics in ways that could make them even more potent. By noticing and surfacing the hidden harmonies in the world around us, and embedding more of them into our surroundings, could we find a more understated kind of joy in our lives?

HOW THE BRAIN TIDIES UP

Looking more closely at the pictures on the *Things Organized Neatly* blog, I realized that they rely on a simple rule to create a sense of harmony among objects: *like goes with like*. Putting objects with similar features together taps into a principle of gestalt psychology called similarity, which says that the brain tends to perceive similar objects as a group. The individual feathers or leaves or toys cease to be seen as independent objects. Instead, they become modules in a larger composition. According to gestalt theorists, the brain does this to simplify and make sense of information coming in through the visual system. After all, similar objects often have a practical relationship to one another, not just a visual one. A group of similar leaves likely belongs to the same plant, and it's simpler to look at a forest and see a hundred trees rather than millions of individual leaves. According to neuroscientist V. S. Ramachandran, the pleasurable "aha!" sensation we feel when we see related objects as a group suggests that the brain's processes for identifying objects may be intrinsically connected to the reward mechanisms in the limbic system. In other words, joy is the brain's natural reward for staying alert to correlations and connections in our surroundings.

This principle helps explain why collections feel so joyful. Even if the individual items don't have much value, our eyes read a collection as more than the sum of its parts. Interior designer Dorothy Draper was well aware of this when she advised readers to "decorate with hobbies" in one of her World War II–era *Good Housekeeping* columns. "Don't sprinkle your collection out of sight in a meaningless jumble," she advised. "Notice how groups of small objects, when they are well arranged, become important and effective." She suggested, for example, placing bird or flower prints in identical frames and tiling a wall with them, or turning a coffee table into a shadowbox to showcase small items like paperweights under glass. Since the eye naturally looks for similar features, if you can find a common thread between objects, you can make them feel like they belong together. The common element can be size, color, shape, or material. In my house, I realized I often had similar things living in different places for no good reason. For example, I had a turquoise vase in my bedroom, turquoise books on the shelf, and a pair of turquoise matchbooks in the kitchen. When

I gathered these items together and placed them on the entryway table, it transformed them from random pieces of junk into a delightful vignette.

I use this principle in my life in many small ways. For example, when I put things on a bulletin board or on a fridge door, I like to use pins or magnets of the same color. This way I can put up a hodgepodge of greeting cards, pages torn from magazines, and other found objects, and they all look as if they're part of a single composition. A small luxury, but one that will last a lifetime, is to buy matching hangers for your closet. This has the effect of unifying the clothes, making them look as coordinated as they do when they're hanging in the store. If you happen to like mismatched things, such as antique dishes or silverware, look for pieces that are roughly the same size to make them feel more like they belong to a set. Many of Marie Kondo's storage techniques rely on this principle as well. For example, her method of storing socks—rolling them like sushi and standing them on end in a drawer—imposes a calming uniformity on a typically messy area of the home.

The same principle can also be applied at a larger scale. Repeating colors, shapes, or textures in different parts of a room helps our eyes view the room as a whole, rather than a mishmash of disconnected things. This is important because research shows that we're attracted to environments with a moderately high degree of complexity, but only if the complexity is well structured. The greater the complexity in an environment, the greater the need for an underlying harmony to bring a sense of order and ease to a space. Because of this, harmony can be a vital complement to the abundance aesthetic. I'm reminded of Dylan's Candy Bar and the ways they use consistent elements to unify the store. While the many types of candy look wildly different, the clear acrylic bins holding them are all the same size and shape. And a rainbow installation groups different kinds of candies by their hues, turning them into a simple spectrum. (What is a rainbow, after all, but an organized set of colors?)

"If you're looking for a sense of unity in your apartment, take it space by space and look at it just as a composition," says interior designer Ghislaine Vinas, who is known for creating vivid spaces with poppy colors that blend influences from her upbringing in South Africa and the Netherlands. She believes you can use color as a bridge between different rooms and eclectic styles. "What color is your sofa? What color are your chairs? Can you connect something that's happening in your kitchen to something in your living room?" She relies on fabrics or pillows that weave together multiple colors to move the eye around in a harmonious way. While I was visiting her one afternoon at her colorful studio, she pointed to a cushion covered in an orange, navy, and green print. The colors pulled the eye from the neon orange chairs in the kitchen to the navy rug and green details in the sitting area. "You don't even know that it's happening, but you're basically creating order." Viñas has also used color and pattern to unify the structural features that break up a space. For example, one client of hers had a tiny bedroom that barely had room for a bed. Viñas painted big horizontal stripes on the walls, covering the door and even the artwork. This unified the different shapes—the rectangle of the door, the square of the painting, the moldings—that would normally divide the walls, making the room feel larger.

THE PARADISE OF SYMMETRY

If I ask you to name a joyful shape, what's the first one that comes to mind? For many people I've talked to over the years, the answer is the circle. Circles have long been used as symbols of harmony and wholeness, in sacred traditions as well as secular ones. Circles describe halos in Christian art, the sun in Egyptian temples, and the festive rangoli made to celebrate Diwali, the Hindu festival of lights. King Arthur's knights convened at a round table because the circle gives equal weight to every position around it. For similar reasons, circles also create a sense of social harmony in business meetings and informal gatherings. Research suggests that people prefer sitting at a slight angle to one another, rather than side by side, and that they will drag chairs into a loose circle wherever possible. The circle's unbroken perimeter and even rate of curvature make it the most stable, complete, and inclusive shape. But the circle is joyful for another reason: it is infinitely symmetrical.

A love of symmetry is one of the best-studied human aesthetic preferences. In 1871, Charles Darwin observed, "The eye prefers symmetry or figures with some regular recurrence. Patterns of this kind are employed by even the lowest savages as ornaments; and they have been developed through sexual selection for the adornment of some male animals." Scientific consensus agrees with Darwin. The human eye is exquisitely sensitive to symmetry. Our brain can recognize symmetrical forms extremely quickly, at less than one hundred milliseconds, much faster than asymmetrical forms. We can detect symmetrical shapes against busy backgrounds, and we notice them even when our eyes aren't directly focused on them. In a 2013 study at the University of Liverpool, psychologists discovered that people unconsciously associate symmetrical forms with positive words like "pleasure," "paradise," and "heaven," and asymmetrical or random forms with words like "disaster," "evil," and "death." Another recent study found that symmetry literally puts a smile on our faces. Looking at symmetrical compositions stimulates a slight contraction of the zygomaticus major, one of the main facial muscles involved in smiling.

One reason we love symmetry may be that it is an outward symbol of inner harmony. Symmetrical faces are typically considered more attractive by members of both sexes, and research has shown that people with more symmetrical features are rated as healthier, more conscientious, and more intelligent than their less symmetrical peers. These judgments may sound superficial, but they have a deeper logic. Facial symmetry has been shown to correlate with increased diversity in a set of genes related to immune response, which confers greater resistance to disease, while people with symmetrical bodies have been shown to have a lower resting metabolic rate, suggesting that they are more efficient users of energy. In studies of reproductive health, women with more symmetrical breasts tended to have higher markers of fertility, while men with more symmetrical bodies had higher sperm counts and sperm motility than their more asymmetrical peers. This view holds that we find symmetry attractive because it signals vibrancy and health in a mate, and it increases the likelihood that these attributes will be passed on to our offspring. Species as diverse as scorpion flies and barn swallows also use symmetry as a benchmark when choosing a mate.

But symmetry's allure isn't limited to sex appeal. Studies of infants as young as four months old show that they, too, prefer symmetrical patterns to asymmetrical ones. Cognitive scientists believe that just as the brain derives pleasure from grouping similar objects together, it also finds pleasure in identifying symmetrical objects, because they tend to be more evolutionarily significant than asymmetrical forms. A human body is more intriguing than a boulder, an apple more valuable than a stone. A symmetrical form suggests the presence of life or something crafted by a living creature, such as a nest, a honeycomb, or an anthill. Perfect symmetry isn't easy to achieve, which may be why it is so often associated with spiritual harmony. For example, the bilateral and four-fold geometries that appear in Navajo weavings are an attempt to create *hózhó*, a word that roughly means "balance" or "harmony." Having *hózhó* results not only in beauty but also in peace and well-being. Notably, when researchers at Michigan State University tried subtly altering versions of classic abstract patterns from cultures such as the Aónikenk, Navajo, and Yoruba to make them asymmetrical, they found that they were consistently rated as less attractive.

Symmetry has been a basic tenet of architecture since antiquity. Geometry was in widespread use in the ancient world, and architects from Egypt to India used it to create temples, palaces, and mausoleums with floor plans based on precise symmetries. Most homes have also historically been symmetrical. When it comes to architecture, symmetry is not only pleasing; it is simple and efficient. After all, a building whose two sides are mirror images needs only half a blueprint, which can be reflected across a centerline.

Yet over the last fifty years or so, asymmetry has crept into our homes and buildings. Architectural critic Kate Wagner traces this shift to the suburban building boom of the blingy 1980s. While the energy crisis of the seventies kept home sizes modest, the Reagan years brought large incentives for the construction industry and a culture of conspicuous consumption that turned houses into status symbols. These luxury homes, dubbed "McMansions," swelled to include all kinds of new features: exercise rooms, home theaters, three-car garages, and grand oversize entryways. Eager to please, developers sacrificed symmetry for scale, producing massive homes that often felt surprisingly awkward. They sometimes looped architects out of the equation entirely, using a modular approach that allowed prospective homeowners to customize their design based on a kit of options. These options included architectural details like arches, moldings, and bay windows, which were then applied haphazardly to the surface rather than integrated into the structure. McMansions are among the most egregious examples of asymmetrical architecture, but they're not the only ones. Many urban apartments have been subdivided and reshaped over the years through renovations, leaving behind spaces with odd proportions that are as far as can be from Grecian temple–like harmony.

If the architecture of your space doesn't give you symmetry, you can create your own. By placing pairs of similar objects, such as chairs or potted plants, on either side of a line that you define, you can make an axis of symmetry where none exists. This axis can be measured from the center of a wall or prominent architectural feature, such as a fireplace mantel or built-in bookcase. Make sure that furniture, rugs, and light fixtures are centered on this axis. Research suggests the most salient axis of symmetry is the vertical, likely because it's the one across which our own bodies are reflected. Mirrors, especially large ones, create instant vertical symmetry because they reflect the space back on itself. We are less attuned to horizontal symmetry, but it, too, can add harmony to a space. Dorothy Draper always recommended lining up the tops of lampshades to the same height in a room, creating a subtle horizontal axis. If that's too persnickety for you (as I admit it is for me), then simply making sure that surfaces are level and artworks are aligned is a good start. Often, it works best to align pictures by the tops of their frames, but this isn't always the case, so when in doubt, trust your eye.

Creating symmetry doesn't have to be a serious exercise. Interior designer Ghislaine Viñas describes a whimsical solution she once found for an unbalanced space. "We had a project where the clients had a piano. This was driving me crazy because everything in the house was completely white and very bright, and then there was this very heavy black piano on this one end. And I did not know how on earth I was going to balance out the room on the other end." She found herself preoccupied by the asymmetry. "It made me feel very uneasy, it just wasn't right." Then one day, her client showed her a picture of a giant lamp in the shape of a horse. It was practically life-size. "And as soon as we put that into the room, it balanced it out." Viñas and her team often tape out the outlines of rugs and furniture on the floor before they commit to a layout to make sure that the space feels harmonious.

Just as we have an intuitive eye for vertical and horizontal symmetry, our eyes also unconsciously gravitate toward the center of an

object or a space. In *A Pattern Language,* Christopher Alexander and his colleagues point out the unconscious impulse we have to place an object such as a bowl of fruit or a candle at the center of a table, and how "right" a table with a centerpiece tends to feel. Similarly, the best-loved public squares and courtyards all have a focal point: a fountain, obelisk, or other object of interest in the middle. An object in the center of a space tends to change the space around it, anchoring a blank expanse. It may be that defining a center heightens the sense of symmetry that helps us get our bearings.

FEEL THE RHYTHM

While researching symmetrical architecture, I discovered a place that happened to be a short detour from an upcoming vacation in Palm Springs, and it didn't take much to convince Albert to come along. Driving through the southeastern corner of the Mojave Desert, near Joshua Tree National Park, we almost missed the white-faceted dome in the dusty surroundings. It was built by a former aviation engineer named George Van Tassel entirely out of wood, based on instructions he claimed he had received from extraterrestrials visiting from the planet Venus. He called it the Integratron. Van Tassel intended it to be an electrostatic generator, cellular-rejuvenation machine, and time-travel device, but he died in 1978 after more than two decades of work on the structure, and its supernatural potential was never realized. Yet the enormous all-wood dome has properties that make it valuable even if it can't transport us back to the age of the dinosaurs. It is a nearly perfect acoustic environment.

We lay on striped cushions gazing at the ribbed vaults above, a thin plume of Palo Santo incense wafting over us. Every murmur was magnified, so that even a whisper across the dome sounded to me as if it had been uttered right in my ear. As people settled into their spots, a hush came over the space. Then a low, resonant tone filled the dome. Soon a higher note played, smooth and pulsing, and then another. The sound emanated from a collection of quartz-crystal singing bowls, but it felt like it was all around us. I now understood what the man who welcomed us meant when he described it as "a feeling like when you see a guitar and just want to curl up inside of it." Here we were in the hollow of a giant string instrument, swimming in rich vibrations of sound.

It was like being suspended between dreams and waking, almost hallucinogenic, full of strange images and thoughts unmoored from reality. It does not surprise me that aficionados of these "sound baths" say that they produce a trancelike state, along with deep joy and relaxation.

Watching musicians caught in a riff, or dancers swept up in a rhythm, you might be tempted to believe that music is joyful because it is so free and unfettered. But underlying the pleasure of music are layers of order: the repetition of sounds, the sequence of beat and rhythm, and, at the deepest level, the quivering oscillations of the sound waves themselves. Our first experience with a beat is in utero, and even outside the womb babies are comforted by the sound of their mother's heartbeat, repetitive sounds, and rhythmic rocking movements. Though Eastern and Western music traditions can sound radically different, adults and children from a range of cultures agree on which tones are consonant and which are dissonant. Certain ratios known as the *perfect fifth* and *perfect fourth* are considered universally pleasurable and appear in the music of most cultures. Even the earliest instruments—flutes carved from the bones of swans and woolly mammoths forty-three thousand years ago—have been found to produce these harmonious intervals. Musicologists say that these intervals sound pleasant to us because the ratios at which the notes vibrate, 4:3 for a perfect fourth and 3:2 for a perfect fifth, create regular intersections between their different wavelengths. On a violin playing a perfect fifth, one string vibrates at a rate of three oscillations for every two of the other strings, meaning that the two wavelengths frequently coincide. Contrast this with an interval called the tritone, which has the distinction of being known as the "devil in music." This interval has a pitch ratio of 42:35, which creates a dissonant, ominous sound. In 1787, a German physicist named Ernst Chladni discovered a way to see these musical oscillations. By covering a metal plate with sand and vibrating it like a drum, he found that symmetrical designs emerged on the surface, revealing a distinctive shape for the timbre of each tone and reminding us that music is essentially patterned sound.

Whether sonic or visual, patterns are a timeless source of joy. One of the reasons we love patterns and rhythms is that their structured repetition of elements quickly establishes a baseline level of harmony. Patterns enable us to experience an abundance of sensation without it feeling overwhelming, and they create an orderly background against which we can detect when something is out of place or awry. This lets our brain relax, rather than having to remain on high alert. To this point, research has shown that the regular beat and melody of music reduces stress better than unstructured sounds like rippling water, and that coloring in a structured pattern such as a mandala can significantly reduce anxiety.

As Darwin observed, nearly every culture on earth uses patterns in its decorative arts, from Scottish tartans to Kashmiri paisleys to the vibrant kente cloths made in Ghana. A remarkable array of patterns can be produced through simple means: by etching into clay or wood, weaving wool or grass, or painting with pigments made from plants or crushed stones. Pattern making doesn't require fancy or costly materials, just practice and patience. Even comparatively poor cultures will invest effort in the creation of patterns, imbuing a water jug or a vest with joyful significance.

On a trip down the Silk Road a few years ago, I found myself plunged into a world of beautiful patterns: ultramarine ceramics and embroidered suzanis in Uzbekistan, red woven carpets in Turkmenistan, and graphic felt rugs in Kyrgyzstan, traditionally used by nomadic herders to adorn their yurts. When I came back, I found I missed the effortless way that the central Asian cultures wove patterns into their lives, so I started to collect textiles with joyful patterns. I find them in antique shops, fabric stores, and markets, at home and when I travel, and though I don't always know how I'll use them, they always find a place— sometimes as a cushion, or a cover for a stool that's starting to wear out, or just draped over a chair. One of the best things about patterns is that they can be joyful while still being understated. White-on-white patterns, such as knits or laces, can bring joy to even the most chromophobic among us!

So strong is our desire to spot patterns that we sometimes see them where none exist. This tendency, known as patternicity, explains the delight we find in spotting constellations in the night sky, faces in clouds, or a melody in the random noise of the street. Patterns tend to contain valuable information, and it has historically been safer for humans to overinterpret meaningless data than to miss a true pattern, like the foliage of an edible plant or a sequence of divots in the mud that might be animal tracks. On the other hand, some patterns are so subtle that we don't even realize they're there. When comparing a forest with an office building, it might seem as if the building is the more orderly scene. Repeating windows and geometric shapes create simple symmetries and mathematical relationships, while the forest seems wild and chaotic. But in the 1970s, a mathematician named Benoit Mandelbrot proposed that many natural objects contain patterns that repeat not in a linear way, like a pattern on a textile, but across different scales of view. Zoom into a tree branch, and you'll find the same fork-shaped pattern that you see in its trunk, repeated in ever-smaller increments. Mandelbrot dubbed these patterns "fractals," and they can be found in many natural objects and phenomena including coastlines, river networks, snowflakes, blood vessels, skylines, and even our heart rates. This type of pattern is also known as expanding symmetry, because the central motif grows as it is repeated. Research suggests that we have a strong preference for fractals with a medium degree of complexity—the kind that happens to be most common in nature. Looking at these fractals stimulates alpha waves in the frontal cortex, a state known to correlate with wakeful relaxation, which may be another reason that we find spending time outdoors so joyful and restorative.

Fractals also appear in certain man-made contexts. Inside Jackson Pollock's swirls of paint researchers have found fractal patterns, which increase in intricacy in paintings over the length of his career. Gothic architecture is rich in fractals, as are some Hindu temples. Entire villages in Africa are laid out according to fractal algorithms. Mathematician Ron Eglash studied villages in Ethiopia, Cameroon, and Mali and found that fractals are widespread across the African continent as an architectural principle and that they underpin many customs and religious rites.

The joy of fractals and complex patterns is a reminder that the harmony aesthetic isn't always something we can see. Just as often, it's something we feel.

FINDING FLOW

Because the feeling of harmony can be so subtle, sometimes a sense of imbalance arises, and even with my design training, I don't always know how to address it. Hungry for more concrete guidance on how to create harmony in a space, I began looking into the history of architecture and design. It didn't take me long to discover that a well-established practice of spatial harmony has existed for millennia: the Chinese art of feng shui.

I had always been a bit circumspect about feng shui. The articles I had read had promised luck and prosperity by following a few simple tips but never shared a rationale for *why* the advice might produce such wonderful outcomes. It seemed more like magical thinking than science to me, a kind of astrology for the home. At the same time, feng shui has been practiced continuously for more than five thousand years. With that kind of staying power, maybe it deserved a closer look.

As I embarked on this exploration, I found a kindred spirit in Cathleen McCandless, a no-nonsense feng shui practitioner whose book, *Feng Shui That Makes Sense*, debunks many of the myths around the discipline's more mystical promises. McCandless began her career as a conservationist studying deforestation in the Amazon basin. When her mother was diagnosed with stage 4 cancer, she returned home and was browsing in a bookstore when she happened upon a book that had a brief chapter about feng shui. She tried out a few of the ideas in her mother's home, and to her surprise, her mother said they made her feel better. After her mother passed away, McCandless devoted herself to translating feng shui's ancient dictums for the realities of modern life.

McCandless told me that when feng shui was invented, China was an agrarian society, set in a highly dynamic physical landscape. Feng shui takes its name from two of the most powerful forces in that landscape: *feng,* meaning "wind," and *shui,* meaning "water." When wind and water flow too fast, the result is destruction: hurricanes, floods, tsunamis. When they flow too slowly, the result is heavy air, murky water, and stagnation. "In their profound wisdom," McCandless says, "the ancient Chinese decided to create a system that would ensure safety and an optimal environment for their people." Because the location of homes and fields could influence people's health, crop yields, and even their survival, feng shui naturally came to be seen as a way to increase one's luck and prosperity.

Curious to understand for myself how feng shui might create harmony in the modern world, I decided to try it out in my own home. McCandless lives in Maui, a location that I'm sure is ideal from a feng shui perspective, but unfortunately a bit too far from my New York apartment to do a consultation. So I turned to Brooklyn-based feng shui practitioner Ann Bingley Gallops. She asked me to send a floor plan of my apartment and fill out a brief questionnaire, and a few days later she visited me at home.

Gallops didn't bat an eye behind her red-rimmed glasses when I declared my skepticism about feng shui. Like McCandless, she believes that its power comes from the way it reframes our relationship to our surroundings rather than from any mystical properties. "It's not magic," she said, "it's just about bringing your attention to each area of your space." With that in mind, we started at the front door and walked around the apartment. While I prattled on about how we were planning to replace the cluttered old shelving unit in the entryway, and how we didn't normally have so many shoes and boxes all over the place, Gallops calmly took in all that was there. Her deliberate manner slowed me down. She opened and closed doors, peeked around corners, and stood back to look at each area from a few different angles. I realized I'd been so busy living in my apartment, I hadn't paused and just looked at it in a long time, maybe not since we moved in nearly three years before.

"The chi feels pretty good in most places," she said. I felt flattered for a moment, then realized I didn't know what she meant, so I asked her to explain. She said that the essential premise of feng shui is that all matter, whether around us or inside of us, is animated by an invisible energy called chi. Acupuncture and feng shui both center around chi; the first seeks to rebalance its movement through our bodies, the second through our surroundings. I must have had an uncertain look on my face, because Gallops followed up with a more practical analogy. "It's almost like having a little pet animal. Can it come in, explore the space, and figure out easily how to exit? That's the flow of healthy chi energy." I pictured a friend's Chihuahua let loose in our apartment and imagined its tiny legs whirring as it scampered into every corner. Like the namesake wind and water of feng shui, good chi flows through a space (and our bodies) in a way that's brisk yet gentle, like a seaside breeze. For example, a long, empty hallway creates a fast rush of chi that may be right for an airport concourse but is uncomfortable in a home. A cluttered room causes the chi to swirl around and get stuck. I wasn't sure how I felt about chi as a life force, but as a concept, it made sense to me. Chi is the circulation of air in a space, the movement of a gaze around a room, the daily orbits of a home's inhabitants. Chi is flow.

Suddenly, I saw the joy of order in a new light. It was like looking at the classic optical illusion of two faces in profile, and in a flash, switching perspectives to see the vase in the negative space between them. The joy isn't about structure or organization per se. It's about the smooth flow of energy that such order enables. The Rockettes' kick line, for example, is shaped by strict rules. Dancers auditioning for the Rockettes must conform to a height standard, between five foot six and five foot ten and a half inches tall. The kick line is arranged with the tallest dancers in the middle, gradually descending to the shortest ones on the ends. All this is critical, but the joy is not in the meticulous rules and alignment behind the scenes. It's in the way that such order enables the dancers to synchronize their movements so that the dance appears like one effortless undulation. Or consider the images on the *Things Organized Neatly* blog. When I talked to Austin Radcliffe, the blog's creator, I learned that the orderly layouts featured on his site have roots in two practices: knolling and *mise en place*. Knolling is a system of placing objects, usually tools, at right angles to one another on a work surface. It originated in Frank Gehry's furniture workshop in the late 1980s and was popularized by the artist Tom Sachs. *Mise en place*, which is French for "putting in its place," is a similar practice used in professional kitchens to set up for a shift by neatly laying out all ingredients and tools that will be needed. Both knolling and *mise en place* are strategies that enable smooth workflow, allowing workers to see and use materials in a fluid way. (Of course "flow" is also the term psychologists use for being completely, joyously absorbed in an activity, whether at work or play.) But the by-product of arranging things for good workflow is that they have good visual flow, too, with no awkward angles and plenty of negative space that lets the eye move around easily.

Knowing how powerful these techniques are, I've started to use them in ordinary moments. When I cut up an apple for a snack, I'll arrange the pieces in a circle rather than piling them messily on the plate. Or I'll knoll my desk at the end of the week so that it looks and feels ready for me when I come back to it on Monday. Even Marie Kondo's tidying up method can be seen through the lens of flow. By removing obstacles in our surroundings, we open up channels for the smooth flow of energy through our lives.

Back in my apartment, Gallops led me to the entryway and said, "The only place I feel like chi is getting stuck is in this area." She told me that feng shui places special emphasis on the entryway because it's the gateway to your home or office. You have to pass through it every time you enter or exit, and it's where you greet guests. If your door sticks or you're always tripping over shoes, then you're going to find friction at a moment when you really want momentum. This is mental, but it is physical, too. Instead of flowing smoothly out of the house in the morning, your body will absorb the force from that friction. This might make you grit your teeth or tense your muscles, which in turn might influence the way you handle traffic on your commute or how you greet your coworkers when you arrive at the office. It's a small moment that can have knock-on effects throughout your day. The same thing happens in reverse when you come home at night. Entering your home through a patch of chaos creates a moment of irritation that affects the rest of your evening. With this in mind, I looked at our pinched entryway piled with boxes and could see that Gallops was right. I marked "Fix entryway" at the top of my list.

The other place that she felt needed attention was the bedroom. Right away, she noticed that our bed was in a corner, which is a feng shui no-no. We had placed it there originally to maximize the space, but Gallops pointed out that it creates an asymmetry in the room. "And," she added, trying not to sound too ominous, "in the relation-ship." One partner has easy access to the bed, while the other has to clamber in awkwardly. According to Gallops, whenever one partner faces greater resistance than the other when going about their daily activities, an imbalance is created in the home. I could see how that imbalance might start out small but could build up to hinder marital harmony. I added "Rearrange bedroom" to my list.

That night, I took Albert through Gallops's recommendations. We decided to reconfigure the bedroom immediately, placing little felt pads on the feet of all the furniture so it slid easily into place. The bedroom felt better instantly, as if it should always have been arranged that way. I spent Sunday at a family event, and when I came back, my eyes nearly popped out of their sockets: the entryway was completely clear! Albert had spent the entire afternoon moving furniture and organizing, and it was like walking into a different apartment. Now that the shelving was gone, there was room to move around. I was able to take off my coat without bumping into anything, and a stool was positioned in just the right place for me to sit down while I unzipped my boots. The first few times I left the house, it was so smooth I almost felt like I was forgetting something.

Feng shui practitioners love to tout the mysterious effects that ensue when clients readjust their spaces. A lonely bachelor finally finds a girlfriend; a struggling entrepreneur gets a big break out of nowhere. I'm tempted to roll my eyes at such stories, but when I overlay what I've learned about feng shui onto the broader science of disorder, these stories start to sound a little bit less far-fetched. If your environment makes you feel stable, balanced, and grounded, you're more likely to feel confident taking measured risks and exploring new opportunities. Other people may notice your calm, unhurried demeanor and be drawn to you. And as we've seen, orderly surroundings also make you less likely to engage in behaviors that can undermine others' trust in you, such as lying or cheating.

No major, life-altering events transpired in the weeks after my feng shui experience. But there was a more mundane kind of magic. A few nights after making our adjustments, Albert and I cooked dinner together. We do this fairly frequently, and most nights we find ourselves a little bit on top of each other. He'll turn on the faucet to wash a bowl just as I'm trying to drain the water from the greens, or I'll try to get to the trash just as he's opening the silverware drawer above it. New

York kitchens are not the most spacious, and I've always figured that this is just *how things are.* But on this one evening, we quietly slipped into a symbiotic rhythm. There was no bumping or crowding, no "Hey!" or "Oops!" or "Sorry!" A fly on the ceiling would have seen us moving in leisurely loops around each other, as if we were tracing arcs of invisible choreography. Even though we were tired, we seemed to have a heightened awareness of each other. I suspected he'd probably want parsley on the fish he was cooking, and I chopped a small pile in anticipation. When he opened the fridge to get the wine, he pulled out the mustard for my vinaigrette and placed it in front of me unasked. It was a simple meal: panfried sole, green beans with butter, salad. But we sat down to it feeling so calm and at ease, it was like the meal arrived via flying carpet.

Strangely, none of our adjustments were anywhere near the kitchen. We have no more space in there than we did before. I think it's simply this: harmony begets harmony. A home is composed of many interdependent parts, and just as we often forget that our environment affects our emotions, we also forget that one part of a space affects another. I like the notion of flow because it reminds us that events in a space aren't defined by neat boundaries. Effects from one room cascade into others. Just as one small moment of chaos can spiral out and create havoc around it, so, too, can small points of order affect the larger sense of flow in our lives.

PERFECTLY IMPERFECT

Harmony is unique in that it's one of the few aesthetics of joy that has truly measurable elements. Energy and abundance are tricky to quantify. With freedom, it's hard to know where you'd even start. But in creating harmony, the ruler, the compass, and the level all find application. Yet this quantitative aspect also carries risks. If we're not careful, the angles and ratios can cause us to fixate on an ideal of perfection rather than an experience of harmony. Tools can be useful, but at the end of the day, they are not the arbiters of joy. You are. This is why I find the feng shui notion of chi, or flow, so important. Flow puts us back in our bodies. It reminds us that the most important tools for assessing harmony are the ones we're born with: our senses and our emotions.

Understanding this is vital, because sometimes harmony shows up in forms that aren't as visually perfect as we might expect. When I first started looking at joyful patterns for this book, I found that while most exhibited impeccable symmetries, others seemed to violate many of the "rules." Ikat, for example, is a woven fabric made by an unconventional process in which the warp threads are dyed before they are placed on the loom. As the weft is woven in, the warp shifts slightly, creating a feathery look that breaks the lines of symmetry. Each module in the pattern looks slightly different, but the overall design retains a soft, dynamic sense of harmony. Or consider that many Islamic artisans believe that true perfection is God's domain, so they secretly embed tiny flaws into their designs to acknowledge that no human should try to rival God's work. These flaws mar the mathematical perfection of the patterns, but our eyes flow easily through them without noticing.

Perhaps the most stunning example of imperfect harmony for me is a set of artworks from a tiny community in rural Alabama. The quilts of Gee's Bend seem to radiate an ecstatic balance while simultaneously challenging all the tenets of pattern and symmetry. I first encountered these quilts on a series of postage stamps, and I was struck by their unusual rhythms even at that size. Gee's Bend quilts don't follow the highly structured blueprints of most quilting traditions. A quilt entitled *Snowball,* by quilter Lucy T. Pettway, features a nine-by-ten grid of circles inscribed in squares, alternating red on white, and then white on red. Yet while some of the red patches are solid, others are made of a red fabric with tiny flowers. The floral patches are clustered near the bottom right and the middle left of the quilt, with one or two appearing in other areas, pulling the eye around the composition. One of the most celebrated quilts, *Bars and String-Pieced Columns,* by Jessie T. Pettway, features three striped columns made of pink, white, periwinkle blue, and yellow pieces, bounded by four solid rivers of red. The pieces that form the columns are not rectangular strips but wavy offcuts, resulting in a look that resembles sedimentary rock. The stitching, too, wiggles along with the piecework, superimposing a second undulating texture on top of the first.

There are few ninety-degree angles in these quilts, few straight seams, few shapes that could be described with Euclidean geometry. But far from being imperfect, the subtle curves and dips induce a powerful sense of motion. They feel musical, and the best analogies for their structures do seem to come from music: syncopation — the rhythmic disruption that makes dance music so enjoyable to move to — or improvisational jazz. Looking at them, I wondered if there might be a form of order to these quilts that I just wasn't aware of, and I decided to see if any of the quilters would share their methods.

Not long after leaving Selma, the road thins from two lanes to one, and my cell phone went from one bar to none. GPS was of no help now, and I double-checked the directions given to me over the phone by Mary Ann Pettway, the manager of the quilt collective. I turned left at the dead end onto County Road 29, and after a few miles, I saw it: a white barnlike building, paint peeling off the sides. I'd arrived in Gee's Bend. I now understood the isolation that kept the Gee's Bend quilts from being discovered for so many years. Nestled into a crook of the Alabama River, the all-black enclave was once a cotton plantation owned by a man named Mark H. Pettway. After emancipation, most of the population kept the name Pettway and stayed on as sharecroppers, often struggling with devastating poverty. Only one road goes in and out of the town (now officially known as Boykin). The main lifeline is a ferry across the river, but service was suspended in the 1960s when residents went across to Camden attempting to register to vote and wasn't reinstated until 2006. Gee's Bend women have been quilting since at least the 1920s, but it wasn't until an intrepid collector named William Arnett began visiting the area in the 1970s that the uniqueness of their quilts started to gain broad recognition. Critics have compared them to works by Henri Matisse and Paul Klee, and many have been exhibited at museums around the country. Most sell for upward of five thousand dollars.

Many Gee's Bend quilts have roots in common patterns. Inside the collective building, Nancy Pettway rattled off names to me, unfurling the quilts to illustrate them. A Housetop features concentric squares. A Log Cabin is similar, but with contrasting colors emphasizing the diagonal lines of the squares. A Nine-Patch is pretty much what it sounds like. But these patterns are less templates than loose structures that enable a joyous kind of improvisation. "This one start off as a Housetop, then end up as a Log Cabin," the round-cheeked Pettway said as she unfolded a quilt and laid it across her lap, where it blended in with the flowered print of her skirt. Often a quilt starts down one path, and then the quilter catches a glimpse of another idea. On the wall, hanging from binder clips, was a quilt that seemed to germinate from a sweet little checkerboard into a wild gambol of blue and red before settling back into a classic Housetop with granny florals. Such improvisation may have originated in part out of necessity, just as quilting itself did. Gee's Bend houses were poorly insulated, and women made quilts for the simple reason that they needed to keep their families warm. When explaining why her mother made her learn how to quilt, Lucy Marie Mingo, now eighty-four years old, said, "Mama told me this, and she told the truth. 'You need to learn how to quilt because when you get married, you don't know how many children you're going to have. So if you know how to make your own quilts, you won't have to buy everything.'" (She ended up having ten kids, not to mention a six-foot-six husband who needed his quilts extra long.) Until the mid-twentieth century, most Gee's Bend quilts were made from worn-out work clothes: denims and corduroys, lightweight cottons, sometimes a bandanna. Shaped first to the human body, most of these materials came with their own contours. One quilter, Polly Bennett, described her quilts as "get-togethers," because they were made from whatever pieces she could get together. The women worked with what they had and sought to pull beauty out of it.

But improvisation thrived in Gee's Bend not just because it was necessary. It was also a source of joy and pride. While most of the quilters' daily lives were occupied with tending crops, raising children, and household chores, quilting offered a rare creative respite. Quilters celebrated one another's ingenuity and shared their techniques. Curious about how these artists developed such harmonious compositions without adhering to strict patterns, I asked Mary Ann Pettway if she could explain to me how she pieced her quilts. With hardly a word, she went to the worktable and began to show me. She emptied out a bag of small scraps of fabric and sifted through it with tape-covered fingertips, searching almost more by feel than by sight. Finding two pieces that seemed to work, she aligned the edges and then ran them through the sewing machine. She cut the thread, then began again. Search, position, sew, snip. She spiraled out like a nautilus, starting with small pieces and then adding larger ones around them, feeling for balance intuitively along the way. Sometimes she laid a piece on one edge, then tried it in a different spot before fastening it in place. It seemed a bit like cooking without a recipe. When there's no blueprint, you rely more heavily on the calibration of your senses. You weigh ingredients with your hands, confirming with your nose. You assess the progress by changes in color and the hisses and burbles coming from the stove. Nothing is measured; nothing is perfect. When I asked Pettway how she knew when the composition was good, she gave me the same matter-of-fact answer I heard from Nancy Pettway and Lucy Mingo: "It just looks right."

If I'm honest, I'll admit that I hoped to find some secret, underlying pattern in these quilts, a bit like the fractals embedded in Pollock's paint splotches. Perhaps one day an intrepid mathematician with a penchant for folk art will find one. But what I left Gee's Bend with is a reminder that harmony lies not just in the perfect, but also in the perfectly imperfect. Outside the car window, I saw patches of grass, mown in uneven, alternating green bands. Fences divided the land into irregular patches. And on the tar-squiggled road, the double yellow lines stretched out like a meandering furrow of stitches, keeping its own rhythm, finding its own flow.

5.

PLAY

I was fifty feet offshore, tucked inside a cove on the western side of Isabela Island, breathless. I pointed my mask down, then spun around, looking for the sea lion. All of a sudden, I saw her swimming, her huge brown body racing toward me at an impossible speed. Fear began to surface in my body again, but I hardly had time to brace myself when just inches in front of me she dove under my feet, leaving me aswirl in bubbles. I pulled my head up out of the water and spat out my snorkel in a laugh that shook my whole body. I'd played with babies, dogs, and kittens, but I'd never experienced a joy quite like being caught up in a game of chicken with a Galapagos sea lion.

Play is one of our greatest means of accessing delight, with deep roots in human life. Archaeologists have found children's toys, such as dolls, spinning tops, and rattles, at various sites across the ancient world. But because children play with all kinds of objects, not just those specifically designed as toys, play is likely much older than the archaeological record suggests. All species of primates play. Among these, it's our closest relatives, chimpanzees and bonobos, that are the most playful. Though it was once believed that only mammals played, researchers have observed playful behavior in surprising corners of the animal kingdom: octopuses playing with Legos, turtles batting around balls, and crocodiles giving each other piggyback rides. Our truest human expression of joy, laughter, likely emerged from play. Scientists believe that it evolved from the panting sounds and "play face" that primates make when immersed in play with one another.

Play was an obvious place for me to start when I first began to research joy, because it is the source of so many people's earliest joyful memories. One friend recalled trying to suppress her giggles while playing "sardines" with her cousins. The game is like hide-and-seek except that only one person hides, and when the seekers find the hider, they quietly cram into the hiding spot like sardines, until the last person finds them, and they all spill out. Another friend spoke fondly about the elaborate cardboard forts he used to build in his living room with his parents. Play etches itself deeply into our memories for a good reason: it is the only known activity that humans engage in solely because it produces joy. We eat and make love because they're pleasurable, but that pleasure exists in the service of greater needs. Eating nourishes us, and sex, without birth control, propagates the species. Work can be pleasurable, too, but that pleasure is usually tied to an outcome: money, mastery, recognition, or the satisfaction of having helped someone or produced something. But the only metric of success for play is how much joy it produces. As a result, play has often been dismissed as frivolous, unnecessary. Like emotion, it has received relatively little attention from the scientific community. Yet in recent years there has been a surge of interest in the study of play, in both humans and animals, and a body of research has amassed that points to its critical role in human life.

It would be hard to find a more exuberant advocate for play than Stuart Brown, the spry eighty-two-year-old founder of the National Institute for Play. I drove out to meet him at his house in Carmel Valley, California, on a sunny autumn day. He came bounding down the driveway wearing an orange sweater and tennis shoes, energetic as a Labrador, and waved me into his home office.

"The need to play is in us," he said after we'd gotten settled, "and if we don't do it, we're in trouble." He came to this conclusion via an unlikely route. Years ago, he had been tasked with studying convicted murderers in the Texas prison system, in an effort to understand whether there were factors that could make a person susceptible to violent behavior. He and his team took comprehensive inventories of the criminals' lives, conducting detailed interviews, consulting their friends and families, and comparing them with a well-matched noncriminal control population. After sifting through all this information, they noticed a surprising common thread. "Nearly all of these violent offenders had deficient or deviant play histories," said Brown. Some had abusive parents with volatile tempers or strict parents who set harsh rules. Others were socially isolated. For a variety of reasons, their childhoods were marked by a severe absence of play.

While violent behavior likely has roots in a range of factors, from genetic predisposition to physical abuse, the potential link to play stood out to Brown because it seemed so surprising. But it began to make more sense as he learned of the many ways that play influences our social and emotional development. Play lets us practice give-and-take, through which we learn empathy and fairness. It also promotes flexible thinking and problem-solving, which increase our resilience and help us adapt to change. When we play, our awareness of time diminishes, and our self-consciousness fades. Play can put us in a powerful flow state, which allows us to let go of everyday worries and be absorbed in the joy of the moment.

For children, unfettered by responsibility, the world of play mingles with real life. A game of peekaboo, a walk in the park, even accompanying a parent on a routine errand can be an occasion for imagination and frolic. As we age, we're told to "quit playing around," we have more homework than recess, and we learn that seriousness is prized over joy. Of course, most of us maintain an inner child who sneaks out every now and then to have a pillow fight, ride a roller coaster, or catch snowflakes on her tongue. But the moments when we let that inner child out are few and far between. In Brown's view, the goal-oriented nature of our society starts to suppress our natural play impulses even in childhood. "If you've had a helicopter parent who's overorganized you, or you've primarily been rewarded for your performance, there's a play debt in there that blocks access to your personal playfulness." Brown has found this "play debt" particularly acute among the elite students he's met when lecturing at competitive universities. He believes students today are more knowledgeable than ever, but less spontaneously joyful. "The culture needs more play," he said, wistfully.

After my conversation with Brown, I began to notice that while the topic of work-life balance comes up frequently in the media, play is largely absent from the conversation. The notion of making more free time has been gaining traction, but most people I know use that extra time to catch up on errands or email, or recharge their batteries through passive relaxation, such as binge-watching Netflix or online shopping. But the most joyful people I know manage to hold a space for play in their adult lives: a recreational sport, an improv-comedy hobby, a band they jam with on weekends, a family game night, or an hour a week set aside to dabble in watercolors. Not only that, these people also bring the spirit of play out of their "playtime" and into the rest of their lives. They play with their friends at dinner parties and with their dogs at the park. They play in business meetings and in their marriages.

"We still have that child in us," said comedian Ellen DeGeneres in one of her standup routines. "Each one of us has that child that we need to play with every day." She joked that insomnia was probably the result of a playful inner child who was bored from being cooped up all day. "I don't know what happens, but somewhere along the way we just get so jaded, and we lose that joy and that bliss." As a remedy, she suggested the following: "Go up to a total stranger tomorrow on the street, just go up to 'em and…go 'You're it!' And just run away!" She envisioned a giant game of tag across the city, everybody playing with their briefcases and backpacks, shouting "Who's it?" "I'm it?" "No, you're it!"

I found Ellen's notion that the child within us is bored, yet otherwise alive and well, to be a big relief. We don't lose our instinct for play, even if we do lose touch with it at times. Stuart Brown agreed. "Play is generated from deep within us as an instinctive, subcortical, primal force. It's in there." But how do we draw it out? A common approach uses nostalgia to inspire playfulness. If we are at our most playful in childhood, the thinking goes, then an environment that transports us back there might stir joyful memories and reconnect us with our impulse to play. In an effort to boost creativity, some organizations, especially technology startups and corporate R & D groups, create innovation spaces inspired by kindergarten classrooms and playgrounds. They feature bright, primary colors and rubber floor mats or plush rugs instead of hard flooring, and they often have colorful beanbag chairs or foam cubes that can be moved around. Some companies even include rock-climbing walls or slides instead of stairs.

This approach can be effective, not least because it brings other aesthetics of joy into a space, such as energy and freedom. Most places we view as playful tend to incorporate these aesthetics, because exuberant energy and unbridled freedom help fuel a spirited, generative sense of play. But the approach also has a downside. For people who haven't connected with their inner child in a long time, such environments can feel overwhelming, even condescending—especially in a workplace context. Play can be profoundly liberating, but it can also make us feel vulnerable. It breaks routines and exposes us to the unpredictable. While lifelong players know that there's no right or wrong way to play, people who don't play regularly might wonder if they're doing it badly. The unfortunate result is that sometimes these adult playgrounds actually foster resistance to play rather than a desire to join in.

As I was thinking about whether there might be another way to approach this, I recalled something Brown had told me about animal play. He said that animals invite one another to play with gestures called play cues. Dogs, for example, will dip their front legs in a gesture ethologists call a play bow. Other animals will gently slap a paw. Among humans, a mischievous smile, a silly face, or a teasing punch in the arm might suggest that play is likely to ensue. These cues are an invitation to enter a safe, joyful space, one that is governed by different rules from those of everyday life. They are, in Brown's words, "fundamental mammal-to-mammal cues that allow pleasure, safety, and nonviolence to occur." What struck me about this was that all of these gestures are nonverbal. Play seems to have its own physical language.

I wondered if there might be a variant of this play language in the inanimate world. Do objects somehow suggest to us through their aesthetics that they'd make good toys? Do certain spaces have embedded cues that make us want to play? I went back to the wall of joyful images I had pinned up in my studio when I first started thinking about joy and cast my eye over the pictures of toys and playrooms, amusement parks and schoolyards. Suddenly, I had a kind of "eureka!" moment. A single shape appeared over and over throughout the images.

THE SHAPE OF PLAY

I took out a highlighter and traced the circle of a Hula-Hoop and the perimeter of a spinning top. I drew along the edge of a kiddie pool photographed from above, a cool blue circle. The Ferris wheel, the merry-go-round, the game of ring-around-the-rosy, all describe circular arcs. Bubbles, balls, and balloons: all round. Aesthetically, the story of childhood is the story of the circle and the sphere.

Round forms are magnetic, especially to children, and often become toys no matter their original purpose. My father learned this the hard way, when I was about six years old. One day I came across a glossy ceramic sphere in my neighbor's yard and couldn't resist trying to roll it down a hill. As it turned out, the "ball" was a sculpture by the artist Grace Knowlton, which I learned only after it had broken into several pieces. Many guilty tears were shed, though fortunately the artist was gracious in piecing it back together and, according to my father, kindly declared she liked the sculpture better that way. But my confusion was easy to understand: circular and spherical objects have been used as toys for thousands of years. A circle made of vines, resembling a modern Hula-Hoop, was used as a toy by Egyptian children as far back as 1000 B.C. Mesoamerican cultures play a game with a rubber ball called *ulama* that dates to at least 1600 B.C., making it one of the oldest continuously played sports in the world. Ball games were also common in ancient Greece and Rome. Break out a ball, and a dog, a chimpanzee, or a dolphin will try to play with it. Sea lions even play with puffer fish as if they were beach balls. "It shouldn't surprise us that a ball in the hands of a highly intelligent, social animal is going to bring out a lot of familiar behaviors," says anthropologist John Fox in the documentary *Bounce: How the Ball Taught the World to Play*. But why do round objects act as such strong and universal play cues?

As children grow, they must navigate between opposing goals: safety and exploration. Learning about the world requires hands-on engagement, but this entails a certain amount of risk. Playful objects help resolve this tension, promoting discovery without subjecting the player to unnecessary danger.

Circles and spheres are the most approachable shapes, with no sharp edges to risk injury. Our emotional brain understands this intuitively and unconsciously prefers round forms over angular ones. Research has shown that people implicitly associate curved forms with safety and positivity, while associating sharp angles with danger and negativity. A 2007 study uncovered a potential source of this response: heightened activation in a part of the limbic system called the amygdala, a small, almond-shaped structure known to be involved in fear processing. Using functional magnetic resonance imaging (fMRI), researchers revealed that the right amygdala lit up when subjects looked at an angular object, such as a square dish or sharp-cornered chair, but stayed quiet when they looked at a curved version of the same object. They speculate that because sharp objects in our environment, such as teeth or thorns, represented potential sources of danger to our ancestors, we have evolved to respond to angled contours with an unconscious level of caution.

As any parent of a crawling infant quickly learns, sharp corners don't make for a playful house. "Childproofing" companies market all manner of stick-on bumpers that new parents can use to swaddle their angular furniture in soft foam. But a home full of angles isn't just hazardous to a child. It sets everyone subtly on edge. Sharp angles slow our movement and increase the sense of formality in a space. You don't break into spontaneous happy dances in a living room where you risk splitting your shin on the coffee table, and you don't do a running jump to join your partner in bed when you might catch your foot on the corner of the bedpost. Because hard angles inhibit joyful movement, they also decrease flow, and I wasn't surprised to find that feng shui practitioners discourage using them in the home. Cathleen McCandless goes so far as to recommend houseplants with rounded leaves rather than spiky ones. While I tend to feel that any plant is better than none, McCandless's advice points to an important nuance. Angular objects, even if they're not directly in your path as you move through your home, have an unconscious effect on your emotions. They may look chic and sophisticated, but they inhibit our playful impulses.

Round shapes do just the opposite. A circular or elliptical coffee table changes a living room from a space for sedate, restrained interactions to a lively center for conversation and impromptu games. A large rubber exercise ball used instead of a desk chair does more than improve core strength and posture. It can also create a sense of playfulness in an office, especially if several workers choose to use them. Pom-poms sewn along the edges of curtains or pillows make them irresistibly playful and tactile, while polka dots and penny tiles do double duty, mixing play with abundance. Even flowers can be playful: a bouquet of pom-pom dahlias or yellow, ball-shaped billy buttons brings play together with the natural textures of the freedom aesthetic.

I've slowly been adding round shapes to my apartment: a spherical light fixture here, a circular mirror there. Of course, sometimes a rectangular profile will work better in the space you have. If you find this to be the case, you can still soften the edges by choosing a design with curved corners. This is a common strategy employed by toy makers: many toys are simply rounded versions of cars, tools, and other everyday objects. But this doesn't have to mean making your house look like a toy store. By using more subdued materials, such as wood or marble, and limiting the use of primary colors, you can incorporate the playfulness of round shapes without the kindergarten feel. My penchant for circles has occasionally backfired. For a period of time I was lobbying Albert to find a place outside the apartment to store his bike, until one day he casually observed, "It's nice having the bike in the house because it has two big circles." I looked over at the wheels and found I couldn't disagree. The bike stayed put.

Safety isn't the only thing that roundness has going for it. Curved objects have a broad range of "affordances," a term designers use to describe the different ways an object can be used. When creating objects for everyday life, designers usually try to limit the affordances so that the object's function is clear to the person using it. For example, a door with a bar-shaped handle has affordances that suggest it can be pulled or pushed. Because both actions look equally possible, manufacturers often have to supplement with a label indicating PULL or PUSH. But when you see a door with a flat metal plate, you know automatically to push, because that's the only action available to you. Everyday objects with limited affordances help us more easily make our way through the world. But because play involves undirected activity and a search for novelty, the best toys are those that can be used in a wide variety of ways. This explains why found objects such as rocks and sticks make such attractive playthings, and why snow is so joyful: it changes the affordances of the landscape, turning an ordinary surface into something that can be scooped, slid across, and shaped into an endless variety of forms.

Of all toys, balls have the broadest affordances. They contact the ground at only one point, thereby reducing friction and making them dynamic and unpredictable. Balls roll, twirl, spin, and bounce. They can be hit or kicked, whacked with a stick or shot through a hoop, volleyed with rackets or bare hands. Two kids with a ball and limited supervision can come up with an entire Olympics' worth of new sports in an afternoon. (My childhood favorite was "pancake-turner ball," a tennis-like game using spatulas for rackets, best played out of the vicinity of rare china and mirrors.) Round objects offer unique potential for discovery and delight.

Perhaps another reason that curves feel so playful is that they echo the movements we make when we play. Children run in swooping arcs, and when engaged in rough-and-tumble play, they signal that they're not dangerous to their playmates by subtly rounding their movements, instead of moving in straight lines. According to Stuart Brown, curvilinear movements send the message that we are operating in the land of the "not real," making it safe to engage. This reminds me of something interior designer Ghislaine Viñas said when I asked her how she would design a playful home. She was silent for a few moments, and then a knowing look suddenly came over her face. "Creating circles in a home — if you can ever do it — is amazing for children," she said. She explained that the layout of her apartment has two hallways that connect the rooms in the front to the ones in the back, creating a kind of closed loop within the home. "When my kids were little, it used to make them so happy to run around this circuit," she said. Memories of houses from my own childhood flashed through my mind. The house I grew up in had a circle on the first floor connecting the kitchen, dining room, living room, and den. My best friend's house was even better, with two connected staircases that we used to run up, down, and around. It's not always easy to do, but if you are renovating, adding an extra doorway can open up playful new possibilities in a home. "It's a magical thing that happens," said Viñas. "If you're living in confined spaces, instead of having cul-de-sacs that you go into and come back out of, the circular form can create so much continuity." As I thought about it, I realized this layout also makes parties more enjoyable. Circular layouts increase movement, reducing the likelihood of guests getting stuck in a corner and making it easier to mingle. It seems circular movement is joyful, even for adults.

CUTE AS A BUTTON

In a 2008 *Saturday Night Live* skit, the actor Christopher Walken plays a mild-mannered gardener with a problematic phobia: he is afraid of plants. Fortunately, he has developed a strategy to mitigate this debilitating fear. As the camera fades in, we see him in a beige apron misting a stand of cacti, each with a pair of googly eyes affixed to it. "Normally, plants don't have eyes," intones Walken, with his characteristic deadpan, "so it's hard for me to trust them." He shrugs. "Hence, googly eyes." It isn't just spiky succulents but also ferns, trees, and even grass that get the googly-eye treatment, though much to his consternation, the eyes don't stick to the tiny grass blades. The shy gardener attributes the success of this strategy to the way it enables him to make eye contact with his plants. But the cartoonish stick-on eyes have another effect, one that is much more subtle: they make even the prickliest cactus look playful and innocent. Though it was a silly sketch, it made me curious. The googly eyes didn't make the cacti any less spiky, so why did they suddenly seem so much friendlier?

A clue arrived in the form of a friend's new kitten. On a recent visit, I was sitting on the floor playing with the tiny tabby when she got

a little overexcited and dug her needlelike claws into my forearm. I yelped and pulled my hand away, but as I did so, the kitten cocked her head to the side and looked up at me with huge round eyes. Though I knew she might scratch me again, I found myself reaching back out to keep the game going. I later discovered there was more to that wide-eyed gaze than I had originally thought. Big eyes are a key characteristic of what ethologist Konrad Lorenz called the baby schema, a set of physical attributes common to juvenile animals of many species (including humans) that lend an appearance of innocence and vulnerability. Compared with adults, baby animals tend to have larger, more circular faces relative to their bodies, rounder features, and less pronounced noses or snouts. These features create an impression of cuteness that is hard to resist.

We've all succumbed to the delight of cuteness at one point or another, whether cooing at a newborn in the grocery store or getting sucked into a video shared on social media about baby otters. But what we don't often think about is that cuteness helps ensure the survival of a species. Because mammals are born in live births, they are typically dependent on their parents for a significant period of time, humans especially so. While a rhesus monkey's brain is 65 percent of its mature size at birth, a human infant's is only 23 percent of its final size. Human babies are born particularly helpless and don't become self-sufficient for several years. And at various points along that journey, as any parent knows, children can be trying, diverting resources from other pursuits and pleasures. Those big eyes and apple cheeks create a spark of joy and stimulate protective, nurturing impulses that help ensure a baby's survival.

Research has demonstrated that infant features are detected by the brain more quickly than adult features and have found that looking at pictures of cute infants stimulates activity in an area of the brain called the medial orbitofrontal cortex, a region involved in feelings of reward and motivation. The attraction to infant features is so pervasive that it holds true for both parents and nonparents, men and women. It even affects children as young as three (perhaps as a defense against jealousy in older siblings). But more than just a caretaking response, cuteness also elicits a playful one. We don't sit back and watch a baby or a puppy from a distance. We get down on the floor and play. We tickle and touch. Psychologists Jonathan Haidt and Gary D. Sherman believe that this response may have adaptive value, because it increases social engagement. Time spent playing facilitates bonding, which strengthens the caregiver's attachment and creates an abundance of sensorial and verbal stimulation for a baby. The soft, rounded features we consider cute function as a particularly compelling form of play cue. They enroll us as helpers in a child's development, and in return, they give us access to our own playfulness.

Given our response to kittens and pretty much any other baby animal, it is obvious that our attraction to cuteness isn't just confined to human babies. But I quickly discovered that cute features don't even need to belong to a living creature to evoke a tender kind of joy. The oversize heads, rounded ears, and downy coats of stuffed animals make them treasured playthings for children worldwide. Cartoon characters from Bambi to Tweety to Hello Kitty are similarly round and evocative. This is no accident. Walt Disney was well aware of the power of cuteness to stir emotion and supposedly taped a note reading "Keep it cute!" above his animators' desks. As a result, cute characters often have even bigger faces and rounder eyes than the most adorable baby animals. It is strange to think that a few curvy lines on a page or a screen can bring on a genuine pang of playfulness and affection. Those lines take advantage of a psychological quirk known as peak shift effect, which can lead us to respond to an exaggerated stimulus even more strongly than the real thing. Many animals are susceptible to this effect. Some birds, for example, will ignore their own nestlings to feed a fake baby bird beak on a stick, as long as the fake beak is redder and wider than those of their chicks. The peak shift effect explains why bobblehead dolls are so delightful and why googly eyes make cacti (or anything else) so terribly disarming. They possess a hyperpotent form of cuteness that we are hardwired to find irresistible.

I soon realized that ordinary objects could piggyback on our natural receptivity to cute features. The Fiat 500 and the Mini Cooper are both terribly cute cars, inspiring deep affection on the part of their owners. A recent study compared images of the fronts of cars with similar images that had been altered to create a more baby-faced look, by enlarging the headlights (usually seen as eyes) and shrinking the grille and air vent (correlating to nose and mouth). Researchers discovered that looking at the cute cars triggered a subtle activation of the zygomaticus major muscle, one of the primary muscles involved in smiling. The cute typeface Comic Sans remains incredibly popular, despite being ridiculed by designers, because of its rounded, childish forms, which seem to take the edge off of whatever message it is conveying. Cute gadgets, sometimes called cutensils, bring this playful feeling to mundane objects such as kitchen tools, tableware, and tech accessories. We owe the proliferation of cute things in our lives in large part to a collaboration between retail giant Target and architect Michael Graves that began in 1999, launching Target's effort to make high design more accessible. The products from that collection, among them a bubbly toaster and a teakettle with a spinning whistle, attracted so many fans that Graves went on to design more than two thousand products for Target, which in turn inspired other designers to adopt a cute aesthetic. After being paralyzed in 2003 by an illness, Graves became dismayed by the spartan, depressing aesthetics of products for the elderly and people with disabilities. In the last decade of his life, he designed wheelchairs, hospital beds, walking sticks, and bathtub grab bars with chubby curves that were both joyful to look at and easier for patients to hold and use.

Despite our attraction to cute things, I've noticed that cuteness sometimes has a pejorative connotation. Just like play itself, it is easily dismissed as frivolous. But research indicates that cuteness actually affects our attention in positive ways. A recent study from Japan showed that people performed better on tasks requiring intense concentration and conscientiousness after looking at cute babies and animals. The researchers speculate that cute aesthetics could be beneficial in applications that demand heightened focus, such as driving or office work. This suggests that Apple may have been onto something when it launched the bubbly iMac in the late 1990s and that a cute task lamp or stationery set isn't just playful, but may be practical as well.

Of course, no place has more cuteness per square foot than Disneyland, which does not so much draw out the inner child as melt the adult around it. Cute boats and cars whisk families on rides through colorful, miniaturized worlds. Big-eyed characters pose for pictures with adoring fans. Round edges abound, and lilting music fills the air. On a recent visit, I met three brothers in their seventies, one of whom was wearing a white collared shirt with the classic Disney characters embroidered across the front. "I'm just a kid at heart," the man told me. "I like color. I like laughter. Where I live doesn't have that, so if I can find it, I go to it." The cuteness may be over the top, but Disneyland is valuable because it is one of the few places where adults give themselves permission to play. As Holocaust survivor Elie Wiesel wrote after a trip there in 1957, "Today, I visited not only Disneyland, but also—and especially—my childhood."

AHEAD OF THE CURVE

"Why to be serious do things have to look serious?" Gaetano Pesce raised a silvery eyebrow and shrugged his shoulders. If the world had an answer to that question, I knew I wouldn't find it here in the Italian designer's SoHo studio, a wild menagerie of whimsical forms. Swirling pools of gem-colored resin folded themselves into chairs, tables, and vessels. A collection of urns reminiscent of sea creatures spilled from a table onto the floor. Quite a few things looked as if they might have been made of sugar. A mannequin wearing a stack of rubbery necklaces, like ropes of gummy candy, kept company with a bowl that had the glassy texture of the clear, hard sour balls my grandfather used to keep on the bench seat of his Cadillac.

I nestled into a semicylinder of red felt lined with quilted turquoise fabric. The felt bent back on itself, creating an adjustable cowl that felt regal and cozy at the same time. Pesce sat opposite me on another of his creations, a sofa made to look like the New York City skyline, the backrest a huge full moon rising behind him. At seventy-eight, he showed no sign of slowing the pace of his creative output—a whiteboard in the studio labeled LISTA PROGETTI (project list) contained twenty-two active items. Nor did he seem inclined to tame the raucous mix of shapes and materials that has made him one of the most celebrated designers in the world. I had come to visit Pesce because he is the rare designer who makes objects that are unapologetically joyful. Yes, like every designer he creates useful things: chairs, tables, lamps, shoes.

But the difference is that Pesce's objects seem first and foremost designed to delight. Joy is their raison d'être, not a veneer applied at the end.

"I've always wanted to make things that help people to laugh," said Pesce. "I try with my work to give a positive feeling, something opposite to the news." For Pesce, this means color, light, and, above all, curves. "There is no joy in the rectangle, the triangle, the square," he said. "I try to create with shapes that are friendly. I draw from a catalog of geometry that is organic and alive." "Catalog" seemed like the right word. In Pesce's studio, I could see a whole palette of playful forms that went far beyond the circle and the sphere. His lines could be loopy, wavy, or wiggly, his structures bulging and bombous or gooey and elastic. I thought of Stuart Brown's observation that the movements of play tend to be curvilinear, and I realized that this is exactly what Pesce does: he crystallizes the motions of play into form. Most of his designs are developed through hands-on exploration with materials, and as I looked at the different objects, I began to imagine the motions that had created them. Twisting lines, squiggly doodles, splats, and splotches—the shapes seemed to brim with energy, as if play might erupt at any time.

Pesce's lighthearted work has made him an anomaly in the world of avant-garde design, where self-seriousness and cool intellectualism reign supreme. His work is like a fit of giggles in an academic lecture hall, a bright burst of humanity amid all the sober philosophizing and pretense. But the whimsy of Pesce's designs belies the fact that they contain serious innovations. I looked to my right to see a prime example, the voluptuous bulk of the *Up 5* chair (also known as *La Mamma*), the first Pesce design I ever encountered. It was in a friend of a friend's apartment, sitting in the corner, covered in a red-and-gold-striped fabric that undulated over its zaftig curves. It was pure joy to sink into that chair, to try to balance my feet on its ball-shaped ottoman, tied to the chair with a thick cord. I sat there most of the night like a princess on a cartoon throne and had to be pulled out of it when it was time to go home. What I didn't know at the time was that Pesce had used new manufacturing techniques to mold the chair entirely out of closed-cell polyurethane foam, with no internal frame. This allowed the chair to be compressed to 10 percent of its size and vacuum sealed into a vinyl envelope so it could be shipped flat like a pancake. When it arrived at your home, it magically rose into shape.

The innovative nature of Pesce's work gives credence to the notion that play can facilitate creativity. Pesce believes, as many scientists do, that when people are able to retain a childlike perspective, they open themselves up to fresh ideas that lie outside of traditional frameworks. But a few months after my visit to his studio, I was intrigued to find research that suggested a more unconscious link between play and cre-

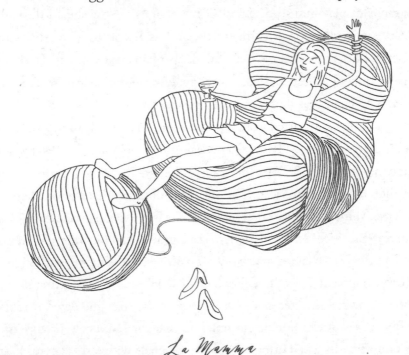

La Mamma

ativity, involving the curving movements so common in play. In a series of studies, people were asked to trace a drawing either with swooping lines that forced their arms to move in fluid curves or angular lines that produced herky-jerky movements. Then they were given a creative task. Participants who moved fluidly were able to generate more ideas for uses of a newspaper, and the ideas they came up with were more original. (For example, a typical use of a newspaper might be to cover the floor with it when training a puppy. An original idea might be to use it to transfer text onto wet nail polish.) Curvilinear movements seemed to unlock a more flexible thought pattern, which in turn heightened creativity. Subsequent studies revealed that curved movements decreased rigidity in other types of thought patterns. Curves made people more likely to believe that racial categories were socially constructed and elastic, rather than biological and fixed, and less likely to make discriminatory judgments about others based on stereotypes.

Games or activities that get your body moving in curvy arcs — playing catch, Hula-Hooping, or even doing the actual hula — could be a way to encourage more innovative ideas and open-minded collaboration in the workplace. It may even be enough to be in a place where you can simply look at curves. In several of the studies mentioned above, participants didn't actually make fluid movements with their arms. Instead, they watched a video of a red circle making curved motions on a screen. While more research is needed, this raises the possibility that spaces with curvy lines might induce the eye to move in ways that prompt fluid thought.

I was originally focused on how the play aesthetic could bring more levity to the home. But this research made me think the aesthetic could potentially have an even-bigger impact on the places in which we work and learn. Most offices, factories, and schools bear no traces of curves. (The signature element of most offices is the exact opposite: the cube.) One reason for this is surely cost. Curved building components, such as doors or windows, tend to be custom-made rather than off-the-shelf, making them more time-consuming to produce and more expensive. This was the reason that the British government gave in 2012 when it banned the use of curves in the design of school buildings. But this doesn't explain why curves rarely appear even as surface treatments in these buildings—in paint or flooring, for example—or in furnishings like desks, chairs, and lighting, where curvy things cost no more than angular ones. I thought back to Pesce's opening question: "Why to be serious do things have to look serious?" I believe we unconsciously abide by this principle because our notion of work is rooted in an industrial economy that values efficiency and structure at the expense of joy and creativity. Our workplaces and learning environments (starting in middle school, if not before) exclude play cues, creating a tangible reminder that work is a serious enterprise where the inner child is not welcome. But as Stuart Brown observes, the separation of work and play is a false construct. "The opposite of play is not work," he often says. "It's depression."

Bringing work and play back together won't happen overnight, but perhaps incorporating playful curves into our workspaces might help start to fuse them. Brown points to the ringlike form of the new Norman Foster–designed Apple headquarters as an example of the way that an innovative company might start to bring aesthetics of play back into the workplace. If a new headquarters isn't in your company's budget, curvy room dividers, circular furnishings, and round carpets could help. If you don't have much control over your workspace, a piece of art featuring a flowing design or some curvy desk accessories could bring more curvilinear elements into your space. I keep a collection of tiny wooden tops on my desk. Whenever I get stuck on a problem, I spin them, and they make me feel like my thoughts are still flowing.

Curves play a vital role in a recently redesigned school, one with a poignant history: the Sandy Hook Elementary School in Newtown, Connecticut. After the devastating shooting in December 2012 that killed twenty children and eight adults, the town decided to raze the original brick building and hire the New Haven–based architecture firm Svigals + Partners to design a new one. The need for security was at the forefront of everyone's mind—a long list of new safety regulations had been mandated by the state—and the resulting building could easily have resembled a fortress. Instead it feels like a pair of arms stretched out in welcoming embrace. The floor plan of the school is curved, with the building's spine bowing gently in toward the parking lot. The curved shape of the school is not only playful but also acts as a subtle security feature, giving staff members in the administrative offices at one end of the building a view into the music and art classrooms at the other, increasing the natural surveillance of the school. A wavy line of two-tone wood cladding runs the length of the façade, and the staggered windows seem almost to bounce softly up and down with it. Squiggly canopies cover the entrances to the school. The curves were mostly inspired by the site's rolling hills and nearby rivers, but Barry Svigals, the founder of Svigals + Partners, also admits a more intuitive inspiration. "Some elements are squiggly because, well, squiggly is fun!"

A big goal for Svigals was to integrate play into the school building itself. He pointed out that the contrast between playgrounds and schools often implies that play can only take place in certain places and certain ways. By giving the school a playful form and keeping the affordances open, the architects created space for kids to exercise their own creativity. He said he often observes spontaneous and surprising examples of play when he visits the school. The curved main hallway, for example, features a few stained-glass panels. "I came out of a meeting a few weeks ago," said Svigals, "and there were kids running in and out of the reflections of colored light from the stained glass onto the floor." He laughed as he recalled it. "I would never have thought of doing that."

* * *

Back at home, I was organizing photos when I came across the pictures of Gaetano Pesce's studio. I noticed something so subtle I had missed it earlier. The ceiling was shaped like a series of waves. It was as if I were looking up at the surface of the ocean from underwater. I looked up at my own ceiling, a large rectangle crisscrossed by rectangular beams. My rectangular apartment had rectangular walls and a rectangular floor. A rectangular window shaped my view, which looked out over the stairstepped skyline of New York City, itself a sea of rectangles. I had added curves here and there, but I couldn't help but wonder what life might be like in a more circular frame.

It's surprisingly difficult to find architects who specialize in round buildings, but after a little research I came upon pictures of an odd-looking house constructed entirely of spheres. Built in the 1970s in France by an obscure Hungarian architect named Antti Lovag, it was intended to be a new kind of dwelling that was more aligned with the movements of the human body. "The motion of human arms and legs traces circles in the air," Lovag has been quoted as saying. "We have a circular field of vision. Conviviality is a circular phenomenon. The circle structures the way human life is carried out." Like Arakawa and Gins, who designed the sensorially stimulating reversible destiny lofts in Japan, Lovag was an iconoclast who believed that architecture was broken. He sought to develop a new way of building and living embodied by a structure he called the bubble house. But while he was dogmatic in his beliefs, he was uninterested in money and idiosyncratic in his approach. When the rare client came to him wanting a bubble house, he would state three conditions: "I don't know what it's going to be like, I don't know when it's going to be finished, and I don't know how much it's going to cost." This freewheeling approach didn't win him much business, but he found a champion in the French fashion designer Pierre Cardin, who bought an unfinished bubble house in 1992 and contracted with Lovag to expand it. The result is a vast, stunning complex of spheres cascading off the Esterel Massif on the southern coast of France. It's called Le Palais Bulles—the Bubble Palace.

I hastily drafted an email to a Monsieur Jean-Pascal Hesse, Cardin's director of communications, and booked a ticket to France.

LIVING IN A BUBBLE

I rented a car in Nice and began the drive along the water to Théoule-sur-Mer, stopping along the way to pick up my translator, Sylvie. We traced blue scallops of coves along the shore, winding through pink and yellow villages, grand hotels, and marinas full of slender masts. It was still early, but umbrellas had been set out on some of the beaches, and late-season vacationers frolicked on the thin strip of sand between us and the water. As we drew close, the road turned up a hill, narrowing as it climbed the rust-red cliffs studded with pines. We parked the car alongside a stucco wall, planted with prickly pear cacti and inset with a steel gate shaped like a giant sun.

Sylvie peered through the gate. "It looks like the Barbapapa house!" she exclaimed, referencing the globular abode of the pink shape-shifting cartoon character that occupies a beloved niche in

French culture. I joined her and caught a first glimpse of the house's organic curves and the distinctive bubble skylights that appeared like eyes across its surface. It certainly looked like a cartoon character would be perfectly at home here. We spotted a narrow gate to the left—a pedestrian entrance—and through this we could see a thin, curving path leading down into the house. I could hardly stand still, I was so excited, but we were early, so I hesitated to ring the bell. Soon we heard a rustling down below. "Bonjour?" I called out. "Bonjour, bonjour!" I heard in response, and presently the tall, bespectacled figure of Jean-Pascal Hesse appeared from around the bend to let us in. He led us down the driveway toward the main part of the house. We entered a large round atrium through a massive oculus that opened by sliding up, like a garage door. To the right an elliptical window offered a view to the sea. Other rounded openings pierced the space, giving peeks into rooms above and below the main room. Hesse whisked us through the house, up and down stairs, along winding pathways, into and out of the many bedrooms, each decorated by a different young artist. The beds were all circular, covered with tailored quilts in shades of raspberry, mint, and periwinkle, each piled with a small mound of pillows that looked like candies. We followed Hesse down a sweeping hallway to the heart of the house, a living and dining space built at a more intimate scale. There was a round living room with a C-shaped sofa, a dining area that held a circular table with a built-in lazy Susan, and, my favorite, a breakfast nook encased in a bubble that could be unlatched and swiveled open for poolside dining. Hesse excused himself to take a phone call and invited us to explore the place on our own.

I began to wander, aiming to retrace my steps and see everything again at a slower pace. But the house took me on its own journey. I started down the path back to the main atrium, but I couldn't resist poking my head through each circular aperture and following each curving branch off the hallway. I ascended a whorl of stairs up one turn to a closed door made of honey-colored fiberglass, convex and shaped like a duck egg. The door was locked, but I paused for a moment to study the curves, like a ball at the top of its arc before it turns back down. Then I was off again, following pathways that wove between inside and outside, snapping pictures of palm trees framed by portholes and round swatches of clouds through the skylights. Near another set of steps, I was stopped briefly in my tracks by a circular window radiating aqua light: an underwater window into the pool. I followed the curve around, up more steps, and into another bedroom, its walls lined with navy-blue carpet and inset with curving shelves that housed glass vases colored like semiprecious stones: amethyst, lapis, turquoise. A strip of salmon-colored carpet patterned with giant dots led me into a sun-filled lounge with a ring of curvy red plastic chairs as glossy as candy apples. A squiggle-shaped ladder caught my eye, and I climbed it. A new path appeared, and I followed it. The house looped me around and around, as if I were playing hide-and-seek with myself.

The language of buildings fails me when trying to describe this house. The spherical volumes felt more like vessels than rooms. They spilled into each other gently, at elliptical intersections that resembled portals rather than doorways. Walls and ceilings met not in hard lines but in soft arcs and gibbous shapes. Rooms didn't stack into levels, but nestled together like soap bubbles in foam. This gentle, undulating structure was a direct result of Lovag's unorthodox method of design and construction. Instead of following the traditional architectural practice of drawing up precise blueprints, he would arrive on-site with a construction crew and no defined plan. He and his crew would create spheres out of steel mesh, the armatures for the various spaces in the home, and then roll them into place like beach balls. It was construction as play, an improvisational process that allowed the architect to try out different arrangements and create the house in a way that responded to the natural contour of the site. He had only one firm rule: *Pas d'arêtes!*—"No hard edges!"—and the power of that simple rule became evident as I settled into the space. I felt embraced by this house, a feeling I can't remember having had in any other structure. Cardin has said of Palais Bulles, "I love this house, as natural as an egg, as a matrix, even if many people find it difficult to imagine living here. It gives you a sense of well-being, and it never hurts you if you bump into it, as everything is round, even the beds." Light behaves differently here, too. The corners of rectilinear buildings collect shadows and cleave light into splinters. Here, the absence of angles keeps the light whole. It pools and swells. As I sat in a half-moon of pinkish light under one of the skylights, I felt as if I were in a champagne bubble, flung aloft on an endless, effervescent spume.

Antti Lovag would say that he wasn't looking for clients but for *jouers* and *aventuriers* ("players" and "adventurers"), and he found both in Cardin, a figure whose lighthearted approach to fashion had been bucking norms since the 1950s. It seems fitting that the two would have found each other, as both shared a deep affinity for the circular form. One of Cardin's breakout hits was his "bubble dress," a silhouette that features a tight waistline with a loose skirt gathered at the hem in a bubble shape. It became an international sensation, cementing his place in the fashion world. Cardin went on to embrace the circle like no other designer. "Everything in the universe is round," he has said, "from planets to specks of dust, from the cells of the human body to the infinity of the cosmos. The circle symbolizes infinity and perpetual movement; in short, it symbolizes life. In fashion, I have sought to attain the perfection of the circle in the construction of my garments, my shapes, and the materials I use." The space age influenced his work tremendously. He brought stylized space helmets to the runways, and circular eyeglasses that resembled goggles. His collections featured coats with giant polka dots, mod dresses with circular pockets, jackets with circles cut out of them, even a dress with two circular patches placed right over the breasts. In one piece, a short coat, he created stiff arcs of fabric, so that when viewed from just the right angle, the coat looks like a perfect circle. The designs are whimsical yet still elegant. They have something fashion so often seems to lack: a playfulness that reminds us that dressing up is a delight, or at least it can be. They are clothes of which the inner child heartily approves.

Of course, the playful quality of Cardin's clothes and Lovag's bubbles is not wholly innocent. As I wandered in and out of hemispherical bedrooms and curvy bathrooms, through meandering passageways and past intimate alcoves, it was clear to me that this was a place for adults to play. Many fashion shoots have highlighted the sexiness of the house, juxtaposing leggy models with its sinuous curves. "It is the body of a woman," Cardin has said. "The bubbles are her breasts; the passages are her insides. It is all completely sensual." But it is a lighthearted sensuality, one that is rare in modern life. The proliferation of pornography and the mainstreaming of the particular mix of eroticism and violence depicted in books like *Fifty Shades of Grey* have expanded the repertoire of sexual discourse, but in the process they seem to have eclipsed a softer, more playful incarnation of sexuality. This isn't a new issue. In 1977, French philosopher Roland Barthes wrote, "Current opinion always holds sexuality to be aggressive. Hence the notion of a happy, gentle, sensual, jubilant sexuality is never to be found in any text. Where are we to read it then? In painting, or better still, in color." But I think it's more likely to reside in curves. It was curves that typified the aesthetics of the free-loving, boundary-blurring, psychedelic 1960s, a decade when experimentation began to melt the rigid forms of modernism and soften many traditional social roles and codes. The liquid forms of Verner Panton, who created trippy interiors made of curved, upholstered foam, the swirling patterns of Emilio Pucci, and of course Cardin's curvy silhouettes — all had a playful sensuality that, like the Palais Bulles, managed to be grown up without losing their whimsy and verve.

I swooped back toward the living room, where I found Sylvie and Jean-Pascal. Water cascaded down through a series of giant clay-colored bowls into the pool. Sylvie remarked that it was beautiful, and I nodded. Jean-Pascal chuckled and made an offhand remark in French. Sylvie translated for me: "You're welcome to swim if you'd like." I was halfway up the path to the car to get my swimsuit before I realized that he might have been joking. After all, who jumps in the pool in the middle of a workday in October? I didn't even have a towel. But if my eager acceptance of the offer to swim was importune, I shrugged it off. I was too full of joy from time spent wandering the house to worry much about propriety.

I sprinted back down the path and wound my way to the nearest bathroom, pulling off my dress in a mad rush that snarled my hair. I left the clothes in a heap, not worrying about how I might find my way back to them. My only thought was that azure lagoon, perched out at the edge of the cliff like a floating ocean. I eased in, watching my legs turn blue-green. Sylvie went looking for the porthole to see if she could see me underwater. The temperature was bracing, but what did that matter? I was in a bubble pool in a bubble palace. I splashed around,

giddy, my heart like a buoy bobbing at the surface of my chest, pulling joy out of every corner of my soul into a big, curving grin.

*   *   *

The shape of our built environment is defined by choices that are hundreds, if not thousands, of years old. As these choices solidified our buildings and roads into a rigid, angular grid, they took us further and further from the curving, undulating landscape within which we evolved. Perhaps in the process, they also took us further from essential aspects of our own nature: playfulness, creativity, sensuality, joy. Perhaps they took us to a place where we forgot that these aspects were part of our nature at all. Antti Lovag called his philosophy of architecture habitology, because he believed that what people needed were not homes but habitats, places that truly supported human flourishing. But while Lovag aimed big, I believe we can start small. A squiggly canopy here, a curvy mural there. A porthole window here, a pom-pom there. Circle by circle, curve by curve, we can round the edges and break out of the rigid frame of our world.

6.

SURPRISE

I sat near the head of a boardroom table in a towering office building in Sydney, my heart fluttering inside my chest. The table seemed to stretch a mile from end to end. All along its edges sat the directors of business units, division heads, and people whose titles start with the letter *C*. Three weeks earlier, full of the bravery and blind optimism of a twenty-four-year-old who had just moved to the opposite side of the world by herself, I had talked my way into a trial run as a brand consultant, a job I had never done before. I had worked nonstop since then on a brand analysis for the client's new business, expecting that my boss would be the one presenting it. But a few days before the meeting, my boss told me he believed that the people who did the work should speak for it and that, despite my lack of experience, he wanted me to give the presentation. So there I was, pale faced and shaky, awaiting the calamity that I was certain would follow as soon as I opened my mouth.

As the last few attendees straggled in, I tried closing my eyes and taking deep breaths, but as I did so, memories of my previous misadventures in public speaking rose to the surface, and I began to feel even more panicked. I snapped my eyes open and looked down at my feet. Out of the corner of my eye, I noticed a burst of color. A pair of rainbow-striped socks peeked out from under a charcoal-gray pant leg. They seemed so incongruous I wanted to laugh out loud. I looked up at the wearer. It was the imposing, no-nonsense head of the digital business. His eyes followed my gaze to the socks. Then he looked back up, smiled, and winked. A moment later I heard my boss bring the meeting to order and call on me to begin the presentation.

Joy has a way of showing up when we least expect it. As we move through the stream of daily life, tiny moments can capture our attention and turn our thoughts in a joyful direction. These moments can be especially powerful in times of stress or sadness. My encounter with the rainbow socks didn't magically transform me into a brilliant presenter, but it did something else that was helpful in that moment: it interrupted my anxious inner monologue, turning my attention from the highlights reel of my past failures to the incredible opportunity I had before me to share my work with an eager audience. It pulled me back into the room and widened my perspective. Suddenly, I found myself wondering what else might not be as it seemed. Maybe hiding inside all those power suits were other warm or funny people. Maybe my boss wouldn't have given me such a big client if he didn't think I was capable of handling it. Maybe I could do this after all. I can't say I wasn't nervous as I stood in front of that room. In fact, I clutched a water glass for the entire two-hour presentation so tightly my boss later said he could see my white knuckles. But despite my jitters, there were moments when I had to admit to myself that I was actually having fun. In the end I did well enough to turn my trial run into a full-time job and gained more opportunities to practice speaking my mind in public.

Years later, I thought about those rainbow socks and began to wonder why they had affected me so deeply. They were such a small detail, but in that sea of gray they felt like a life raft. I began to take note of moments like this, where a small, unexpected burst of joy seemed to have an outsize effect on my mood. For instance, one day I left work feeling a bit down, only to see a cluster of ice-blue balloons tied to a fire escape with curling ribbon. Against the backdrop of stone and steel, it looked like a giant blue raspberry, and I had to smile. Another day, Albert and I had been arguing in the car. We were coming out of a toll plaza when, as the green light illuminated, we noticed that a smiley face had been drawn over it with black marker. It was so out of context that we burst out laughing, a moment of relief in a tough conversation.

That unforeseen pleasures had such power to shift a bad mood made sense after I did a little bit of research into the nature of surprise, one of the six primary emotions identified by psychologist Paul Ekman. Surprise has a vital purpose: to quickly redirect our attention. It acts

like a warning bell for the brain, alerting us to a gap between what's happening in front of us and what we had anticipated. In stable, predictable situations, the parts of the brain that attend to our environment slip into a kind of background mode. Our awareness of our immediate surroundings recedes while our conscious mind thinks through a problem, carries on a conversation, or daydreams. But an unexpected noise or tap on the shoulder brings the mind and senses into a state of sudden vigilance. This can be seen in the distinctive expression of surprise: widened eyes with dilated pupils that take in more of the visual field and an open mouth that facilitates respiration. If the event was particularly jarring, there may also be an activation of the sympathetic nervous system, which enables the "fight or flight" response. These physiological changes focus our attention and heighten arousal, preparing us to react in case of sudden danger. But not all surprises are threats. Often, they signal opportunity, and the increased alertness and arousal of the surprise response can also prepare us to take advantage of joys that come from out of the blue: serendipitous events (e.g., Ryan Gosling shooting a movie down the street), unlikely windfalls (ooh, free ice cream!), or changing circumstances (say, an early spring) that could influence our happiness for the better. While these moments of joy might seem fleeting, they can have lasting effects because they help to promote upward spirals of positive emotions. Joyful surprises bring our attention away from ourselves and back out into the world, prompting us to approach and engage. They incite curiosity, spur exploration, and increase the chances we'll interact with others in ways that keep the positive vibes flowing.

Surprise also intensifies our other emotions. It acts like a magnifying glass for joy, imbuing tiny pleasures with heightened significance. Though we rarely think about it, the unconscious mind is a bit like a bookie at the track, constantly calculating the odds of various events happening to us as we move through the world. These predictions help us manage our energy and our emotions, allowing us to brace ourselves or build anticipation for future events. A study of Olympic athletes illustrates this well. Researchers looked at medal ceremonies at the 2000 Summer Games and evaluated the athletes' emotions. Then they compared those emotions with predictions made by *Sports Illustrated* magazine about the athletes' chances of winning. They found that athletes whose performances exceeded their expectations were more jubilant, even if they were standing in a lower position on the podium. A bronze medalist who hadn't been expected to place displayed more joy than a silver medalist who had been favored to take home the gold. An unanticipated misfortune is especially painful because as it takes place, we don't have time to adjust our expectations. Likewise, when we encounter joy we didn't expect to receive, it feels a bit like luck or grace, as if a benevolent universe is looking out for us.

I began to wonder if there might be ways to design more delightful surprises into our lives. It sounded implausible on the face of it. After all, isn't the whole point of surprise that you don't see it coming? But as I started to think more about it, I realized that not all surprises are as sudden as a friend jumping out from behind a corner and shouting "Boo!" Many surprises are more subtle: the pastel color of an Easter egg hidden in a bush, the music emanating from a new restaurant opening in your neighborhood, the particular size and shape of a thank-you note among the junk mail. I began to look for aesthetics that could heighten these kinds of gentle surprises and weave them more deeply into everyday life.

A STUDY IN CONTRASTS

One day I was walking down a street near my Brooklyn neighborhood when I noticed that the poles of all the parking meters had been covered with colorful knit sleeves. It was a charming sight, so incongruous with the gray urban landscape that I slowed my typical New Yorker's walk to a stroll. I had been down this street so many times. I knew its banks and delis, its ash-colored sidewalk and wrought-iron railings—but it felt transformed. The colorful stripes and soft textures gave the parking meters a Candy Land sweetness. Around them the whole street felt friendlier, more welcoming, more alive.

Magda Sayeg, the artist responsible for those parking meters, and the founder of a movement variously known as graffiti knitting, yarn bombing, or guerrilla knitting, says in her 2015 TED talk, "All I wanted was to see something warm and fuzzy and humanlike on the cold, steel, gray façade I looked at every day." So she wrapped the door handle to her Houston boutique with a soft knit cozy in pink and blue yarn. The reaction to this simple gesture stunned her. People stopped their cars to get out and take a look at the knit handle. Emboldened by these early responses, she began covering pieces of public infrastructure—the post of a stop sign, a fire hydrant, the squiggle of a bike rack—and invited other knitters to join in. The appeal was contagious, and soon Sayeg's collective was joined by other groups of like-minded guerrilla knitters in cities around the globe. Like graffiti artists, yarn bombers "tagged" in public areas, often without permission. But whether because their work was easily removable or because it was just so bright and cuddly, they rarely faced issues with law enforcement. According to Leanne Prain, one of the authors of *Yarn Bombing: The Art of Crochet and Knit Graffiti*, knitting has a disarming effect on people. "Nothing is intimidating about knitting. It's soft and fuzzy. It makes people want to come closer."

As yarn bombing took off, I often encountered pieces of knit graffiti in the wild, and if I wasn't in a hurry, I'd stop to observe the faces of passersby. Sure enough, there was a flash of the signature wide-eyed, openmouthed expression of surprise, followed quickly by a smile. People might exclaim, "Look!" and nudge a companion. Some would impulsively reach out to touch the piece. Clearly these scraps of yarn were surprising to people, but I wondered what exactly made them so.

I learned that the human brain is extremely sensitive to difference and contrast. From the age of just three months, infants are able to detect a different-looking object within a group of similar ones. The brain is so adept at spotting differences that contrast makes an object appear to pop out from the background. This capability is related to the gestalt principles that underpin the harmony aesthetic. Just as we feel pleasure in being able to visually group similar items into a larger whole, we also delight in noticing when something is unusual. It's for this reason that harmony and surprise pair so well together. Consistency and repetition help to set clear expectations, which makes a surprising element more likely to stand out. This pairing is often used in music, where composers build the listener's anticipation with a repeating melody and then disrupt it with a swift change in key or tempo. Used together, harmony and surprise create a tension that highlights the advantages of both.

If the essence of visual surprise lies in the contrast between an object and its context, then to intensify the surprise, we need to amplify the contrast. I found inspiration for this in a small, extravagantly colored jungle bird, the male Wilson's bird of paradise, which performs an unusual mating dance on the rainforest floor. But first, he cleans up. Not wanting his suitor's eye to be distracted, the bird chooses a thin sapling and proceeds to remove all of the detritus from a few square feet of ground surrounding it, taking special care to clear away all of the green leaves. When a female answers his call, she perches above him on the sapling and looks down as he suddenly fans out his neck feathers, which form a striking semicircle of emerald green against the smooth brown canvas. The knitting on the parking meters was a similar study in contrasts, introducing soft textures into hard spaces, domestic artifacts into public places, femininity into a masculine sphere. The installation leveraged other aesthetics of joy, such as energy and abundance, but the added contrast meant that only a little of these aesthetics was needed. Surprise acts as a kind of force multiplier for other aesthetics of joy. When placed in an unlikely setting, a few patches of energetic color or abundant texture act like a concentrated tincture spreading rapidly through a glass of water.

Soon I began to discover other artists who were creating tiny interventions aimed at bringing joy to urban spaces. The German artist Jan Vormann traveled around the world patching up crumbling buildings with colorful Lego bricks. In London, Steve Wheen was creating "pothole gardens," filling pitted roadsides with flowers and moss, and occasionally tiny chairs or wheelbarrows. The Detroit duo Gina Reichert and Mitch Cope of Design 99 were lashing together pieces of scrap plywood, painting them with geometric designs, and placing them in the broken windows of abandoned buildings. Known as *Sculpture Security Systems,* they were designed to protect derelict structures from squatters while calling attention to the problem of urban blight. These initiatives seemed emblematic of a broader shift in street art, from an act of vandalism aimed at destroying the city to a kind of joyful activism whose goal was to address the harshness of urban life by suffusing forlorn spaces with little sparks of joy. Speaking about yarn bombing, Leanne Prain said, "Leaving your creations is like gifting them to the public." It's this generous, constructive spirit that has moved street art from being an illicit activity to a welcome one. Now, rather than self-funding their projects and working surreptitiously, many of these artists receive sponsorship from public arts organizations or business improvement districts, along with big publicity for their efforts.

Obviously Legos don't fix crumbling infrastructure, nor do a few plants in a pothole fix run-down roads. But small, surprising interventions can be gateways to broader community engagement. Surprise functions like a spotlight, illuminating a problem in a joyful way. The poet Mary Oliver writes, "Attention is the beginning of devotion." The moment that something captures our attention, we cease to become detached from it. We see it, we engage with it, and perhaps we become involved. Leanne Prain told me that sometimes she has revisited a piece of knit graffiti to find that someone has woven daisies through it or added what she calls an appreciation tag—an additional piece that builds on the first one. Surprises open apertures in which the city becomes tender, personal. They can be icebreakers in a broader conversation about how to improve the world around us.

The same principle of contrast can be used in other contexts, to animate overlooked areas and shake up tired experiences. One day I was walking up Elizabeth Street in Manhattan when I saw a station wagon that had a jumble of bright, magnetic letters on the back, like those from a child's play set, out of which someone had spelled the words SOCKS, WOW, and ADVENTURE. The letters turned the back of the car into a game for people walking by and gave the owners the surprise of seeing what new words were spelled out whenever they returned to their car. In Paris, a pizza place called Pink Flamingo gives customers a pink balloon when they order a pie to go. Customers can go find a picnic spot on the nearby Canal Saint-Martin, and Pink Flamingo will deliver their pizza right to them and their balloon, a process far more poetic than being handed one of those buzzing, blinking coasters they give out at most chain restaurants.

I learned a few ways to bring this idea of contrast home from Ghislaine Viñas, the Dutch–South African interior designer, for whom surprise has become a hallmark. Like the yarn bombers, Viñas often introduces soft textures in unlikely places, collaborating with a fiber artist to cover a basic hard chair or a lamp with crochet. Other times, she'll take a simple black chair and dip it in neon-green paint so that it appears as if it's wearing brightly colored socks.

When I visited Viñas's studio, I noticed a white ceramic vase that had a ring of neon-pink masking tape around it. She told me that the vase had broken and that this was her way of fixing it, rather than just throwing it out. This was a technique she used often when things broke, and it reminded me of the Japanese art of *kintsugi,* or "golden joinery," a method of repairing cracked pottery with a vein of lacquer mixed with gold or silver. A plausible origin story dates this art to the fifteenth century, when Japanese shogun Ashikaga Yoshimasa broke his favorite tea bowl and sent it back to China to be repaired. It was returned with ugly metal staples, prompting the shogun to order his craftsmen to find a more aesthetic means of repair. I love the idea that an accident can be an occasion to make something more delightful, not less so. There are many other ways to practice this art of joyful repair. For example, one of my friends never worries when a button falls off her clothes. She just replaces it with a similar button in a different color, giving her clothes a small but surprising twist. A relatively new product called Sugru, a colorful, moldable glue, makes it easy to repair all kinds of things in a joyful way.

These small surprises can do a lot to break the monotony of everyday routines. A few months ago I realized that though I loved our white dinnerware, I was getting a bit bored with it. But rather than consider buying a new set, I ordered two extra pink plates in each size. The pink dishes make the whole stack of plates seem more appealing, and when laid out on the table for a dinner party, they're like joyful punctuation marks. Similarly, the "accent nail" trend, which involves painting the thumb or ring fingernail in an atypical color like lemon yellow or turquoise, offers a simple way to make a manicure special.

One of my most amusing yet poignant lessons on the value of the unexpected happened a few years ago. Albert and I had begun to consolidate our finances and needed a joint credit card. As I removed the credit card from the envelope, I discovered it was identical to the one I used for my own personal spending. To tell the cards apart, I put a sticker on the face of the new one: a tiny illustrated llama. I didn't think much about it until a few days later when I was paying for groceries. The cashier took the card from me and then burst into a giggle. "Is that a llama?" she asked. "How fun!" Since then, at least half the time I use my "llama card" I'm greeted with a big smile or a laugh. In the brusque, plastic world of finance, a furry llama is about as unexpected as can be. It sounds silly, but the surprised reactions people have to the llama always jostle me out of my type A, impatient mind-set. They slow me down, prompt an exchange of names and pleasantries, and shift what are often impersonal transactions into joyful moments of conversation and connection.

PEEKABOO

While I love the outdoors, I am not a huge fan of carrying a large backpack, so when Albert said he wanted to go spend a week in the woods my reaction was "Have fun!" But when I realized we wouldn't be able to talk to each other at all during the trip, I burst into tears. We had been married for less than a year, and I knew I would miss him badly. I went to sleep the night he left feeling lonely and unsettled.

The next morning I opened the fridge, and on a bright pink

Post-it note were written the words "I love you so much!" I nearly burst into tears again, this time from joy, at the surprise of feeling Albert's presence in a moment of absence. Later, I went to get my scarf from the rack, and as I was arranging it around my neck, I heard a crinkling sound. I felt for the nape of my neck and pulled off another pink Post-it, this one with a heart drawn on it. I yelped with delight. Every day that week I seemed to find another pink love note. One fluttered out of the pages of the book that was sitting on my nightstand. Another was tucked inside the cover of my notebook. It was a joyful way to make me feel like he was with me, even though he couldn't be there physically.

Albert's sticky notes were incongruous little surprises that popped up in places I'd never expect them. But they also made use of another technique for creating surprise, one that underpins many children's games and toys, from peekaboo to scavenger hunts to the jack-in-the-box: *hide-and-reveal*. We tap into this pleasure when we wrap presents in colorful paper and ribbons and when we buy scratch-off lotto tickets. Many holidays include rituals centered around revealing something previously hidden. At Passover seders, a piece of matzo known as the afikomen is hidden for the children to find. Many people use Advent calendars in the days before Christmas, counting down each day by revealing a small sweet or trinket. The breaking of a piñata and the search for the baby figurine in a piece of Mardi Gras king cake are other well-known hide-and-reveal holiday traditions.

Hide-and-reveal taps into our innate human curiosity, which spurs us to explore our world. When we see windows, we peek into them. When we come to doors, we open them. When we find containers, we look inside them. Though to my knowledge no scientist has studied this, it must be adaptive. Nature is full of hidden treasures: oily nutmeats concealed in thick shells, eggs laid in camouflaged nests, fruits sheathed in inedible wrappers. Surely we must descend from inquisitive ancestors for whom the impulse to look around, under, and into things meant a better chance at a good meal.

One of the great joys of the surprise aesthetic comes when we surprise others, and hide-and-reveal is a fun way to do this. Annie Dillard writes that as a child she used to love to hide pennies along the sidewalk for strangers to find, nestling them in between tree roots or in a crack in the pavement. Then she would draw arrows in chalk pointing toward the pennies' location with the words SURPRISE AHEAD or MONEY THIS WAY. Jordan Ferney, author of the blog *Oh Happy Day*, suggests hiding a mix of small, brightly colored balloons inside a friend's mailbox, fridge, or car in order to give them a delightful moment of surprise. Another way to surprise a friend is with a mystery vacation or excursion: tell them how long you'll be going for and what they need to pack, but don't reveal the destination until you both arrive at the airport. Surprising someone else can be doubly delightful because it often tempts them to return the favor just when you least expect it, creating a joyful circle of surprise.

Hiding things also enables us to do something that seems impossible on the face of it: surprise ourselves. A few years ago, when the first chilly day of fall arrived, I put on a coat I hadn't worn in six months. When I stuck my hand in the pocket, I felt a trio of shells, collected on a winter beach walk the previous year. Since then, I often hide small souvenirs—stones, acorns, ticket stubs—from my adventures in my coat pockets and handbags, knowing that when I find them later they'll feel like little gifts. After my grandmother died, I inherited one of her evening bags. Inside was an invitation to a gala in Boston she had attended many years ago. I was suddenly flooded with memories of my elegant Nana, her blond hair piled high in an updo, and was so grateful that she had left the invitation in her bag. I still keep it there, because it brings me joy every time I rediscover it. I've since learned that I'm not the only one who secrets away mementos in hidden places. My friend Danny keeps one of his son's toys in his pocket during the workday, usually one of whatever he is playing with at the moment. "Currently I have Wolfman," he wrote to me. "Last week I had a little musical calculator."

It goes without saying that having clothing with pockets facilitates hide-and-reveal endeavors—the more, the merrier. Clothing can also conceal other joyful surprises. I once had a pair of pants that had yellow piping inside the waistband. I only saw it when I put them on and took them off, but it was like having a really fun secret, and I kept those pants well after they had gone out of style. Later, when the lining of my favorite coat was ruined, I had a tailor replace it with bright red silk. Such details can be a way to add joyful color to your wardrobe even if you're reluctant to wear anything too bright. A pop of neon under a collar or stripes on a rolled cuff can be just enough. Or you could wear your color underneath your clothes, with underwear and socks in vivid hues. These drawers are the first ones you open every morning—why shouldn't there be a rainbow of color in there to greet you?

A similar joy can be created by tucking vibrant patterns into out-of-the-way spaces. One of my favorite recent design trends has been the rise of colorful restaurant bathrooms. At a restaurant called Dimes in New York, the bathroom is covered floor to ceiling with tiles hand-painted with brushy strokes of color by ceramicist Cassie Griffin. Compared with the relatively subdued décor in the restaurant, the bathroom is like a detour into another world. Other restaurants I've visited recently have bathrooms with bold-patterned wallpaper or gallery walls filled with tons of different artworks. The same joyful approach can brighten up a half bathroom, which tends to be a less frequently used space in the home. On a smaller scale, painting the insides of closets or cabinets a bright color or using patterned paper to line drawers creates a renewable hit of surprise every time you open them.

Hide-and-reveal is also used in the digital world. Many developers have embedded joyful displays, colloquially known as Easter eggs, in the code of various applications so that they appear when users perform specific actions. For example, in the 1997 version of the spreadsheet program Microsoft Excel, developers embedded a flight simulator that popped up only when users pressed a particular sequence of keys. On Google, searching the word "askew" will tilt the page's results, and searching the peculiar phrase "zerg rush" will create an apparently unwinnable game where the *o*'s fall out of the Google logo and begin attacking the search results. Unlike most software features, Easter eggs have no practical function. They are pure delight, made for users to stumble upon and to share with friends.

Hide-and-reveal can introduce a playfulness into many ordinary experiences, from getting dressed in the morning to typing up a document. But its impact extends beyond momentary pleasure. By hiding delightful things for ourselves and others to discover, we become a bit like squirrels, caching joy so that we can reap its rewards at a future date. Our world becomes layered. It contains joys that can be seen and others that lie just below the surface of everyday life. And with each joy we uncover, we are reminded that we are the architects of our own delight, the makers of our own luck.

A HOME FOR SURPRISE

Mandy and Kevin Holesh had only lived in their Pittsburgh apartment for about five months, but they were getting "itchy." The apartment was beautiful, in a bustling area of town, and it was the first one they had lived in since getting married. But they kept thinking about a trip they had taken not long after their wedding, in a pop-up camper borrowed from Mandy's aunt. As they had traveled around the southern United States, staying in state parks and exploring new towns, they found it was surprisingly comfortable, even with their two dogs in tow. They had often joked, "What if we just stayed out here like this—indefinitely?"

Now back in the city where they had both grown up, they were surrounded by friends who were also getting married and settling into their first homes. The temptation to buy a house was strong—all their peers were doing it, and they nearly fell for one cute little place. But their hearts weren't in it. They both loved traveling, and both worked for themselves, Mandy as a wedding photographer and Kevin as the developer of a mobile app called Moment, which helps you track and reduce your screen time. They started fantasizing about life on the road again, scanning listings for campers for sale. Two months later they bought one.

The Keystone Cougar 276 was a fixer-upper for sure, with old blue carpets, lots of heavy, dark wood, and a funky smell. But it was five thousand dollars, under their budget, leaving them money for a renovation. They parked the camper in Kevin's family's driveway, and for two weeks, they set about ripping up the old carpet, reupholstering the daybed and breakfast nook, and giving every surface a coat of fresh white paint. They winnowed their possessions down to the bare minimum, put the rest in storage, and hit the road.

One of their requirements in choosing a camper was to have a lot of windows, because, as Mandy said, "If we were going to do this, we really wanted to be able to see where we were." The model they found has big round-cornered windows on three walls. Not only did this feature make them feel immersed in each location they visited, but it also had a way of bringing serendipity into the heart of their home. As if to prove the point, during our Skype conversation Mandy suddenly burst out, "Oh my God, there are dolphins out there!" Kevin turned his head to look. "Oh wow, are there? Seriously? That's so cool," he murmured, shaking his head. They apologized for the interruption, but it was actually a perfect view into their lifestyle. When your home goes anywhere you want it to, your windows become kind of like a dynamic wallpaper, with an ever-present possibility for surprise. This is accentuated by the fact that the Holeshes usually "dry camp" in nature rather than park in an RV park, which allows them to wake up in wild places like seashores and state parks, where the scenery is more unusual.

Knowing they were going to be trading in a 1,200-square-foot apartment for a 188-square-foot camper, Mandy had the challenge of trying to make the place feel like a home without adding clutter. To do this, she kept her design touches small and nestled them into unexpected spots. Kevin laughed as he recalled Mandy sending him out to the store one day for potatoes in varying sizes. She cut them in half, dipped them in black paint, and used them to stamp a quirky set of organically shaped polka dots on the wall behind their bed. "Because the camper is arranged like a long hallway, you can see this wall from the whole space," said Mandy. "So I didn't want just a basic wall, but I also didn't want anything that made it feel more cramped." She bought some pom-poms and strung them together into a garland to hang over the bay window. "The bay window is my favorite spot in the camper," she said, "and I didn't want to block it with curtains." But the draping of the garland created a similar shape to curtains, softening the window's edges and adding a festive pop of color without obscuring the view. Another spot where Mandy knew she wanted to do something fun was on the two steps leading up into the bedroom. She had traveled in Spain and loved the colorful tiles from that region, but because of the weight restrictions on the camper, she was trying to avoid heavy decorations. So she found sticker versions of colorful Spanish tiles and applied those to the risers to draw the eye to a place that people don't normally look.

The Holeshes' camper showed me that a home could be a venue for daily experiences of surprise, allowing its inhabitants to regularly rediscover the joys of their own personal space. It reminded me of the words of the French architect Le Corbusier: "The home should be the treasure chest of living." Mandy and Kevin's home isn't just a place to rest their heads. It's a portal to new experiences, and while they're not opposed to settling down eventually, for now their plans are as open-ended as the road in front of them.

WEIRD AND WONDERFUL

For the Holeshes, the decision to buck the tradition of settling down after getting married and instead embrace a nomadic lifestyle met with more than a few quizzical looks from friends and family. Most have since come around, but it got me thinking about how surprising choices can often be acts of bravery. When we pursue a path in life that contradicts others' expectations, whether it's our choice of career or partner or even just how we wear our hair, we find ourselves outside the comfortable norm. Sometimes it can feel safer to stay on well-trodden paths. Ruth Lande Shuman, the founder of the nonprofit Publicolor, which paints New York City schools with vibrant hues, put it this way: "I think many of us hide behind an idea of good taste," she said, "because we're afraid to really be ourselves."

Shuman's words stayed with me for a long time. I had lived much of my life behind good taste's high walls. Throughout my teens and twenties, I read a raft of design magazines every month, studying the editors' picks as if they were gospel. I stuck to tailored clothes that were deemed flattering to my body type. I admired the flashy and the frou-frou only from a safe distance. Of course, good taste has a seductive promise: as the name implies, it confers not just style but *goodness*. It suggests that we can go to the store to purchase a chair, a dress, an artwork, and, if we choose right, we might enjoy a healthy dose of approval and belonging as well. But the god of good taste demands sacrifices, and it's always the weird, quirky, awkward parts of ourselves that are first to be thrown on the pyre.

Yet the weird, quirky, awkward parts are where the surprises lie and, therefore, a great deal of joy. The flamingo, for example, is an improbable bird, with its outlandish pink color, bendy neck, and toothpick legs. While many birds are endearing, the quirky flamingo is the only one to have been mass-produced in plastic and scattered across thousands of suburban front lawns. Similarly, the ball-shaped allium is a strange flower, the first I would plant if I had a garden. With its giant, fluffy head resting atop a slender stem, it looks more like a plant from a Dr. Seuss book than a real one. Perhaps the best illustration of the joy of quirkiness is the good old-fashioned dog show. I caught one on TV recently and was struck by the way the voices of the commentators changed when different dogs were in the ring. The sleek, flawless breeds drew serious commendation, as if the announcers were discussing paintings in a gallery. But for the lovable oddballs—the absurdly fluffy Tibetan mastiff; the squat corgi, legs whirring like mad to keep up with its handler; and the mop-like komondor, its eyes hidden under heaps of dreadlocks—their voices brightened, as if they were smiling.

While good taste wants things to be simple and normal, joy thrives out on the edges of the bell curve. This is a different manifestation of the surprise aesthetic, one that disrupts our expectations of how things should look and behave. It has a rebellious insouciance, and I wondered what it might mean to add more of this offbeat spirit to our lives.

I didn't have a ready answer, but I had an idea of where to look. Starting in the mid-1990s, a burgeoning design movement took root in the Netherlands that gleefully challenged established conventions around furniture and decorative objects. Full of verve and unbridled inventiveness, Dutch designers began pushing and pulling at traditional forms, playing with our expectations of scale and proportion in whimsical ways. A lamp or a vase might become huge, the largest thing in the room, while a table might shrink down so small as to feel elfish. Old wooden chairs were yoked together with elastic sheaths, yielding surprising new silhouettes. Vases and urns were cast in silicone instead of ceramic, resulting in vessels that resembled traditional Dutch pottery but could be dropped without breaking. For designers, this was an electric time. After years of pumping out refined and tasteful furniture, the industry was being poked full of holes and a fresh wind was blowing through it.

"The thing you call surprise—some people call it wit, some people call it humor—I'd call it lightness." Marcel Wanders ran his fingers through his silver-gray hair and looked off into the distance, reflective. A propulsive force in Dutch design, first as a member of the upstart collective Droog, and then as founder of his own studio and furnishings brand Moooi ("beautiful" in Dutch, with an extra *o* for emphasis), Wanders is responsible for some of the movement's most striking creations. Describing his designs is a bit like trying to explain objects that appear in one's dreams. Take, for example, one of his signature pieces, the *Knotted Chair*. The chair resembles the net of a hammock, made of rope tied in an intricate macramé pattern. But unlike a hammock, it isn't just the seat that is woven. The whole chair is made of rope, even the legs. The first time I came across one, I bent down to look underneath it. There were no wood braces, no hidden steel supports. It wasn't at all clear how the chair was holding itself up. I sank into it, holding my breath. The chair held my weight easily. It felt solid, yet I looked like I was floating in midair. In fact, the flimsy-looking rope had a carbon core wrapped in aramid fibers, a strong synthetic material used by the military for body armor and for the casing that surrounds a jet engine. After being knotted, the rope was dipped in epoxy resin to stiffen it into the shape of a chair. It was as solid as any chair made out of wood or metal, yet it continued to intrigue me long after I'd figured out its secret.

I soon learned there's a method to Wanders's madness. "If you look at one of my pieces, there are usually two things present," he said. "One, it's kind of related to something you know. If it is a chair, it's got four legs." He paused, smiling wryly. "I don't do chairs with eighteen legs. I do things that in a way are familiar to you, that you can recognize from afar. I first make you feel comfortable. But then there's something...," and here he made a noise like a car stopping short, and his eyes flashed as he gestured an abrupt left turn with his hand. "Something a little weird, something that surprises. We call that an *unexpected welcome*. It is a bit of a surprise, but it's a welcome surprise. It is a way that we instill a sense of lightness in products."

The Knotted Chair

I thought about other Wanders designs I had seen. There was an enormous paper lamp that glowed softly, like a giant mushroom, and a circular carpet that was embellished with a pattern borrowed from Delft blue china, making it look like a giant plate had been laid on the floor. Another example: *Sponge Vase,* an object that might look just like a natural sea sponge if you saw it from afar. In fact, it once was a sponge, until Wanders dipped it in clay and fired it in a kiln. The sponge burns off, leaving behind a porcelain replica with a well inside to hold a flower.

The unexpected welcome is a contradiction, a tension that pulls the mind in opposite directions: between the strange and the familiar. Pure strangeness can be alienating on its own. But weird becomes wonderful when it is tethered to an element we recognize. The flamingo delights us because for all its peculiarity, it is still a bird with two wings, a beak, and feathers. Its "birdness" is a reference point by which we can measure its eccentricity. Similarly, we measure things in our surroundings against the yardstick of our own bodies, so giant lamps or miniature cupcakes transform our sense of ourselves, making us feel like Alice at the bottom of the rabbit hole or Gulliver among the Lilliputians. By nestling his wild ideas in a mantle of familiarity, Wanders takes us on fantastic voyages while simultaneously anchoring us on safe ground. Of course, objects don't need to be as wild as those of Wanders's imagination. Slight asymmetries, or small adjustments to proportions, like those common in handcrafted objects, can create a gentle quirkiness that makes the surprise aesthetic more accessible for every day.

I soon realized that this simple idea could take us far beyond creating delightful moments in our homes. It could also challenge stereotypes and preconceptions in a joyful way. The contradictions inherent in the unexpected welcome trigger what psychologists call a need for accommodation. Surprises puncture our worldview, forcing us to reconcile new information with previously held beliefs. When we're stressed or anxious, we become less tolerant of ambiguity and risk, which in turn makes us more likely to reject things that are strange, offbeat, or new. But in a state of joy, our mind-set becomes more fluid and more accepting of difference. Studies have shown that positive emotions decrease an effect called the own-race bias, whereby people tend to recognize faces of their own race more quickly than those of other races. Other studies have shown that positive affect makes people less likely to cling to an initial hypothesis when presented with conflicting evidence. This suggests that joyful surprises might help disrupt harmful stereotypes, increasing the chances that we'll see difference as delightful, rather than threatening.

Consider, for example, what happened when three-dimensional printing began to revolutionize the world of prosthetic limbs. Traditionally, prosthetics have been designed to mimic the body parts they are replacing. Matched to skin tone and featuring lifelike details, these devices seek to comfort amputees and those with birth defects not only by restoring functionality but also by creating as natural an appearance as possible. Three-dimensional printing of limbs began as a way to address the problems of accessibility in prosthetics, particularly for children. Prosthetic devices are complex and expensive, and children grow so quickly that it has rarely been possible to justify the cost of fitting them. So most children with missing hands or fingers have simply had to do without. But the advent of 3-D printing has enabled volunteer designers to create custom-fitted prosthetic hands for children that can be assembled by families like Lego kits, often for less than fifty dollars (compared with thousands for a traditional prosthetic). These prosthetics have radically increased accessibility for children, but they have also had an unexpected benefit: they often look more like accessories than prosthetics. Fashioned in bright colors like red, blue, and purple, they feature visible joints and elastic bands that function as tendons to enable grasping. Kids discover that hands can be made fluorescent or glow-in-the-dark. Eleven-year-old Jordan Reeves, who was born with a left arm that stops just above the elbow, designed a prosthetic arm that shoots glitter. She is currently working on an interchangeable design that lets a user switch between attachments, swapping out the glitter shooter for a hand or whatever else is desired in the moment.

Rather than aiming to blend in, like traditional prosthetics, these new hands call attention to themselves. And in doing so, they disrupt the common perception that a disability is a disadvantage. Some parents report that while their kids used to be teased or bullied, now other kids admire their child's superhero-like hands. By framing difference in a joyful way, these 3-D-printed prosthetics give children a surprising new freedom to be themselves.

* * *

All children live in a world rich with surprises. Each new thing, no matter how ordinary, inspires a sense of wonder and delight. But novelty naturally declines with age, and our surroundings begin to dull with familiarity. Psychologists call this phenomenon hedonic adaptation. I imagine that hedonic adaptation is much worse in the modern era than when we were nomadic hunter-gatherers, out in nature with all of its dynamism. Our solid, unchanging indoor environments don't harbor surprises unless we put them there. The danger of hedonic adaptation is that it sparks a kind of desperate materialism. Hungry for novelty, we often throw out functioning objects that have lost their luster and replace them with shiny new versions. In fact, hedonic adaptation is often known as the hedonic treadmill, because the cycle can repeat endlessly without bringing us any closer to happiness.

The surprise aesthetic can be a tool for cultivating a more emotionally sustainable relationship with our things. When the objects in our lives continue to surprise us, we don't want to trade them for new ones. We rediscover their joy again and again, and we fall a bit more in love each time. By restoring a sense of whimsy and unpredictability to our surroundings, small bursts of surprise also change our relationship to the world as a whole. Surprise destabilizes us a little, just enough to introduce a new idea or a different perspective. It brings back a bit of that childlike freshness. By snapping us out of our habitual thought patterns, a small surprise can reset our joy meters and allow us to see with new eyes.

7.

TRANSCENDENCE

We'd barely gone to sleep when the alarm rang: 3:15 a.m. Albert and I slid into our clothes, grabbed a couple of energy bars, and dashed out of the hotel into the moonless night. The drive was short—just twenty minutes—but the parking lot was already almost a third full by the time we arrived. Soon the gates swung open, and we headed into a long arcade lined with food stalls and souvenir kiosks. It was still hours before dawn, but the place had a carnival atmosphere. White-haired couples, their jackets covered with commemorative enamel pins, strolled down the arcade holding steaming cups of coffee. People shouted breakfast orders to food vendors while their kids wandered off to look at displays piled high with light-up toys, whirligigs, and floppy hats. The smell of fried dough filled the air.

We bought egg sandwiches and found a spot to perch on while we waited for daybreak. It felt like the theater before the curtain comes up, a cheerful kind of restlessness. Just as we were beginning to get impatient, we heard a long "Ooooh!" sweep through the arcade. The chatter hushed and the entire crowd swiveled to face the field. For a few seconds, we saw nothing. But then there was a flare of orange light, and the rounded form of a hot-air balloon quietly floating up toward the stars. Soon, two more balloons began to rise. They ascended silently, a pair of inky shadows in the blue-black sky, until their burners flicked on to reveal their distinctive patterns. We stood rapt, watching them pulse like fireflies. As they drifted away from the field, more balloons began to take to the air. They jittered slightly as they lifted off, the way a bubble clings to the end of a wand before it floats away. A thin wedge of light appeared over the Sandia Mountains, and the sky began to blue. The Mass Ascension had begun.

For ten days every year in October, the Albuquerque Balloon Fiesta draws thousands of hot-air balloon enthusiasts from all over the world to this spot in the New Mexico desert. More than five hundred balloons launch at once on weekend mornings during the festival in a spectacle known as the Mass Ascension. It is the largest simultaneous launch of hot-air balloons that occurs anywhere in the world. The spectacle is so joyful that many people come to the festival just to see it from the ground. But this being my first Mass Ascension, I was curious to see it from above as well, so I had reserved two spots in a balloon piloted by a twenty-year Balloon Fiesta veteran named Jon Thompson.

Our balloon was bigger than a house and covered with patches of yellow, pink, blue, and green. Around it, an ebullient crowd had amassed to see us off. Kids showed off their collections of baseball-style trading cards featuring glossy photos of balloons gathered from pilots around the fair. Parents vaulted small children onto their shoulders to give them a better view. Albert asked me, "Have you seen anyone who isn't smiling?" I looked around. At most festivals, you can scan the crowd and find at least one scowling grump or child on the verge of a meltdown. But there was not one in sight.

When Thompson gave the cue, we climbed a step stool into the basket, and with a nod from one of the festival's air-traffic controllers, the crew let go of the basket, and up we went. The sun had just risen, shining a lemony light, and a low sash of clouds glowed pink in the new day. We drifted along in the flotilla of balloons, watching them gently rise and fall. They were everywhere: right and left, above and below. Gazing out over the scene, one of our fellow passengers said, "It looks like someone just hung a bunch of Christmas ornaments in the air." Occasionally a "special shape" floated by: Yoda, a penguin, a goldfish wearing a top hat. "Look, an egg with pants!" I shouted. Albert turned to where I was pointing. "You mean Humpty-Dumpty?" he said, laughing. In the spaciousness of the air, familiar things looked new to me.

When I asked Thompson why he had continued to fly balloons for so many years, his face lit up. "It's so peaceful," he said. "You're just

The Mass Ascension

floating along, seeing things people don't normally get to see." He said he finds a deep pleasure in other people's reactions, especially first timers. "The grins get real big," he said, with a grin to match.

Many of the balloonists I talked to at the festival were once airplane or helicopter pilots, and while they love all kinds of flying, they find a special joy in the balloon. Balloons are not the most practical of aircraft. They can't carry heavy loads, and they can't be steered. (While we were descending, Thompson's crew radioed to ask where he thought we might land. "As far as I can tell, on the ground!" he quipped.) But though the balloon lacks utility, it more than makes up for it in delight. "What makes ballooning unique is the fact that you can just go up and effectively stand there silently without a motor or an engine," said Bryan Hill, a balloonist from Page, Arizona, whom I had met a few years ago and reconnected with at the festival. Unlike a plane or a helicopter, a balloon has no booming propulsion system, no beating whir of blades. Just the pure, contemplative joy of floating freely above the earth.

This kind of joy is inscribed within our language. Walking on air. Being on cloud nine. Feeling swept off your feet. We feel uplifted or in high spirits when joyful, down or in low spirits when sad. Research suggests that these associations are unconscious and automatic. For example, people recognize positive words more quickly when they're shown at the top of a computer screen, and negative words more quickly when they appear at the bottom. In a study done in the 1920s, when people were shown pictures of different kinds of lines and asked to choose one that looked "merry" or "cheerful," they overwhelmingly chose lines that sloped upward, while downward-sloping lines were judged as sad. Upward movements also seem to correlate to joy, as evidenced by a recent study in which researchers asked people to recall memories while moving marbles between two trays. The people who moved the marbles upward, from a low tray to a high one, recalled more positive memories than the people who moved the marbles down.

Why is it that our emotions seem to lie along a vertical axis? Cognitive linguist George Lakoff and philosopher Mark Johnson believe it starts with our own bodies. A smile curves the mouth up; a frown bends it downward. A joyful body is an ascending one, as Darwin observed: "A man in this state holds his body erect, his head upright, and his eyes open. There is no drooping of the features, and no contraction of the eyebrows. . . . The whole expression of a man in good spirits is exactly the opposite of one suffering from sorrow." Just as metaphors for joy have an upward dimension, so do those for health and vibrancy ("the *peak* of health," "being in *top* shape"), while those of sickness move downward ("*falling* ill," "coming *down* with a cold"). Lakoff and Johnson assert that because the physical experience of joy and well-being has an upward quality, upwardness has become a metaphor for positivity in our lives.

This explanation makes sense, but I suspect that there's an even-deeper logic to the connection between emotion and verticality. Our spinning earth hugs us toward it so constantly and pervasively that we rarely think about it, yet that embrace gives rise to the most significant force in our world: gravity. Every movement we make is constrained by gravity's irresistible pull. Though we roam freely in the horizontal plane, without technology we're unable to rise above the ground. We can run, swim, dive, and jump, but we cannot float or fly on our own steam. It shouldn't be surprising, then, that upward movement feels joyous and that the sky is the universal province of dreams.

Humans have long been obsessed with the idea of breaking free from the restraints that gravity imposes on us, though for most of recorded history, flight was a capability reserved for deities and angels. By the second century B.C. the Chinese had invented the kite, which they used to carry fishing lines away from the shore and to signal during battles. Throughout the Middle Ages, people experimented with gliders, makeshift wings, rockets, and propeller toys. But it wasn't until the invention of the hot-air balloon in 1783 that people were able to soar above the earth untethered. The first flights were scenes of almost indescribable joy and wonder. At one of the early balloon trials in Paris, thousands gathered along the Champs de Mars to catch a glimpse of the launch. Historian Richard P. Hallion reports the following comments from an observer: "The idea that a body leaving the earth was traveling in space was so sublime, and appeared to differ so greatly from ordinary laws, that all the spectators were overwhelmed with enthusiasm. The satisfaction was so great that ladies in the latest fashions allowed themselves to be drenched with rain to avoid losing sight of the globe for an instant." For the first aeronauts, the joy was even greater. Jacques Alexandre César Charles, the inventor of the hydrogen balloon and pilot of the second manned-balloon launch, wrote of his first flight, "Nothing can compare with the joy that filled me as I flew away from the surface of the earth. It was not a pleasure, it was blissful delight.... [A] majestic spectacle unfolded before our eyes. Wherever we turned our gaze, we saw the heads of people, above us a sky free from cloud and in the distance the most alluring view in the world."

Getting up above the ground changes our relationship to the earth and to the lives we live on it. Worries and petty disagreements seem to shrink along with the houses and cars. Of course, flight is now a routine occurrence for many people. You may even be reading this while sitting in an airplane en route to a business meeting or a visit with family. Yet the hassles of commercial air travel—the crowded airports, the jostling and competing for baggage space, the cramped seats—often overshadow the wonder of flight. My hot-air balloon experience reminded me that elevation can be magical in its ability to clear our minds and open up space for joy.

But do we have to befriend a balloonist to find this joy? And does the pleasure have to be so fleeting? As we drove away from the balloon festival, I wondered whether there might be other ways to access this feeling of lightness and cultivate an aesthetic of transcendence in our everyday lives.

TREEHOUSES AND TOWERS

Travel through Europe, and at the highest point in every old village you'll see a church or a fort with a lookout tower offering a bird's-eye view of the area. Its original purpose was to provide a way to spot potential marauders at a distance. Yet these towers survive on token contributions from tourists because people have a nearly universal desire to see new terrain from above. This upward pilgrimage also takes place in large cities worldwide. Most skyscrapers have observation decks, purpose-built to satisfy our longing for an elevated view. Helen Keller, who was famously deaf and blind from a childhood illness, visited the newly built Empire State Building just after its opening in 1931. Asked what she "saw" from the top, Keller wrote an affecting letter with the following description:

> The little island of Manhattan, set like a jewel in its nest of rainbow waters, stared up into my face, and the solar system circled about my head! Why, I thought, the sun and the stars are suburbs

of New York, and I never knew it! I had a sort of wild desire to invest in a bit of real estate on one of the planets. All sense of depression and hard times vanished, I felt like being frivolous with the stars.

For Keller, the skyscraper's observation deck brought on a giddy lightness, a bit like, well, being high. When I read her letter, it made sense to me that the word "elation," which describes an intense feeling of joy, comes from the Latin *elatus*, meaning "raised up" or "elevated."

Over the years, people have crafted ingenious structures to access the elation of elevation. Zip lines let us careen among cliffs and trees, funiculars ascend steep inclines, and revolving restaurants spin slowly to reveal panoramic views. The Ferris wheel debuted in Chicago in 1893 at the Columbian Exposition, with the hope that it would offer a whimsical answer to the Eiffel Tower. A clever fusion between play and transcendence aesthetics, it proved to be a spectacular success, with more than 1.4 million people paying to be vaulted 264 feet into the air during the course of its four-month run. Now a fixture at amusement parks and county fairs, the Ferris wheel's cheery circular form projects joy far and wide.

The most expensive real estate occupies the highest points in a city; the most coveted apartments perch on the lofty penthouse floor. But one of the most joyful elevated structures is also the most humble, tucked away in many a suburban backyard: the simple treehouse. I've found that just saying the word "treehouse" causes people to smile, no matter their age. It is like a password to the inner child's sanctum, a place both exotic and familiar, a place of memories and dreams. The treehouse doesn't bring us to the highest elevations. It doesn't offer the broadest vistas. Yet even a shabby, ramshackle tree shelter—a few old boards held together with bent nails and a rope ladder—will radiate more joy than the swankest hilltop estate. Why does the treehouse hold such sway over our imagination?

If anyone knew the answer to that question, I suspected it would be Pete Nelson, the exuberant star of the show *Treehouse Masters,* a man who brings a child's enthusiasm and a master carpenter's craft to building the most unique and daring treehouses in the world. Nelson's catchphrase is "To the trees!" but he almost seems to be from the trees, with his tall, broad-shouldered frame, bark-colored hair, and habit of bounding around the forest in big, loping strides. The first time I watched his show, I was on a plane, and his infectious joy seemed to expand beyond the boundaries of the small screen. Nelson hugged the trees, kissed them, conversed with them like old acquaintances. His expressive face lit up with delight and wonder as he started to form a vision of each treehouse taking shape before him, and he had his own lexicon of jubilant exclamations: a low, reverential "Wooooow!" when admiring his team's clever craftsmanship, a loud "Ayayeeee!" yelped at the discovery of just the right tree, an owl-like "Ohhoohooo!" hooted from the threshold of a new treehouse. I wasn't surprised to discover that Nelson is so beloved that fans send him handmade gifts and that a whole wall of the company's headquarters is papered with drawings of fantasy treehouses—crystalline treehouse castles, spaceship-style tree pods, and multistory masterpieces ringed with spiraling slides—sent in by children around the world.

Like those children, Nelson has always had grand visions for his treehouses. He was six years old when he first attempted to build one. "My plan was to have a zoo in the trees," he said, as we settled into a pair of knobby wood chairs at Treehouse Point, the bed-and-breakfast Nelson runs with his family in Washington State. "It was going to be a *really* wonderful place." His ambition being a bit larger than his skill, however, that first attempt fell short, and his father came to the rescue to help him build a treehouse in a trio of maples next to the garage. Years later, when Nelson moved with his young family to Fall City, Washington, he imagined they would live in a Swiss Family Robinson–style compound: a fifteen-by-fifteen-foot central treehouse that would later be augmented with satellite bedrooms and rope bridges. ("It was going to be Tarzan-land," said Nelson, eyes flashing.) But his wife, Judy, raised the sensible objection that their three children were still quite small for running around in the treetops. So that treehouse became his office, and Nelson poured his treehouse-building energy into his business. At first, he built regular homes to pay the bills and treehouses on the side. He couldn't fathom that building treehouses could be a full-time occupation for a father of three, but after a friend advised him to raise his rates, he decided to try. He scheduled a treehouse-building workshop that filled almost overnight, and a few months later, he found the plot of land that would become Tree-house Point.

"The treehouse is so iconic, not just in our culture, but around the world," Nelson said. He had traveled to see treehouses and collaborate with treehouse builders in countries from Norway to Brazil, Japan to Morocco. When I asked him why he thought the treehouse had such universal resonance, he said, "To have a shelter in nature, literally in the boughs of the trees, you get a great feeling of safety that cuts across all cultures." Of course, this shouldn't be too surprising. We descend from tree dwellers. Long before hominids walked upright through the grasses of the savanna, our primate ancestors swung from the forest canopy, and still do. All great apes build sleeping platforms high in the trees, except for the male gorilla, which grows too big and heavy to do so. A few cultures, mostly in tropical areas of South Asia, still use treehouses as their primary dwellings because they keep inhabitants safe from flooding, snakes, and other dangers. In the trees we feel held by nature, secure and hidden from view.

Yet at the same time, the treehouse also offers a certain wild freedom. For a child, a treehouse is often the first place of independence, a hideaway out of the range of the parental gaze, where kids make the rules and determine who comes in and out. (Nelson remembers being so stringently territorial about his treehouse that his younger sister had to go build her own.) The treehouse sits apart from the civilized world in two ways. First, it lies *out* in the woods, away from houses and towns and cars and buildings. And second, it stands *up* in the trees, above the swirl of everyday life. "You look out the window and there's a chickadee," said Nelson. "You're in the birds' area. And that to me was always magical and inspiring." He led the way into one of his treehouses, a two-story beauty with a wooden sign reading TRILLIUM outside it. Two clear walls of paned windows wrapped around the façade, and a staircase spiraled around the big western cedar that held it. The house jostled slightly as we moved through it. Nelson smiled. "You really do feel it when a good gust comes through," he said. "It's like being on a boat." That swaying movement made me feel like I'd become a part of the forest and increased my sense of distance from the world on the ground.

We tend to assume that the treehouse is a space for children, but, in fact, treehouses have a long history of being used by adults as places for relaxation and recreation. One of the first references to a treehouse

comes from Pliny the Elder in the first century A.D., who described one built in a plane tree for the Roman emperor Caligula. Treehouses were also popular in the Renaissance (the Medici family had several) and the Romantic period in France and England. In the 1850s, a band of enterprising restaurateurs inspired by Robinson Crusoe created a cluster of treehouse restaurants and bars just south of Paris. High in the branches of chestnut trees were gazebo-like dining rooms laced with rambling rose, where patrons ate lunch and drank champagne hoisted up in baskets on pulleys. At the phenomenon's peak, there were ten different restaurants and more than two hundred huts among the trees. Nelson has found that adults are rediscovering the joy of treehouses, primarily as spaces to pursue their hobbies and passions. He and his crew have built a recording studio, an art studio, a spa with a hot tub and sauna, and a Zen meditation retreat, all high up in the trees.

"Our culture is so competitive," said Nelson. "Trying to make a living in this capitalist world on your own is hard. It's sink or swim, and it means constant motion. And this is where the treehouse comes in, because when you're up there, you're cut off from all that. It does help you disconnect almost instantly from that constant motion of what we need to do to feed ourselves." Treehouses make ideal spaces for reflection because they pull us out of the hustle of our lives and give us perspective. "I don't know why just getting twelve feet off the ground makes you feel different, but it does certainly take you away from the everyday," said Nelson. "Who doesn't dream about being away from it all?" On that note, Nelson had to leave for a meeting, but he kindly invited me to linger in the Trillium treehouse for as long as I'd like. I sat in one of the chairs surrounded by windows, looking out at branches covered with moss, scribbling in my notebook to the rushing sound of the nearby creek. In the cool, quiet air, my often-cluttered mind was capacious and still. On my way out, I flipped through the pages of the guest book. "Thank you for choosing this life!" one grateful guest had written. "Like a dream," wrote another, "only when you wake up, you're still in the trees!"

The shift in perspective we feel in a treehouse isn't just in our imagination. Research has found that gaining elevation can lead us to focus more on the big picture and less on the details of a situation. For example, when told that someone is painting a room, people who had just walked down a flight of stairs were more likely to think about the specific actions involved ("applying brushstrokes"), while people who had just walked up the stairs were more likely to think about the broader purpose behind the actions ("making the room look fresh"). This ability to think abstractly has been shown to promote creative thinking and help people adhere to their values when making complex decisions and resist short-term temptations that might sabotage long-term goals.

Perhaps this is why Nelson's treehouses weren't the only ones I encountered in my search for joy. When I visited Stuart Brown, the psychiatrist we met in chapter 5, who specializes in the study of play, I noticed a treehouse in his front yard, which he uses as a guesthouse. Ellen Bennett, the founder of the colorful apron company Hedley and Bennett featured in chapter 1, has a treehouse-like structure inside the company's Los Angeles headquarters that serves as her office. The new Sandy Hook Elementary School includes two play areas that resemble treehouses on either end of the second-story corridor, projecting out over the greenery that rings the school. "They are spaces that have no prescribed use," said architect Barry Svigals. "They're places where kids can look out and feel special." The treehouses are treasured by the kids, Svigals said, and "have become the darlings of the school." At Chez Panisse, the iconic farm-to-table restaurant in Berkeley, there is a small, much-coveted seating area in the front of the second floor that feels like a treehouse. Even though it's only a step above the rest of the dining room, the wraparound windows fill with foliage from the trees outside, making it reminiscent of those nineteenth-century French treehouse taverns.

Seeing these treehouse-like structures integrated into traditional architecture made me wonder: How high do we really need to go to achieve a measure of transcendence? After all, the researchers who studied the effects of elevation on mind-set used a simple staircase, and even a lift of just a few feet can double our height relative to the earth. I thought about the way that people tend to seek out mezzanines, landings, and bay windows, structures that provide a subtle sense of perspective. Bunk beds and sleeping lofts, too, offer an elevated view while also making good use of small space. My best friend had a loft in her room when she was a child, and it was such a joy to sleep over at her house, knowing we were tucked away at the house's pinnacle.

Certainly the feeling of transcendence we find in a loft or on a balcony isn't the same as the one we find at the top of a skyscraper. Most likely, these experiences lie along a continuum, with the breathtaking feeling of flying or summiting a mountain at one end and the gentle elevation of a staircase on the other. Yet while the intensity of the feeling varies, experiences all along the spectrum can help to evoke a joyous shift in perspective, raising us up above the plane and scale of our everyday existence.

LIGHTER THAN AIR

Through my years of studying joy, I've noticed that people seem to have a natural attraction to things that float and fly. Most insects attract little interest, but when a butterfly appears and flits around the garden, it becomes a cherished visitor. People happily spend all day birdwatching or flying kites or gliders. And on summer afternoons, when the picnic basket has been emptied, the iced tea and lemonade all drunk, there is little more tempting to do than to recline in the grass and watch the sky parade its cotton menagerie overhead. Floating things offer a vicarious kind of transcendence. As we watch them swoop and sail, we feel our spirits rise even while our feet remain firmly planted on the earth.

Yet as mobile devices have come to permeate our lives, our attention is increasingly pulled downward. We spend so much time looking at our phones that we are beginning to suffer from serious neck strain; research suggests that when we look down at our phones, we increase the stress on our necks by as much as 500 percent, making it as if our heads weighed sixty pounds! At the same time, in a culture that embraces busyness, taking time to gaze up at the sky feels like a guilty pleasure, a pursuit reserved for loafers and daydreamers. In defense of this indolent pastime, the British cloud enthusiast Gavin Pretor-Pinney has crafted a field guide to clouds called *The Cloud Collector's Handbook* and convened a Cloud Appreciation Society with more than forty-three thousand members.

"I see engagement with the sky as the perfect antidote to all the pressures of the digital age," said Pretor-Pinney. I reached him on a cloud-filled April morning, the blue sky crowded with fluffy examples of the cumulus variety. "Our day has fewer and fewer of those spaces when the brain can flip into idle mode and coast, and I think that's a time when very valuable activity takes place," he said. He cited fMRI research that indicates that the brain is as active during daydreaming as it is during focused thought. In fact, not only is the brain active while the mind is wandering, but studies show that daydreaming engages two networks of the brain whose functions were once thought to oppose each other: the "default network," which is involved in internally focused or self-generated thought, and the "executive network," which is recruited when we tackle demanding tasks or pursue external goals. The researchers note that this pattern of neural activity resembles that of creative thought and that, while daydreaming may hinder our ability to complete tasks in the moment, it can help us devise novel ideas and think through issues with long-term, rather than immediate, ramifications.

Pretor-Pinney views cloud gazing as a kind of meditation, and he

is fond of quoting the Greek playwright Aris-
tophanes, who described clouds as "the patron
goddesses of idle fellows." He believes that cloud-
spotting lends a bit of legitimacy to the act of doing
nothing that can help us carve out space in our days for daydreaming.
"It needn't be for a long time," he said. "It can be just for a few moments.
But it's a kind of disengagement, a decoupling from the other stuff
down here." I heard in this idea an echo of Pete Nelson and his observation that the intensity of daily life eases with a brief escape to higher
elevation. The beauty of clouds is that they offer this escape from anywhere. "Clouds are the most egalitarian of nature's displays," said
Pretor-Pinney. "You don't have to live in an area of outstanding natural
beauty to look up at outstandingly beautiful skies."

These words reminded me of my conversation with Hilary Dalke,
the London-based color specialist featured in chapter 1, about her work
in prisons. For security reasons, the windows of prison cells are usually
positioned high up and covered with bars. Dalke knew she couldn't
remove the bars, but she was determined to make them less depressing.
"One of the first things I did was to say that the bars on the windows
should all be painted a pale color," she said, "so they wouldn't look like
very dark bars up against the sky." It was a small gesture, but a poignant one, acknowledging the power of the sky to inspire hope even in
the most dismal of settings.

As I thought more about clouds and other floating things, I realized
that it isn't just their elevation that makes them joyful. It is also a sense of
 lightness. Like elevation, the quality of
lightness appears to be a universal meta-
phor for joy. When I asked multilingual
friends for words like "lighthearted" and

"heavyhearted" in their native tongues, I received examples in languages as diverse as French, Swedish, Hindi, German, Hebrew, and Korean. Research conducted in China affirms this association, showing that people identify positive words more quickly when they are presented after an image of a lightweight object (such as a balloon), and they identify negative words more quickly after seeing a picture of something heavy (such as a rock). This got me thinking: How could we bring a sense of lightness into the dense and solid structure of our world?

Bubbles seem to create a lightness wherever we encounter them. Once, as I waited for the subway at Canal Street in Manhattan, I saw a plume of bubbles make its way out over the dark ironwork of the tracks. It was a luminous glimmer of transcendence in a dank, subterranean world, and it sparked my imagination: What if the impending arrival of a train were always preceded by bubbles, rather than a staticky announcement through a loudspeaker? A few years ago, I heard from a friend whose father was in charge of the entertainment for the Portland Marathon; he had hired a team of bubble blowers to stand at a bend in the course. I'm sure many runners' heavy legs lightened when they rounded the turn and saw the sky filled with bubbles.

We capture a bit of the lightness of bubbles in a type of architecture that flourished briefly in the 1960s. Inflatable structures were first developed for the US military in the mid-1940s as a temporary shelter for radar antennas. The inventor, an engineer at Cornell Aeronautical Laboratory named Walter Bird, eventually began to look for more quotidian applications for his technology, creating inflatable swimming-pool covers, greenhouses, and storage sheds for suburban homes. Inflatable architecture took off as plastic technology improved and the rise of environmentalism prompted architects to question the impact of standard methods of building. Inflatables opened up futuristic visions of architecture that would be cheap, portable, and transcendently light. With no heavy steel supports and no concrete foundation, they are literally buildings made of air.

The dream of inflatables turned out to be overblown. People soon discovered that air bubbles made suboptimal dwellings. The pumps required to maintain the air pressure were noisy and hot, and you couldn't exactly open a window. But inflatables have found joyful application as energy-efficient temporary structures for festivals and art installations. A giant air bubble appearing out of nowhere elicits a certain delight, especially in winter when it can transform a chilly outdoor space into a balmy indoor one. Nowadays, the most compelling uses for inflatables are playful ones. We find the airy legacy of pneumatic architecture in the bouncy castle at a child's birthday party, the inflatable slide at a county fair, and the pool floats on which we while away summer afternoons.

But what to do if you wish you could live in a house of air instead of one made of brick or stone? I thought back to that Chinese study, where just looking at pictures of balloons and rocks created an unconscious priming effect, and it reminded me of a concept designers call visual weight. Visual weight describes how heavy things look to our eye, and it doesn't always correlate to the actual mass of an object. For example, light colors have less visual weight than dark ones. Translucent materials appear lighter than those that are opaque, and slender objects appear lighter than bulky ones. Negative space is also tied to visual weight, so objects with perforations or spaces appear lighter than solid ones. Knowing this, we can imagine ways to create a space that borrows some of the lightness we find in bubbles or clouds. By using light colors and sheer fabrics, leggy furnishings and translucent accessories, we can bring some of the lightness of the sky down to earth.

LOOKING UP

My adventures with balloons, treehouses, and clouds showed me how experiences of transcendence can create feelings of lighthearted joy and heightened mental perspective. But I'd also noticed another effect, a feeling that is harder to define. Some people express this in religious or spiritual terms, as an awareness of a divine or numinous presence. Others describe a more secular sense of peace and purpose, a feeling that all is right with the world. It reminds me of the way a scene of profound harmony, like a perfectly balanced rock formation or an intricately patterned Islamic carving, can suffuse ordinary matter with a sense of the sacred.

As I was thinking about this aspect of transcendence, a friend shared with me a paper by psychologists Dacher Keltner and Jonathan Haidt describing a little-studied emotion called awe. They defined this emotion as a response to an experience of vastness, something so great or powerful that it lies outside our usual frame of reference. Immense canyons, towering mountains, or celestial phenomena trigger our sense of awe, as do great works of art or music. "Awe transcends our understanding of the world," says Keltner, who has led much of the research on awe over the last fifteen years and has been a guiding force for how emotions show up in popular culture, advising companies like Facebook on their "Reactions" feature and Pixar on the film *Inside Out*. Just as in a moment of surprise, awe brings us to attention and prompts a strong need to understand the magnitude of a scene and incorporate it into our worldview. But the feeling is more intense and more durable than surprise. Awe overwhelms our senses. It is not a passing flutter, but a wholesale immersion.

This intense state can affect us in profound ways. In a study led by researcher Yang Bai, tourists at Fisherman's Wharf in San Francisco and Yosemite National Park were asked to draw pictures of themselves. When the researchers compared the resulting drawings, they found that people drew themselves as much smaller when immersed in the grandeur of Yosemite than in the hubbub of San Francisco. This study offers a striking illustration of the experience many people have in moments of awe: the feeling of being "small or insignificant." Keltner calls this phenomenon the small self, and while it may sound unpleasant, in fact for most people it comes with a euphoric feeling of resonance and oneness with other beings. People in this state often say that they feel the presence of a higher power and that day-to-day concerns recede from their attention.

Glimpses of transcendence are vital in giving our lives meaning and purpose, yet with the decline of religious belief in Western society, we have seen the ebb of structures and rituals that traditionally provided these moments. The result, according to psychologist Abraham Maslow, is a kind of yawning spiritual gap in modern life, a "state of valuelessness" that he describes with words like "emptiness," "rootlessness," and "anomie." While traditional spiritual teachings aim to remedy this state through inward-looking activities such as prayer and meditation, I find the research on awe powerful because it suggests that we can find a way to access the sacred side of life by looking around us. I've met many people who believe that the spiritual world is closed to them because they are agnostic or atheist, because they don't feel special or chosen, or because they aren't disciplined enough to maintain a regular spiritual practice. Recognizing that we can find transcendence in our surroundings liberates the sacred and allows us to rediscover our connection to it, regardless of what we believe.

Any kind of vast setting can trigger a moment of awe, but some of the most profound experiences of this emotion come from looking up. Gazing at the snowcapped peak of Kilimanjaro, the giant sequoias of Northern California, or the twinkling of the Big Dipper, we feel the contrast between our own scale and the immensity up above. When I asked Keltner about this, his eyes brightened. "One of the striking things about awe is how upward it goes," he said excitedly. "Awe comes from big things: parents, trees, churches." Even the gestures of awe have an upward cast. "I had a team go to Namibia to work with the Himba," Keltner said. "Twenty thousand people fairly untouched by Western civilization. We had them tell stories about awe, and their bodies would go like…" Here he broke off and raised his arms and eyes in a gesture of wonderment, his hands just above his forehead, slightly turned in as if he were receiving something passed down from a high shelf.

Perhaps this is why houses of worship are often so tall. Rather than culminating in simple flat or peaked roofs, they incorporate elements such as domes, arches, and vaulted ceilings to accentuate the feeling of elevation. Patterned tiles or painted frescoes cover the ceilings of churches, temples, and mosques to draw the eye upward. Even some religious music has an ascending quality. One Sunday morning I dragged Albert out of bed at six o'clock to accompany me to a Gospel service in Harlem. As the choir began a buoyant rendition of "Great Is Thy Faithfulness" and invited the congregation to join in, the energy soared within the church. Later, Albert (who comes from a family of musicians) pointed out that each verse was sung in a progressively higher key, creating a feeling of upward movement in the room.

Awe is often relegated to the edges of our lives—religious holidays and camping trips—but there's no reason that everyday places can't offer pockets of transcendence. Designed well, museums can be cathedrals of learning, sparking wonder as a way to open the mind and invite shifts in perspective. In New York City's American Museum of Natural History, for example, a life-size model of a blue whale hangs suspended from a ceiling of artificial blue skylights in the Hall of Ocean Life. Grand Central Station, with its vast open atrium and ceiling etched with constellations of gold stars, offers commuters a space for contemplation between home and work. And the soaring ceilings and skylights of the Washington, D.C., Eastern Market make the ordinary act of shopping feel like a transcendent excursion. Many transcendent public spaces are historic buildings, but there are a few modern examples, too. The glassy Seattle Public Library, for one, provides an elevating, light-filled oasis in the bustle of downtown, free and open to all.

While the proportions of most homes don't lend themselves to awe, exactly, we can still create spaces that feel more uplifting by highlighting the vertical dimension of the space. If you're lucky enough to have high ceilings, you can draw attention to them by adding decorative moldings, wood beams, or painted details. Eye-catching light fixtures or sculptures can also draw the eye upward, though take care to keep overhead elements light; heavy details can create a looming feeling that is the opposite of transcendence. If your ceilings are on the lower side, you can make them feel loftier by choosing low-slung furniture, especially big pieces like sofas, beds, and dressers. The conventional wisdom that light-colored ceilings feel higher has been borne out by research; painting the walls a light color can increase the effect. Tall plants, vertical stripes, built-in bookshelves, and long curtains hung near the ceiling can also accentuate the height of a room. These small gestures can have surprising effects, revealing that, even in modest settings, the transcendence aesthetic can help create room for spirits to rise.

SEEING THE LIGHT

We stood around, wondering what to do. Only a handful of people were allowed in the gallery at a time, and we had each waited hours in the February chill to get inside. Now we found ourselves standing in a white room with a slick, glossy floor and a bright, illuminated wall on the far end. It looked like a projector screen that stretched from edge to edge, filling the wall with an even plane of white light. It was nice, but I wasn't sure I needed ten whole minutes to look at it.

A woman began walking toward the wall. She drew close to it, so close I was sure a word of warning would come from the gallery staff, but there was only silence. Then she took another step—and I watched, bewildered, as she walked straight through the wall.

Those of us who had hung back looked at one another with big eyes. Suddenly, it became clear that we had been looking not at a wall of light but into another room. Pulled forward by curiosity and amazement, I walked toward it, hesitantly crossing the threshold into the peculiar light room. Inside, I found my eyes unable to fix on a single point. They slipped into soft focus as I walked forward into what seemed an infinity of light. Much like walking through a dense fog or skiing in a whiteout blizzard, I felt a strange blend of exhilaration and calm. The chaos of the city receded, and joy rushed in to fill the space it had left behind. This was true transcendence, as if instead of entering a room I had inadvertently stepped into the sky. I floated this way, unmoored and euphoric, until an abrupt signal from the docent snapped me back into my body. The visit was over. I peeled off the white Tyvek booties they had given me and, still dazzled, threaded my arms through my coat sleeves. What I had thought would be nine minutes too many had turned out to be hundreds too few.

As I puzzled over this experience, I wondered what it is about light that leads to such transcendence. It wasn't until a few months later, walking through the angled shadows of skyscrapers in midtown Manhattan, that I understood: light, too, lives along a vertical gradient. Light streams down from the sun, filtered by clouds, leaves, and buildings on its way to us. Shadows appear on the undersides of things, and the consistency of this principle helps our brain unconsciously make sense of the shape and position of the objects in our surroundings. As we look up or rise above the ground plane, the shadows recede, and we begin to enter a world of light. In this way, light becomes an aesthetic not only of energy but also of transcendence.

Not surprisingly, the inherent verticality of the light-dark spectrum lends itself to spiritual metaphors. Heaven is light, hell dark and umbral. In Genesis, God's first act after creating heaven and earth is to make light. When we have a spiritual or intellectual awakening, we are said to "see the light." The desire to bring more light into cathedrals was one of the driving forces behind the birth of Gothic architecture, which used innovations like flying buttresses to absorb the stresses of the high walls and allow for a lacy abundance of windows. Light seems to raise us up to be closer to the divine.

But many transcendent experiences of light are artistic, not religious. The light-filled room I had visited was an installation by Doug Wheeler, one of the founders of an artistic movement known as Light and Space, which arose in California in the 1960s. Working with natural and artificial illumination and materials that are transparent or reflective, these artists aim to create moving experiences of pure light.

Wheeler's "infinity rooms" seem simple, but they are really a product of intricate craftsmanship designed to eliminate any possible seam or shadow. To do this, he works with a team of fabricators to sculpt the far end of each room into a concave shape, like the inside of an eggshell, with fiberglass panels, resins, and paints. Then it is lit from various sources to create the illusion that all its depth has disappeared.

Naturally, many Light and Space artists find inspiration in the sky, and it often feels that their work is an attempt to bring the variations of lights and colors above us down to earth, where we can get close to them. James Turrell, another artist who works with light, creates minimalist rooms that feature a perfectly square or elliptical aperture cut into the ceiling, like an enormous skylight without glass. Inside these "sky spaces," all peripheral distractions fall away, and we are left in simple communion with the deep blue space overhead. Skylights and clerestories, the term for windows placed above eye level, offer a way to bring a similar delight into our own spaces. This kind of joy is now available even for apartment dwellers. An Italian company named CoeLux has created a realistic (yet pricey) faux skylight that uses nanotechnology to create the feeling of sunlight entering a room from above.

As with the energy aesthetic, color influences light and vice versa. The light walls and ceilings that make a room seem taller are also naturally more reflective, mimicking the diaphanous quality of light at elevation. Gradient washes (also called ombré) in pale colors evoke the way the sky's hue naturally fades toward the horizon. Blue, as the color of the sky, is especially conducive to creating a transcendent feeling. The town of Chefchaouen in Morocco has taken this idea to the extreme. Nearly all of the walls, doors, and alleyways inside of the medina, or old city, are painted in dreamy shades of blue. It's said that the tradition was started by Jews who resettled in Chefchaouen after fleeing the Spanish Inquisition in 1492, but there remains vigorous debate about this. Some believe it was a practical decision, as blue has been known to repel flies. But others think it was a spiritual choice and that blue, the color of the sky and heaven, was meant to inspire a life of holiness and transcendence.

STARGAZING

By day, the sky forms a radiant canopy overhead. But at night, the stars that coruscate in the darkness pull our attention toward worlds beyond. Less than two hundred years after *Homo sapiens* first invented a way to soar above the earth in a balloon, mankind figured out how to venture beyond the planet's atmosphere entirely. Astronauts have long reported a transcendent feeling known as the overview effect, an intense version of awe that brings about a sense of the interconnectedness of life and the dissolving of boundaries such as nationality and culture. Neil Armstrong probably was experiencing the overview effect on his voyage to the moon when he wrote, "I put up my thumb and shut one eye, and my thumb blotted out the planet Earth. I didn't feel like a giant. I felt very, very small." Other astronauts have said they have felt a strong spiritual consciousness rise within them, coupled with an awareness of the fragility of life on our planet.

Now our transcendent longings draw us ever deeper into the vast unknowns of the universe. Space tourism is on the horizon, planets that may be habitable have been found orbiting nearby stars, and talk of forming a colony on Mars is no longer confined to science fiction novels. But just as important as what we find out there is the perspective we gain on life down here. While orbiting the moon on one of the early space expeditions, the crew of the Apollo 8 space shuttle caught sight of the blue-and-white swirled earth rising in the dark sky. Astronaut William Anders leaped for his camera, capturing the first portrait of our beautiful planet in its entirety. Anders's photo, dubbed *Earthrise,* marked the first time that the vast majority of humans who would never venture into space could view the earth in the same way the astronauts did: a tiny thing, floating in endless emptiness. The awe and wonder evoked by that photograph have been credited with raising awareness about the finite nature of our planet's resources, helping to launch the modern environmental movement.

Transcendence detaches us from the world, lofting us up above the currents and eddies of our routines. Yet paradoxically, instead of distancing us from what we care about, it seems to bring us closer. Closer to others, closer to what feels truly important, closer, even, to ourselves.

8.

MAGIC

One of my favorite movie scenes from childhood is from *Sleeping Beauty*, the 1959 Disney animated version. To protect the Princess Aurora from the curse placed on her by the evil Maleficent, the three good fairies—Flora, Fauna, and Merryweather—have been raising her in a tiny cottage in the woods with no knowledge of her true identity. It's Aurora's sixteenth birthday, the day the curse is supposed to expire, and the fairies decide to celebrate by giving her a surprise birthday party. But to keep up their low-profile existence, they try to do it with no magic whatsoever. Fauna, who has never baked before, has grand visions of a fifteen-layer cake covered with forget-me-nots, while Flora, who cannot sew, attempts a pink gown "a princess can be proud of!" The cartoon fairies set about their projects with an industrious mirth, whistling and singing as they work.

A few minutes later we return to see their progress, and as you can probably guess, the results don't quite match the fairies' elaborate hopes. The cake slumps to one side, blue frosting dripping off it, while the dress looks like a present wrapped by a five-year-old, with ragged edges and an odd collection of bows. "It's not exactly the way it is in the book, is it?" muses a disenchanted Fauna. Eventually, they accept that they've reached the limits of their mortal capabilities, and Merryweather retrieves the long-hidden wands. In a haze of white sparkles, the eggs, flour, and milk jump into the bowl, and the cake pours itself into an elegant tiered form. The pink fabric swirls into an exquisite ball gown. The mop and bucket come to life and begin to dance around with the fairies, trailing small bubbles as they clean up the cottage. With the addition of a little magic, big dreams are suddenly within reach, and the dull world gains an irresistible luster.

Magic — and the permission to believe in it — is one of the true joys of childhood. We spend our early years steeped in fairy tales and fantasy films that brim with mermaids, unicorns, and superheroes: strange creatures and characters with extraordinary abilities. These magical worlds blur with our own through myths like those of Santa Claus and the Tooth Fairy, whose stealthy generosity feels perfectly consistent with that of the fairy godmothers in our bedtime stories. As we get older, we learn the truth behind these fanciful tales, and we begin to draw a line between the mythical and the real. By the time we are adults, we are expected to keep both feet firmly planted in the rational world and to leave magic behind entirely.

Yet we don't lose our sense of enchantment. Uncanny coincidences, like running into a friend on the streets of a foreign city, or lucky breaks, like when the bus pulls up just as you get to the stop, make life feel somehow charmed. A mathematician would explain these events through probability, but most of us can't help but find greater significance in them. Astronomical events, too, can seem magical, as anyone who has felt sleepless on the night of a full moon can attest. Belief in the power of cosmic happenings to influence our fortunes is so prevalent that it can affect financial markets. Researchers have found that stocks on both US and Asian exchanges reliably dip in the days following a solar or lunar eclipse. Under the right conditions, even ordinary experiences can be infused with a sense of the supernatural. The milky rays of sunlight that beam through a storm cloud, an early morning encounter with a wild animal, or a spiral of dry leaves blown into the air by a gust of autumn wind: such fleeting glimpses of beauty are often interpreted as signs of destiny or the divine.

A belief in magic may be irrational, but according to Matthew Hutson, author of *The Seven Laws of Magical Thinking: How Irrational Beliefs Keep Us Happy, Healthy, and Sane*, magic can be valuable because it imbues life with a deeper sense of meaning. "Magic fights the cold sense that we're alone in the universe, that we're just a collection of atoms that happens to have evolved into an organism that sits and wonders about things," says Hutson. "It weaves a story where there's an ultimate purpose, and the universe is looking out for us, or at least cares about what we care about." This quality of purpose is vital to human well-being, increasing self-esteem, longevity, and resilience. Hutson points to research that people who believe that a devastating event is "meant to be" or part of a loving God's plan tend to recover more fully from trauma than those who see such events as meaningless and random. Magical thinking can fuel our optimism about the future. "If you expect that there's a silver lining," he says, "you'll look for it." Psychologists who study paranormal and religious beliefs have observed that people who believe in magic tend to find more pleasure in other aspects of their lives, while those who don't can suffer from anhedonia: an inability to enjoy life at all.

Because magic is so deeply connected to meaning, it incites our sense of spirituality, whether religious or secular. Brushes with the mystical are a frequent component of what Abraham Maslow called peak experiences, euphoric moments that affirm our faith in God or a higher power. In this sense, magic is like transcendence. But while transcendence can feel elevated and distant, magic is all around us. Like surprise, it hides beneath the surface of everyday things. Encountering pockets of magic can make the whole world feel more sentient and vibrant and, in turn, more joyful.

Yet magic isn't easily accessible in modern life. We find supernatural beliefs nestled inside religion, in the mystical lore of prophets and angels and the practice of rituals and prayer. But in most faiths, these are not considered "magical," and to call them such is almost an affront. We perpetuate the stories of Santa Claus and the Man in the Moon and line up to enter Disney's Magic Kingdom because it's joyous to create a magical world for children, to watch and share in their wonder and delight. But we stand outside of these worlds, not within them. We may consult a psychic, or buy crystals, or light a smudge stick to "cleanse" a new home, but these are guilty pleasures, ones we admit only with reluctance. With few exceptions, magic in modern culture appears as either juvenile and primitive or dark and occultist. A bright, benevolent, mature aesthetic of magic is missing from our adult lives.

Or at least I thought it was, until I came across a survey conducted in Iceland in 2007 that revealed that 58 percent of that country's population believed in the possible existence of elves. (A further 21 percent said it was unlikely but refused to rule it out.) This seemed so extraordinary, I had to read it twice. A joyous form of magic was alive and well on a small island in the North Atlantic, just a short flight away. What accounted for this blithe embrace of the supernatural in Iceland? I set off in search of an answer, hoping that what I learned might give me ideas for how to bring the joy of magic back into everyday life.

IN SEARCH OF ELVES

If I was going to search for elves, I needed to know where to look. So I decided to pay a visit to the Icelandic Elf School, where, over a snack of pancakes and fresh cream, headmaster Magnús Skarphéðinsson promised to explain what the elves look like and where they live. In a small, slightly stuffy room filled with ceramic figurines, Skarphéðinsson shared stories of elf sightings with relish, as if we were around a campfire. I learned that there are actually two kinds of nature spirits that people claim to see in Iceland: *álfar* (elves), who are smaller and less common, and *huldufólk* (hidden people), who are closer in size to humans. Both are typically spotted in nature, sometimes with a translucent appearance, often wearing old-fashioned clothes.

"There is no doubt in my mind that elves do exist," said Skarphéðinsson in a serious tone. He has interviewed more than eight hundred Icelanders who claim to have seen them. Halfway through the lesson, he brought one of these people in and invited me and my fellow classmates to pepper him with questions. A shy-looking man in his fifties wearing bright green pants, a mint-green shirt, and a brown velveteen jacket stepped into the room but did not sit down. He had rings on every knuckle, and around his neck hung four crosses and a feather. He wore no shoes, only socks: one black and one white. His blue eyes watered behind round, bronze-rimmed glasses.

Skarphéðinsson introduced the man, and then asked him, "When did you first see the elves?"

"When I was six years old," the man responded in Icelandic, with Skarphéðinsson translating.

"Did you know what they were?"

"Yes. I had heard them talked about before. My mother sees them, too."

"Where do you see them?" a woman asked.

"The hidden people — close to the sea. In unspoiled nature as far away from houses as possible. But I have seen elves in my garden. The smallest ones, flower elves, live in the flowers." The right-hand corner of his mouth curved up as he said this.

"What time of day do you see them?"

"When it's bright out. Never at night."

"What are they doing when you see them?" I asked.

"I've only seen them playing. Chasing each other. They're always happy." He smiled another half smile.

"Do they make noises?"

"No," he said, drawing out the syllable. "When I've seen them, it's almost as if there is a wall between us. I can see that they are talking, but I can't hear what they're saying."

"Do they age?"

He thought about this for a while, as if it were a question he had not considered. "I've seen the same elves, up near where my mother lives, fifty years apart," he said. "They aged maybe a little, but very slowly."

It was all very matter-of-fact, as if we were talking about his neighbors rather than mythical beings. In a lull in the questioning, the man asked each of us where we were from, and when it was my turn I said New York.

"Gorgeous city!" he said with a flash in his blue

eyes. I nodded, but observed that there were probably no elves there. He laughed, but then his face turned pensive. "That's true," he said. "I didn't see any when I went to New York."

* * *

Though only 5 percent of Icelanders claim to have seen elves outright, and few discuss it openly, the tacit acknowledgment of these otherworldly creatures exerts a quiet yet pervasive influence on Icelandic culture. More than a few large-scale construction projects have been canceled or diverted due to concerns about the destruction of elf habitats. One such road in the north of Iceland curves around a large landmass, because, as locals say, the bulldozer mysteriously broke on the first day of work and did not function again until an altered plan was agreed upon with representatives from the elf community. (Developers sometimes hire interpreters for this purpose, who, unlike the man I met at the Elf School, converse with the local hidden people and can negotiate changes to a proposed design or the moving of elf settlements that might be disrupted by new roads or buildings.) On another street, a group of boulders has its own house number, indicating that the elves who inhabit that terrain are as much a part of society as anyone else.

Iceland's belief in *álfar* and *huldufólk* seems a puzzling quirk for a highly educated country where one out of every ten people is a published author. But after a few days immersed in Iceland's strange and wild terrain, the need for magical explanations begins to seem rational. Steam wafts from snow-covered fields. Milky salt pools appear in the middle of nowhere, and double rainbows span vast waterfalls that run white with force. One day I found myself stripping down to a bathing suit to soak in a tiny geothermal lagoon in the middle of a frozen lava field, endless whiteness in every direction. The sun barely rose above the horizon, and when it set the whole sky glowed pink like cotton candy.

Mundane moments can suddenly turn magical. A few days after Christmas I took a trip to the Snaefellsnes Peninsula, in the west of Iceland. The guide had planned for our group to be back in Reykjavik by early evening, but a farmers' choir was singing at a local inn, and there was a bonfire and spiked hot chocolate. No one wanted to leave. By the time we got on the road back to the city, the snow had turned to rain, and the road became a cloudy slick of ice. It was well past midnight, and in the slippery conditions the truck could only inch along.

Our guide mumbled something to the driver, and the truck edged to a stop at the side of the road. He wordlessly slipped out into the snow. We looked at one another, wondering if perhaps there was a problem. Were we low on gas? Was there a flat tire? But he was gone only a minute before poking his head back in the door. "There are *crazy* northern lights above us," he said, "and you can see them through a hole in the clouds!" We were all frozen momentarily in shock. Though the news had reported a big solar storm, which made the aurora likely, the clouds had formed a dense blanket all day and we hadn't even considered that it would be visible. "Come on!" he shouted. We scrambled for hats and gloves and jumped out of the truck.

For seven perfect minutes, we huddled together on that iced-over roadside, necks craned toward the sky, eyes wide with wonder. At first, I nearly mistook the aurora for a moonlit cloud. But then, like vapor, it moved, shaping itself into folds of luminous ribbon. It glistened like a cat's back in the sun, arcing and stretching. It pulled apart like taffy and then congealed again. Above a low, thick crescent of orange moon, a moon that would be its own attraction on another night, the light formed pink and green feathers. Its ghostly movement was both too fast and too slow, too broad and too fine, to capture with a camera. It was an ungraspable joy. I stood still, listening to the gasps of delight and ecstatic "Oohs" that chased the shifting light in waves. Like primal creatures, we were reduced to sounds and murmurs. We laughed together in disbelief.

I didn't find any elves in Iceland, but I did find plenty of magic. "Magic is in a sense the power that lives in the landscape that's being personified," said Terry Gunnell, a professor of folkloristics at the University of Iceland and the researcher behind that 2007 study of Icelanders' supernatural beliefs. Gunnell is originally from England, but his wife is Icelandic, and they settled here. He has long, charcoal-colored hair and a beard flecked with gray and a low, lyrical voice that makes him sound like a narrator in a fantasy film. We met in his office at the university, a room that was lined with wooden shelves and smelled of old paper. For Gunnell, the lore of the *álfar* and *huldufólk* emerged directly from Iceland's volatile terrain. "This is a country where your house can be destroyed by something you can't see, in the shape of an earthquake," he said. "You can be knocked off your feet by the wind. You can go to a glacier and hear it growling. You go to the hot springs and you can hear them talking to you. So the land is very much alive. The way to deal with it is to talk to it."

This squared with what I had learned from Matthew Hutson, which is that situations rich in ambiguity tend to spur magical thinking. When we witness something mysterious, it disrupts our sense of certainty about the world and our place in it. We reach for explanations, and inevitably, some of those explanations will be magical. Imagine what it must have been like for a primitive human trying to make sense of this landscape. Some elements were firmly in the grasp of her senses: the rocks, trees, and moss that surrounded her, the fruit and meat with which she nourished her body. Yet amid the comforting solidity of these objects were also strange happenings: mysterious lights, colors that shimmered and shifted, changes in temperature, movements from unseen sources. Overlaid on the material world was an invisible one full of hidden energies, some benign, some dangerous. Without an understanding of these phenomena, it's not surprising that she might have suspected the influence of clandestine creatures.

*   *   *

Some of the most original stories for explaining natural phenomena come from places with similarly extreme landscapes. In Australia, many Aboriginal peoples believe the world was created by spirit ancestors in a prehistoric period called the Dreaming. One of the main creation myths explains that the earth was flat and cold until the rainbow serpent writhed across the land, creating the rocks and valleys, lakes and rivers. To this day, some Aboriginal groups view the appearance of rainbows as a sign that the rainbow serpent is moving from one waterhole to another.

In Mexico, there are networks of freshwater pools that connect underground through limestone caverns, eventually meeting the sea. According to science writer Matt Kaplan, the Maya believed these were gateways to the underworld and used them for offerings and sacrifices. He speculates that while diving in these pools, the Maya likely encountered the transition points between fresh and salt water, known as haloclines, which can create strange swirling effects that resemble magic portals.

Magic has offered a salve for the anxieties of the unknown since before the beginning of civilization. Historian Alfred W. Crosby describes a fifteen-thousand-year-old grave uncovered in Siberia that held a child laid to rest. Inside was a stash of treasures, including a necklace, a bird figurine, a bone point, and blades, suggesting that those who buried him or her believed that these objects might be useful in a spirit world beyond our own. Just as we turn to doctors and psychotherapists today, medieval people regularly consulted diviners, astrologers, and spiritual healers. But beginning in the sixteenth century, the scientific revolution brought a cascade of discoveries that filled in once-mysterious spaces with knowledge. Empirical demonstrations of forces such as electricity, gravity, and magnetism established a world governed not by the whims of spirits but by definable natural laws.

Yet what I learned in Iceland is that scientific knowledge doesn't always preclude magical interpretation. Even if we understand the logic behind the magnetic disturbance of the aurora or the geothermal cauldron of the hot springs, encountering them in certain circumstances can open a gap between our cognitive understanding and the sensory reality before us. Into this gap, magic flows.

UNSEEN ENERGIES

One evening a few summers ago while we were visiting family in upstate New York, Albert called me over to the edge of the lawn where the forest began. A thin fog had settled in between the trees, and for a second, I saw nothing. But then a firefly lit up, and then another, and another. The fog amplified the glow, holding each phosphorescent pulse reflected in the air. As my eyes adjusted, I began to see more and more fireflies flashing deep in the forest, illuminating the dusk. It was an ordinary backyard, but at that moment, it was the most magical place on earth. We can court enchantment by bringing ourselves closer to the mysteries that surround us. Catch the wind with a kite or a sailboat. Surf the waves or float in the tides. Watch a lightning storm (from a safe place, of course) instead of a movie. Sleep outside on the handful of summer nights when meteors litter the sky with shooting stars.

In a way, magic acts as a counterpart to the energy aesthetic, complementing its focus on the visible manifestations of energy (namely, vibrant color and bright light) by surfacing all the other kinds of energies around us: the ones we rarely see and don't quite understand. Air, for example, often appears to us as empty, but place a wind sock or a pinwheel in a garden, and it reveals that the air isn't empty at all but has a mass and movement all its own. A mobile can do the same thing. Inside the new Sandy Hook Elementary School in Connecticut is a set of mobiles created by an artist named Tim Prentice. "They are made of little pieces of aluminum like leaves in a tree," said architect Barry Svigals, "and when the air-conditioning comes on they move ever so slightly. They reflect light down onto the floor. It's hard to describe the mystery and delight and wonder of those mobiles as they play with the air currents." Wind chimes and bells also come alive on the breeze to magical effect. I've noticed that a few companies sell wind chimes as sympathy gifts for people who have lost loved ones. The dance between the chimes and the invisible winds reminds the bereaved that a deceased loved one is still present in spirit, if not in body.

Another favorite magical object of mine is the prism, which reveals the spectrum of colors hidden in ordinary sunlight. I keep one on my desk and have seen people hang faceted prisms called suncatchers in their windows. At certain times of day when sunlight hits the prism, it scatters tiny rainbows across the room. You can buy prisms online from scientific supply stores or use old chandelier crystals, which can often be found in antique shops for a dollar or two. Ridged or etched glassware can have a similar effect, creating rainbows from a glass of water. Some architects have even used prismatic glass to create windows or skylights that bathe a space in rainbow reflections.

Wind and sunlight are not the only ambient sources of magic. Depending on where you live, you might find specific conditions that give rise to unique effects. One dry night in February I climbed into bed in the darkness and saw flickers of yellow light in between the covers. It was the static electricity created by the friction between my pajamas and the sheets, but it felt as if I had discovered a hidden mystical power. Each night I rustled around to re-create the spectacle until the cold snap passed. If you live in a rainy area, you might find magic by installing a rain chain, an alternative to a typical downspout, which hangs from the edge of the roof and channels water to the ground through a series of metal cups or links. Rather than concealing the flow of rainwater inside an aluminum gutter, the chain celebrates it, turning a storm into a small waterfall. The extreme temperatures of the desert can produce magical mirages: illusory images that appear in the distance due to the bending of light as it passes through fields of hot and cold air. And of course, high latitudes with cold winters afford many opportunities for magic: seeing frost etch crystalline patterns on a window, blowing bubbles and watching them freeze into icy spheres, or stepping out onto a frozen pond—literally walking on water. Winter has often been accused of being the least joyful season. But though it is not as liberating or vibrant as other seasons, it is certainly the most magical. As the writer J. B. Priestley has observed, "The first fall of snow is not only an event, but it is a magical event. You go to bed in one kind of world and wake up to find yourself in another quite different, and if this is not enchantment, then where is it to be found?"

ILLUSIONS OF GRANDEUR

The email said to arrive between 8:00 and 8:15 p.m., "no earlier, no later." It suggested bringing an extra layer for warmth and provided an address in San Francisco's Mission District with a peculiar street number that ended in .5. "You will not find this address on a map," the email said. "Google won't be of much use. But common sense will."

That night, my friend Ashlea and I were running late. We quickly scanned the block for the strange address, but only whole numbers presented themselves. We slowed down and walked the block again, calling out the numbers as we saw them. Nestled in between buildings, we caught sight of a narrow metal gate with a tiny placard affixed to it, bearing the mysterious address in art deco–style numbers. I gave it a tug. It swung open, and we bounded through the alley. At the end we found a tiny lobby decorated with vintage diagrams of card tricks and covers of *Abracadabra* magazine in gilded frames. We joined the small line for the box office, and when it was our turn, we gave our names to the woman in the red dress manning the booth. Cash was exchanged, and we stepped out onto a small terrace.

The atmosphere outside was part local playhouse, part garden party. At the front of the space stood a stage framed by a carved wooden structure, a red curtain drawn across it. Three short rows of café chairs were lined up, enough for about forty guests, and people milled about, smiling as they jostled one another on the way to their seats. In the back, a crowd had gathered around the bar sipping cocktails called Disappearing Donkeys. A soft soundtrack of indie folk music played, and string lights crisscrossed overhead, holding the group together in a cozy intimacy. After a few minutes, I realized we were actually in a residential backyard. Flowering vines spilled from planters along walls clad in blue vinyl siding. One of the spotlights was bolted to a fire escape. As dusk fell, lights began to flick on in the windows of the surrounding houses, and the angled outlines of their gabled roofs shaped the sky. Soon the music died down, and we heard a cue to take our seats.

So began my adventure at the Magic Patio, a speakeasy-style magic theater hosted on summer evenings by illusionist Andrew Evans. Barely thirty, Evans has already been performing magic for more than half his life. He received a magic kit as a gift when he was a kid, and before long he had checked out all the books on magic from the school library, found a job at a local magic shop, and convinced neighborhood parents to let him perform at their children's birthday parties. He had his first professional magic show at age twelve. After graduating from high school, he chose to attend Brown University, not realizing until he was there that its library contains one of the world's largest collections of books and manuscripts on magic, some dating back to the sixteenth century. There, he began unearthing blueprints for devices used by history's great magicians and building them. The show we were about to see, *Illusions of Grandeur,* included modern versions of these vintage tricks.

The curtain parted, and Evans took the stage in dark jeans and a crisp white shirt, sleeves rolled up, with a gray vest and tie. His brown hair was neatly cropped, but he wore a scruff of a beard, and he grinned like he was about to have a really good time. He began with a trick involving a rope, "a completely normal piece of rope, just like you'd find in any bedroom," he deadpanned. The rope of course proved to be anything but normal. Evans invited an audience member to examine it and then, pantomiming a scissor motion, proceeded to slice the rope into two pieces with just his fingers. The rope split easily, drawing an "Ahhhh" from the audience, but Evans wasn't happy with the uneven lengths. He scratched his head and looked at them for a moment, then folded them up and recited the magic word "Stretch-o!" and suddenly he had two equal pieces. But this wasn't what he'd originally wanted to do, he insisted. So he bit the rope with his teeth, and two small pieces popped off, while the rest of the rope was suddenly fused into an unbroken loop with no apparent knots. It wasn't a flashy trick, yet it was satisfying in its simplicity, and I heard a few soft "Wows" from the seats near me.

I had always found stage magicians to be either cheesy or macabre, but Evans was neither. He had a sunny California energy, and he maintained a genial patter with the audience that made his magic feel upbeat and delightful. Even when he sawed a woman in half, it wasn't eerie. The cheerful assistant acted as if being cleaved in two was the most natural thing in the world; she had not a hint of worry on her face. Most routines contained other aesthetics of joy, like surprise and abundance. In one trick, Evans played a generous host, offering to pour audience members a beverage of their choice from his mystical cocktail shaker. He asked people to call out the names of their favorite drinks, and then one by one he poured them out: a margarita, chocolate milk, orange juice, a White Russian, a green smoothie, red wine, a Negroni, scotch. Before his final bow, he plucked a rose from a candle flame and tore one of its petals into small pieces. He took a paper fan in one hand and began to drop the petal pieces onto the fan with the other, and as he bounced them into the air they multiplied, leaving the magician enveloped in a blizzard of confetti.

Of all the tricks I saw that night, there was one so extraordinary I still find myself thinking about it. Evans brought onstage a small table covered with a thin satin tablecloth. He held on to the edges of the tablecloth and took a breath. Slowly, the table rose up into the air. The raucous laughter and cheers that had greeted other tricks were hushed, and the crowd sat in quiet amazement. I looked at Ashlea with an eyebrow raised and saw that our faces mirrored each other's. As Evans pulled gently upward on the cloth, the table rose higher and seemed to come alive, spinning around him in a circle and attempting to whirl out over the heads of the people in the first row of the audience, until Evans reined it in with a tug and set it back down. People craned their necks in search of supporting wires, but there was nothing to see overhead except the winking light of a plane traversing the dark blue sky.

The mood was buoyant and the audience bright and chatty as we dispersed into the night. On the way out, I noticed a quote scribbled on a chalkboard that I hadn't seen on the way in. It was from a play by Oscar Wilde: THE SECRET OF LIFE IS TO APPRECIATE THE PLEASURE OF BEING TERRIBLY, TERRIBLY DECEIVED.

* * *

The next day I came back to meet Evans, hoping for a bit of insight into the magician's art. I had my first lesson when I arrived at the address he gave me, which was just adjacent to the one from the night before. Evans answered the door in a neon tie-dyed T-shirt and invited me into a typical-looking apartment. But then he opened a door near the kitchen, and I found myself back in the small lobby of the Magic Patio, except that behind the "box office" a bed was visible, and the walls that had seemed to be made of brick were thin and movable. "Yep, this is my bedroom," said Evans with a sheepish smile,

pointing out the Murphy bed (his own design) and giving an affection-ate "Hello" to Paddy, the parakeet he was training for a future role in his act. We stepped outside onto the patio, already set up for another show that evening, and sat on the floor of the stage while I surreptitiously looked around for hidden mechanisms.

"You can say there are only a finite number of magic tricks in the world," said Evans. "Appearance, disappearance, levitation, teleporta-tion, transformation, penetration [where one solid object disappears into another], restoration [where a broken object is put back together as if new], prediction, and escape," he said, counting them out on his fin-gers. All in all, he listed nine basic types of tricks that he said make up the entire repertoire of all the world's stage magicians.

"Only nine?" I asked. "Why so few?"

"Well, if you break them down, they're all defying some funda-mental law of physics," he said. "Levitation negates gravity, appearance and disappearance contradict the law of conservation of mass. Penetra-tion violates the law that two things can't be in the same place at the same time. These are things that we just know through our experience make the world go around."

We rarely think about these laws, yet we owe the smooth func-tioning of our lives to the fact that all matter on earth obeys them. Imagine trying to walk around if the earth's gravity fluctuated depend-ing on the day, or trying to keep track of your things if they could van-ish and reappear elsewhere of their own accord. Magic happens when those inviolable laws that govern how matter behaves seem to be chal-lenged. Superheroes and wizards break these laws at will, with flying capes, invisibility cloaks, and other fantastical props. But they can only do so in storybooks and on screens. Stage magicians create the illusion that they are violating natural laws right before our eyes.

Natural laws are so universally true that when we see something contradicting them, we respond not just with surprise but with *wonder*. Descartes counted the feeling of wonder among his six basic passions, defining it as an emotion "that brings [the soul] to focus on things that strike it as unusual and extraordinary." Wonder overlaps with awe and both emotions elicit a similar wide-eyed, jaw-dropped expression. But unlike awe, which has both positive and negative strains, wonder is nearly always used to describe a joyous feeling. It often arises when we find ourselves in new surroundings, which helps explain why travel can be so magical and why childhood prompts such a blurring between magic and real life. Everything is new for children, and so everything is wondrous. Evans doesn't perform for children under the age of six because the tricks often fall flat. "Young children are as enthralled by garage-door openers as they are by levitation," he said. "It's kind of beautiful, when you think about it. Everything is magical to a kid."

What about those of us on the opposite end of the spectrum, who have had enough life experience to be jaded about the magician's feats? According to Evans, our wonder is heightened when we embed the magical within an ordinary context. "If I'm Andrewini the Great making someone float on a stage with ornate sets and an orchestra," he said, "it feels like theater. And then you say to yourself, 'This is just a character with some awesome tech and special effects. I can't see the wires, but I know they're there.'" Through this lens, the choice to situate the Magic Patio in a regular backyard under an open sky, with neighbors poking their heads out of their windows, is significant. It brings magic out of the controlled context of the theater, where we believe anything can happen, and into the real world, where we know it can't. "This isn't a set, it isn't a theater," he said. "It's very exposed." He gestured up in the air, at the open sky above the spot where the table had been floating the evening before. For magic to be truly magical, we need to remain tethered to reality while the implausible spectacle unfolds before us.

Magic becomes even more wondrous when it leaves the stage and blends in with real life. Here Evans has a unique perspective, because while by night he is a magician, by day he's a product designer at IDEO, working to bring wonder into everyday experiences like driving, shopping for groceries, and riding the bus to school. Evans believes that designers can create effects that seem magical by pushing against the same natural laws that magicians play with. For example, when the Japanese company Seibu asked architect Kazuyo Sejima to design a new express train, she imagined an invisible train speeding through the countryside. She created this effect by covering the surface of the cars in a translucent mirrored material that seamlessly reflects its surroundings, making the train seem to disappear. The Dutch company Crealev has developed a magnetic technology that makes household objects levitate. Designer Richard Clarkson, a former student of mine, worked with this technology to create a cloud-shaped speaker that floats on a mirrored base like an object out of a surrealist painting.

Science fiction writer Arthur C. Clarke's well-known third law states, "Any sufficiently advanced technology is indistinguishable from magic," which explains the confusion that can occur when people encounter a new innovation for the first time. While the eighteenth-century Parisians who watched one of the first hot-air-balloon launches were elated by the spectacle, the country people who witnessed the balloon descending in a field a few miles away thought it was the work of demons and attacked it with knives and pitchforks. (After this incident, aeronauts supposedly took to carrying bottles of champagne with them as peace offerings for suspicious farmers.)

But while technology can create a sense of magic, it can also be a moving target. Some technologies are delightful decades after their first appearance (think of Polaroid photos, still a fixture at weddings and parties despite the fact that smartphone cameras are ubiquitous), while others become a banal part of the background (like Wi-Fi or GPS). An innovation greeted with joy and wonder often seems humdrum once it has reached saturation in the world around us and eventually becomes quaint.

After talking to Evans, I think I have a better understanding of why this happens. The tech industry can be preoccupied with seamlessness: making all the points of friction in an experience disappear. This certainly creates a feeling of convenience, but in the process it makes us blasé about what we're witnessing. A state-of-the-art elevator that shoots to the top of an office building in a few seconds is technically remarkable, but it's a dull ride. On the other hand, a glass elevator that travels all of three stories can be downright enchanting: by letting us see the changing view as we rise, it reminds us that being lofted into the air at the push of a button is its own kind of magic. We are living at a moment when technology is redefining our world at an unprecedented rate, creating more opportunities to be dazzled but with a greater risk of fatigue. Our best defense is to maintain a juxtaposition between the high tech and the mundane. Technology is most magical when it reminds us of the boundaries of our existence, even as it shatters them.

INSTRUMENTS OF WONDER

It was early still, and the Versailles gardens were quiet as I wandered the gravel path between the parterres. The flower beds were planted with annuals in red, gold, and violet. It smelled of marigolds and geranium leaves. I walked down the curving stone steps, past a fountain tiered like a wedding cake, adorned with gilded frogs and turtles spewing water from their mouths. Topiaries pruned into bulbous shapes stood sentry along the edges of the promenade. Yellow-brown sycamore leaves crunched under my feet. I veered right, winding through the groves along trellis-lined paths, dwarfed by tall hedges. Every route in this neatly manicured forest led to an immaculate courtyard centered on a fountain, a colonnade, or a sculpture of a Roman god in flowing robes of bronze or marble. But not this one. From the end of the path I saw a mass of pure white that filled the clearing. A terrestrial cloud.

As I drew closer, a structure began to emerge from the blur. A large circle of metal pipe rested on vertical standards about twelve feet high, a slender echo of the classical pavilions found elsewhere in the garden. Mist billowed from the top of the ring in thick white strands and rolled in translucent curls throughout the glade. A boy in an orange coat ran in and out of the heart of the cloud, fading and reappearing as if he were a cinematic ghost. Off to the side a woman stood in the cloud's fringes, her lower half obscured, calling out to the boy that it was nearly time to go. But the boy had no interest in leaving and made his mother chase him as he ran giggling through the fog, pulling wisps of it out toward the tree line. I strolled to the center of the ring and put out my hands. It was wetter than I expected, the vapor cool on my fingertips. The grass and clover appeared almost white with dew, and small drops of water clung to my hair and eyelashes. I spun around, collecting droplets, until my wool coat glistened like the grass and I felt slightly dizzy.

I had come to Versailles in search of yet another type of magic, an elemental sort that seemed like it emanated from nature yet was entirely man-made. The cloud apparatus, titled *Fog Assembly*, was part of a series of temporary installations by the artist Olafur Eliasson. I first encountered his work at the Museum of Modern Art in New York, which he packed with curiosities like a waterfall that flowed upward, an immense sparkling kaleidoscope, and, in a darkened underground room, a luminous drizzle threaded with rainbows. Perhaps his most famous work is a giant illuminated sun, which he installed in the winter of 2004 in the vast atrium of the Tate Modern museum. Visitors spent hours sprawled out on the floor, basking in the amber glow like vacationers on a sunlit beach. In another one of his installations, a curtain of fat water droplets fell from a pipe suspended from the ceiling, illuminated periodically by a flashing strobe. The raindrops seemed to stop momentarily in midair, as if time were hiccuping rather than flowing in a smooth line.

Eliasson's installations are not so much artworks as instruments of wonder, designed to manifest the abstract forces that shape our lives in tangible ways. Through the flow of water, we feel the passage of time and are able to ponder its often-turbulent nature. In the haze of an artificial sun, we are reminded of how intimately we are affected by nature's rhythms. It shouldn't be surprising that Eliasson is part Icelandic and spent a portion of his formative years steeped in that country's strange landscape. Like a conjurer, he harnesses its mercurial forces and places them in implausible contexts: clouds in a garden, rainbows in a basement. These contrasts have the effect of reintroducing mystery into the built environment, and it's not uncommon to see people emerge from one of his installations blinking, as if the film of age has been washed off their eyes and the whole world appears new again.

Yet for all the magic of Eliasson's work, his mechanisms are curiously unmysterious. His pieces regularly feature visible spigots, tubes, and supports. He makes no attempt to camouflage these components, leaving them exposed for visitors to examine. And his materials are so commonplace they sound more like restock orders for a hardware store than an artist's media. "Steel, water, nozzles, pump system" reads the list for *Fog Assembly*. Is that all it takes to manufacture a cloud? And for that upward-facing waterfall, the inventory was similarly terse: "scaffolding, steel, water, wood, foil, pump, hose." At least half of these are things most people have lying around the garage.

Eliasson's ability to wring the ethereal out of simple materials inspired me to look for ways that we could do the same for ourselves, albeit on a smaller scale. For example, while magnetic levitation technology is striking, we can create a similar illusion with plain old fishing line. Visual merchandisers, designers who create the eye-catching displays in store windows, often use this trick to suspend objects so that from a distance they appear to be floating in midair. Similarly, mirrors can be used to transform ordinary spaces into magical ones. One of my favorite Eliasson installations is simply a room with a gigantic circular mirror attached to the ceiling. I went with my friend Maggie and her mom, and the three of us lay down on the floor beneath it. After a minute or so we felt our sense of space invert. Were we on the floor looking up at the ceiling, or on the ceiling looking down at the floor? The sensation switched back and forth multiple times, and when we stood up a few minutes later, I almost felt like Spiderman, walking sticky footed in an upside-down world. Mirrors invert space, making it seem as though reality has been flipped or folded. The magic of mirrors is particularly evident in small spaces. A large, floor-length mirror can expand a space or even create the perception of an extra room. A mirror placed behind a light source makes the light appear to glimmer.

Positioning a pair of mirrors so that they face each other creates a kind of endless reflection known as an infinity mirror.

One of the simplest ways to create magic is with optical illusions, which use repeating lines, shapes, or curves to create an impression of depth or movement. The desire to explore the strange wizardry of illusions spawned an artistic movement called op art (short for "optical art"), which flourished in the 1960s. For a dramatic statement, op art wallpapers can create a space with walls that seem to vibrate; geometric tiles can be used in an op art–style floor. Posters and rugs can lend this effect on a smaller scale. Optical illusions are also becoming an increasingly common form of street art. Recently a mother-daughter pair of Indian artists, Saumya Pandya Thakkar and Shakuntala Pandya, used the technique to create crosswalks that look three-dimensional to drivers, creating the illusion that pedestrians are walking on a series of floating islands in the middle of the road.

Another optical phenomenon with ancient roots and modern appeal is iridescence, a flecting play of colors that can be found on the surface of an oily puddle, the wings of a butterfly, and the inside of a mussel shell. Iridescent materials have long been considered magical, likely because of the way that the colors shift and transform. The Maya used paints mixed with mica, a pearlescent mineral, to paint one of their temples so that it glimmered in the sun. Some ancient Egyptians wore eye shadows made of sparkling pigments in honor of Horus, the god of the sky. As it turns out, the makeup had a strange side effect: the ground minerals contained ions that stimulated the skin's production of nitric oxide, which in turn boosted the immune system's response to bacteria. Researchers speculate that this may have protected the wearers from infections they could have contracted from river water during the Nile's annual flooding. The tradition of "magical makeup" continues in the many online tutorials for unicorn- and mermaid-inspired makeup looks, which use iridescent pigments to create a lustrous glow.

Aside from cosmetics, iridescence is more often associated with children's products, such as fairy-princess dresses and sticker books, than with products for adults. But this luminous effect also has a sophisticated side. Since the seventh century, artisans have used contrasting warp and weft threads to weave color-changing fabrics that seem to shimmer, even though they are made of ordinary wool or cotton. These fabrics often make an appearance in hotel interiors or red-carpet gowns. Many crystals have iridescent effects, which may explain why we often see them as imbued with magical powers. One of the oldest iridescent materials is called dichroic glass, which consists of glass mixed or coated with a thin film of metal. The Romans used it in the fourth century, and NASA further developed it for the space shuttle. Now it is used by Eliasson in his kaleidoscopes and by designers to make light fixtures, coffee tables, and jewelry with an opalescent sheen.

Whether it's the illusory movements of an op art canvas or the colors of a peacock feather, magical elements have an elusive quality that feels out of our control. The inherent ambiguity of magic draws us into a liminal space between emotions, one that can be delightful or eerie depending on the situation. Imagine you are standing in a field, alone and far from shelter. An enormous black cloud-like apparition hovers on the horizon. How do you feel? Now imagine yourself in the same field, but replace the cloud with a rainbow-colored ring in the sky. How do you feel now? Both events are strange and mysterious, yet one inspires fear, the other wonder. Tempering magic with other aesthetics keeps it reliably on the joyous side of the line. When playing with iridescence and illusions, use elements of the energy aesthetic: keep tones light and bright. When working with mirrors, incorporate elements of harmony and play. Distortions, like the ones found in funhouse mirrors, quickly become creepy. Symmetry makes reflections feel balanced, while round edges keep them from becoming jagged or sharp.

WONDERS NEVER CEASE

Magic can be captivating, sparkling, and sublime. But what makes it so compelling is that it ruptures the membrane between possible and impossible, igniting our curiosity about the world we live in. "Wonder" is a marvelous word to describe our response to magic because it is both a noun and a verb. When we feel wonder (noun), it prompts us to wonder (verb) and then to go in search of an answer. It pulls us forward into learning and exploration.

During my research I was surprised to find that magic has played a pivotal role in fueling innovation and progress, though history is often silent on this point. Oxford historian Keith Thomas notes that the curiosity fueled by astrology inspired people to search for better methods of measuring the movements of stars and planets, giving shape to the science of astronomy. The father of modern chemistry, Robert Boyle, was originally an alchemist. His first experiments weren't aimed at proving the existence of atoms; he simply wanted to turn lead into gold. Nikola Tesla, whose work with induction motors led to the system of alternating current that powers our houses and buildings, had his curiosity about electricity piqued by a magical incident in his childhood. During a cold, dry spell, he found that as he stroked the family cat, its back turned into "a sheet of light" and began to spark. The sight was so alarming that his mother insisted he stop playing with the cat in case it caught fire. Tesla said this brief experience was so striking that it continued to fuel his interest in the study of electricity eighty years later.

In the cult of productivity and efficiency that rules our waking hours, magic seems like a luxury, much like daydreaming or play. But far from being a diversion, it's often a catalyst for discovery. The joy we find in magic stems from a deeper impulse toward the expansion of the mind and the improvement of the human condition. At the root of our love of rainbows, comets, and fireflies is a small reservoir of belief that the world is bigger and more amazing than we ever dreamed it could be. If we are to be creative and inspired, then giving ourselves permission to feed this reservoir is vital. As the English writer Eden Phillpotts once wrote, "The universe is full of magical things patiently waiting for our wits to grow sharper." Wonders never cease, as long as we are willing to look for them.

9.

CELEBRATION

Every day, big red buses trace loops around the island of Manhattan, carrying sightseers on an efficient tour of the city's most joyful destinations. They stop at the Empire State Building and Rockefeller Center, Broadway and Times Square. They stop for the dioramas and dinosaurs at the Natural History Museum, and the sweet shops that line the streets of Little Italy. They stop at the Central Park Zoo and Carousel, and at the pond full of toy sailboats that children pilot by remote control. But the most joyful place in the city isn't any of these well-loved landmarks. It won't be found in guidebooks or on bus tours, yet to spend a morning there is to be immersed in the most infectious joy the city has to offer. Located at 141 Worth Street, this place is the Office of the City Clerk, informally known as city hall.

On weekday mornings you'll find couples of all ages and backgrounds lined up here to get married, surrounded by beaming friends, proud parents, and little girls hopping around in sateen dresses. The brides wear long gowns and short ones, saris and kimonos, maternity dresses and jumpsuits. Vendors on the street make bouquets of flowers and have rings for sale in case you've forgotten them. For several years, my commute took me past this bustling scene, and on summer mornings if I wasn't running late I would linger to watch the revolving doors spin open, releasing a newly married couple into the world. Some couples threw up their arms as friends showered them with confetti. Others kissed dramatically for a photograph. One day I passed by just in time to see a brass band parade a pair of newlyweds from the courthouse steps to a nearby restaurant where they'd celebrate over lunch with their families.

Celebrations mark the pinnacles of joy in our lives. We celebrate marriages and partnerships, victories and harvests, growth and new beginnings. At these moments, our joy seems to overflow, and we have an irresistible urge to bring others together to join in our delight. Whether in a crowd of hundreds at a hotel ballroom or with a small cluster of family members at a picnic in the park, joy's highest highs draw us into communal experience. We pause our daily activities to toast and dance, feast and frolic. We set aside individual preferences, wishes, and anxieties to immerse ourselves in a tide of collective joy.

Why do we do this? From an evolutionary perspective, celebration seems quite frivolous. All that feasting and frolicking expends valuable resources and energy, while at the same time taking us away from productive endeavors. Yet all cultures celebrate, and so do some species of animals. When elephants are reunited after being separated, they stamp around excitedly, urinating, clicking tusks, flapping ears, and entwining trunks. They spin around each other and fill the air with an ecstatic din of trumpets, rumbles, and roars. Wolves are also known for their noisy reunions. They howl exuberantly when the pack comes back together after splitting up for a hunt, with harmonic choruses that can last for two minutes or longer. The most celebratory of all animals may be our closest relatives, chimpanzees. Primatologist Frans de Waal describes a typical chimpanzee celebration, marking the delivery of bundles of fresh blackberry, beech, and sweet-gum branches to their enclosure. When the chimpanzees spot the caretaker carrying the food, they break into loud hooting that draws in every animal in the vicinity. This is followed by a wild rush of kissing and embracing and a one-hundred-fold increase in friendly body contact among the animals. Afterward, they sit down together to enjoy their bounty. The rigid hierarchies that define chimpanzee social life temporarily ease, and every animal participates in the feast.

That our penchant for festivity is shared by these highly intelligent species raises an intriguing possibility. Perhaps celebration isn't just a pleasurable indulgence but instead serves some deeper purpose in life. What makes celebration unique is that it is a distinctly social form of joy. While we do sometimes celebrate alone, with a happy dance or a glass of champagne, more often celebration is something we do with others. At its best, a celebration cultivates an atmosphere of inclusive delight. The celebrants brim with euphoric energy, casting a halo over all who are present and connecting them to the larger outpouring of jubilation. The result is a state of belonging and attunement, where for a few moments every individual is united in the same effervescent joy.

This emotional resonance brings us together, strengthening a community and enhancing the bonds within it. Research shows that celebrating positive events with others increases our feeling that they will be there for us if we encounter tough times in the future. And not only that, but celebrating with others boosts our own joy. People who regularly celebrate positive events with others are happier than those who keep their good news to themselves; and couples who celebrate each other's good news are happier in their relationships. We're even more likely to laugh in the presence of others. As Mark Twain put it, "Grief takes care of itself; but to get the full value of a joy you must have someone to divide it with." Celebrating together propels the joy of a happy moment even higher.

Yet as the heart of our social lives has migrated online, we find fewer moments and spaces in which to experience this kind of joy. Many celebratory occasions have been reduced to a Facebook post reading "Congrats!" or "Happy birthday!"—accented by champagne and confetti emojis if the sender isn't too late for a meeting. In the crush of balancing work and family life, and with the simulacrum of connection provided by social media, it's easy for people to let opportunities for celebration slip by unheeded. I can't help but wonder what we are losing when we cede these moments of celebration to the virtual world. What is it about the physical experience of rejoicing with others that smooths out the rough edges of life in a community? And how can we use aesthetics of celebration to cultivate more shared joy in our daily lives?

COME TOGETHER

For architect David Rockwell, the importance of celebration became clear at a young age. He lost his father when he was a child, and after his mother remarried, the family moved to a small town on the New Jersey shore. Some of his earliest joyful memories revolve around an empty space above the garage that served as a hub for festive gatherings in his small community. "It was constantly being used for things like dog shows that I would do with all the neighbors' dogs," he said one recent afternoon, "or a spook house for Halloween, or a rabbit run around Easter, or a carnival to benefit muscular dystrophy." Using mostly found objects, he and his four brothers would transform the space into radically different backdrops for these festivities. "You know those roller blinds for windows?" he said. "Taking those rollers indoors, we were able to make a mobile floor and a conveyor belt. Strings and buckets could create a landscape overhead. It was the epitome of my idea of joy."

These early lessons in the power of communal experience continue to resonate with Rockwell, after more than thirty years of designing lively places where people gather: restaurants such as Rosa Mexicano and Union Square Cafe, hotels like the Andaz in Maui and the New York Edition, and theater sets for Broadway shows such as *The Rocky Horror Show, Kinky Boots,* and *Hairspray.* "I learned early on with the death of my dad and our move that there were certain things that weren't controllable, and that creating places for the expression of a single moment was joyful," he said. It was a surprising statement from a member of a profession that aims so strongly toward permanence. Yet as Rockwell pointed out, celebrations can leave long-lasting impressions—sometimes longer than buildings.

Creating an ambience of celebration was top of mind for Rockwell when in 2008 he was asked to design the sets for one of the glitziest and most anticipated celebrations of the year: the Academy Awards. "If you look at the Oscars in 1935," he said, "what was amazing about them was they celebrated the community." Those early ceremonies weren't held in theaters but in grand hotels, and while they were large, they had a convivial atmosphere. Attendees sat at tables sipping champagne rather than in seats facing a stage. But over time, the production moved into theaters and became increasingly designed for television.

"What happened was that the show was onstage, while the community was out here," said Rockwell as he sketched a perspective drawing of the theater, tracing the gulf between the stage and the audience with a ballpoint pen. "The ceremony became just a ritualized thing that didn't really acknowledge the audience." This made it feel more like a performance and less like a party, a situation made worse by the fact that people were constantly leaving the theater during commercial breaks to get drinks, and stars who lost often left just after the winners were announced. By midway through the evening, the theater was half full of seat fillers.

"So we ripped up the six hundred seats in the orchestra and tiered it so that the performance and the experience was about the audience." Now only four steps separated the audience from the presenters. The front of the stage was made circular, and the rows of seats radiated out from it in concentric rings. This brought the presenters out into the audience and gave the whole production a more communal feel. It also cleverly reflected the conventions of amphitheaters and sports arenas, where seats are arranged in the round to provide a view of both the action on the field or stage and the spectators in the stands. Rockwell also suggested putting a band onstage to play during the breaks and keeping the house lighting low, like a nightclub's. The result was that people actually wanted to be there, and many more stars stayed through the evening.

Rockwell's work at the Oscars underscores the fact that the most important ingredients in any celebration are the people. Emotions are naturally contagious, and joy especially so. We "catch" it from one another through facial expressions, tone of voice, and gestures. (I think this helps explain why a photo booth is such a joyful addition to a party, especially if you display the photos as they're printed: it calls attention to the joyful faces of the group.) A good party not only has a lively guest list but also creates conditions that capitalize on the inherent tendency of joy to spread.

If you're hosting, say, an Oscars-watching party instead of the Oscars, how do you do this? My conversation with Rockwell made me realize that physical closeness is vital. In large crowds, such as at a parade or a festival, people naturally bump up against one another. But smaller groups don't gel unless they're in reasonably close proximity. If you've ever attended a middle-school dance in a massive gymnasium and stood awkwardly on the edges while waiting for enough brave people to get the dance floor going, you know what this feels like. You don't want people to be squished and uncomfortable, but you do want interactions to become inevitable. This should be comforting for anyone who thinks their space is too small to entertain. In fact, the real problem is having a space that's too large. A few years ago, I helped host an event in a space that was much too big for the crowd that was going to occupy it. Fortunately, a talented architect I worked with figured out a way to shrink the space in half by using simple screens and potted plants. The room felt buzzy and alive rather than sparse and cold.

Another idea comes from filmmaker and writer Nora Ephron, who considered a round table essential for a dinner party because it brings a group together in a single conversation. It also allows guests to see one another's facial expressions, much the way the amphitheater-style seating did at the Oscars. A related trick is to position a large mirror in the room where you entertain most frequently. The mirror reflects the group and amplifies the joyful vibe.

If you don't have a physical way to make a space feel more intimate, Rockwell says it's possible to achieve this transformation with light. "Lighting defines the boundary of your world," he said. As we've seen with the energy aesthetic, light draws people in, so creating a strong contrast between light and dark can create an artificial perimeter that holds the party together. You can do this with pendant lights hung low over a dining table, for example, or string lights that delineate the boundaries of an outdoor celebration.

Just as the space can promote a feeling of unity, so can attire. Sports fans wear jerseys and paint their faces in team colors. Graduates wear caps and gowns. Bridal parties wear matching dresses and ties, bouquets and boutonnieres. Even an ordinary gathering of friends can be made into a festive occasion simply by adding a theme. When everyone is standing around in 1980s clothing or ugly Christmas sweaters, there is a sense of visual harmony that makes people feel instantly a part of something larger than themselves. As the crowd adopts a shared identity, individuals begin to treat one another differently. Studies have shown that when we believe we are among others who share a group affiliation, we're more comfortable with less personal space, and we exhibit greater trust. We behave less like strangers and more like members of a tribe.

SONG AND DANCE

It was the summer after I turned twenty-one, and I was walking on air: for three months I would be living and working in Paris. I spoke hardly a word of French when I arrived, and while it was a thrilling adventure, it was also surprisingly lonely. After work, I would wander the streets in the long twilight, peering into cafés and people watching in the park. Then one June evening, I left the office to find the city brimming with music. There was an old-timey jazz band in Saint-Germain and a choir outside of Saint-Sulpice, a classical quartet in a small garden and a reggae band in front of a café. And there were other musicians, too — not professionals, just people who happened to have an instrument and knew how to play it. They brought out their guitars and accordions and fiddles and perched on street corners, filling the air with a joyous cacophony of sound.

The festival I had stumbled into was Fête de la Musique, a celebration of the summer solstice that turns the longest day of the year into the city's largest party. The streets reverberated with melodies and laughter. People swayed and sang along. Older couples turned a cobblestone square into a dance floor, whirling around each other with practiced steps while children bounced around in between them. Soon I was dancing, too, alongside countless others that night. And though I was among strangers, I suddenly didn't feel so alone.

"Music washes away from the soul the dust of everyday life," wrote the German novelist Berthold Auerbach, capturing the way a few notes can transform an ordinary setting into a celebration. Rhythms flow through our muscles, triggering the urge to dance or sway in time with the vibrations around us. In fact, just listening to music activates the motion centers of the brain, even when our bodies are still, which is why we often find ourselves snapping or tapping along to a beat without even realizing we're doing so. When infused into a social situation, music produces even-more-mysterious effects. In a study sponsored by Apple and Sonos (two companies that admittedly have an interest in promoting music consumption), footage from video cameras placed in homes revealed that household members sat 12 percent closer to one another when music was playing in a room. And when neuroscientists monitored guitarists playing a short melody together, they found that patterns in the guitarists' brain activity became synchronized. Similarly, studies of choir singers have shown that singing aligns performers' heart rates. Music seems to create a sense of unity on a physiological level.

Scientists call this phenomenon synchrony and have found that it can elicit some surprising behaviors. In studies where people sang or moved in a coordinated way with others, researchers found that subjects were significantly more likely to help out a partner with their workload or sacrifice their own gain for the benefit of the group. And when participants rocked in chairs at the same tempo, they performed better on a cooperative task than those who rocked at different rhythms. Synchrony shifts our focus away from our own needs toward the needs of the group. In large social gatherings, this can give rise to a euphoric feeling of oneness—dubbed "collective effervescence" by French sociologist Émile Durkheim—which elicits a blissful, selfless absorption within a community. Through the joy of belting out a favorite tune or breaking it down on the dance floor, we become more generous and attuned to the needs of those around us.

This fact goes a long way toward explaining why music and dance are such essential and enduring aspects of our celebrations. According to historian William H. McNeill, the pleasure of "keeping together in time" with others played a critical role in enabling humans to form large, cooperative societies—a role that was perhaps even more important than language. Words allowed our ancestors to communicate their needs and agree on shared rules and goals. But when it came to building emotional rapport and motivating people to prioritize the needs of the group over personal desires, language was woefully inadequate.

Song and dance instilled a sense of community on a visceral level. By being united in the same rhythm, people didn't just think of themselves as part of a group; they saw, heard, and felt a harmony that stretched beyond the boundaries of their own bodies.

Sound waves and dance steps don't leave fossils, so it's hard to know exactly when and how our ancestors first began to come together in this way. But anecdotal evidence suggests that festive ceremonies featuring singing and dancing were taking place well before the advent of writing, perhaps as long as twenty-five thousand years ago. Research by Iegor Reznikoff, a scientist who studies acoustics at the University of Paris, suggests that many cave drawings from the Upper Paleolithic were used as backdrops for ritual celebrations. Reznikoff was humming one day while touring a prehistoric site and noticed that the spots with the highest concentrations of paintings produced resonant echoes not unlike those of a Romanesque chapel. By systematically measuring the number and duration of echoes at different places in caves across France and the Ural Mountains, he confirmed that the most decorated locations also produced the most significant echoes, indicating they may have been scenes of primitive rites, chosen to amplify the group's songs and chants.

Though today we distinguish between religious rituals and secular festivities, in prehistoric life, most celebrations likely had elements of both. Anthropologists believe that by the eighth millennium B.C., such gatherings were a well-established part of life among the early civilizations of the Near East and southern Europe. Hundreds of wall paintings and pieces of pottery from the Neolithic period feature depictions of dancing figures with arms outstretched and legs raised. Usually arranged in a circle, sometimes holding hands, the figures' matching body positions and even spacing suggest that they are moving to a common beat. Some wear masks or headdresses or wave sticks or leafy branches, in early indications of the kinds of costumes and sacred artifacts that often define ritual gatherings. Israeli archaeologist Yosef Garfinkel notes that these depictions of dances are the oldest and one of the most prevalent motifs in Neolithic art. If people weren't devoting significant energy to dancing during this time period, they certainly were spending a lot of time thinking about it.

Why did depictions of dance suddenly become so popular in those early days of civilization? It just so happens that the Neolithic dance craze coincided with one of the most significant transitions in the history of human life: from living in small bands of hunter-gatherers to large agrarian communities. No longer limited by what they could carry, our ancestors began to amass property, and this gave rise to social and economic stratification. By settling down, societies gained wealth and security, but along with these benefits came a host of destabilizing forces—inequality, jealousy, isolation, distrust—that hunter-gatherer societies had largely managed to avoid. At this profound inflection point in the evolution of human civilization, Garfinkel suggests, dancing may have been a joyful kind of glue that kept these new societies intact.

To this day, the act of dancing or making music together has the power to connect us to others. You can see this at weddings, where two disparate groups of friends and relatives come together as one on the dance floor. You can see it at festivals, as I did that night when I danced with strangers on the streets of Paris. It even happens at protests, when people chant and sing in unison. The traditions of singing "Happy Birthday," dancing the hora, or starting a conga line at parties can seem cheesy. But we repeat them over and over because they make us feel connected on a visceral level. The essence of celebration is that it is a participatory form of joy, not a passive one. Music and dance engage our whole bodies in the act of rejoicing, drawing us off the sidelines into the center of the action.

BURSTING WITH JOY

A few months ago, I was driving through a run-down area in northern New Jersey when a flash of lime green caught my eye. It was one of those inflatable tube men, basically a long wind sock with arms and a smiley face, dancing on the corner outside a car dealership. It bent back like it was doing the limbo and wiggled its arms in a disco-style shimmy. It folded into itself and then popped up again, arms joyfully outstretched. At the end of each arm, a tuft of ribbons waved like jazz hands. It was tacky and ridiculous, but its energetic movements made me laugh. Amid the dingy strip malls and endless lots of old cars, it was the most joyous thing in sight.

A quick Google search revealed that I wasn't the only one who found the inflatable tube man to be a source of delight. Countless You-Tube videos show people dancing next to tube men, trying to mimic their curiously fluid moves. Some even wear inflatable-tube-man costumes to show their appreciation. But what I couldn't figure out was why. What was it about the tube man that caused its peculiar exuberant-yet-kitschy brand of joy? I puzzled over this whenever I saw one, but it wasn't until I learned their strange provenance that I began to understand their charms.

The tube man is only about twenty years old, but to understand its genesis we have to go much further back, to the late Middle Ages, when authorities within the Catholic Church were attempting to quell what they considered to be an excess of festivity in local churches. Early Christian services had been lively affairs. Dancing was often on the agenda, and even priests participated in the revelry. As Barbara Ehrenreich notes in her book *Dancing in the Streets*, early medieval festivals took place inside churches, which didn't have pews, leaving plenty of space for dancing and making merry. Church leaders had tolerated these behaviors more or less throughout the medieval period, but in the twelfth and thirteenth centuries, they decided to try to curb the rowdy behavior and impose a more sedate form of worship. But they knew they couldn't get rid of celebration entirely. Instead, they designated certain days as feast days and allowed people to revel as much as they wanted to—not in the church, but in the streets. Freed from the oversight of the clergy, for a few days each year people were able to escape the strict rules and hierarchies that governed feudal life, and an atmosphere of unbridled hedonism prevailed.

So Carnival was born, and so it remains: the wildest of festivals, celebrated each year in hundreds of cities in the days leading up to Lent. Today, one of the most exuberant Carnivals can be found in the small island nation of Trinidad and Tobago. In the capital city of Port of Spain, rivers of dancers cloaked in fantastical costumes flood the streets, their bodies animated by lilting calypso and soca music in a local tradition known as mas. Short for "masquerade," mas is a kind of living sculpture that exists for the sole purpose of enhancing celebration. One year, the parade was filled with more than three thousand dancers wearing enormous butterfly wings in every imaginable color, flapping joyously in time to the rhythm of the steel drums. Another year people danced under a rainbow canopy that seemed to stretch for miles, undulating with the movements of the dancers below it. They wore huge layered collars made of white fabric that surged around their bodies like white water.

Though these parades feel spontaneous, the most intricate ones can take months of careful planning. This means that for some mas artists, Carnival is less a moment in time and more a way of life. The most famous mas artist is a man named Peter Minshall, who began his career as a theater designer, leaving Trinidad as a young man to study in London. In 1973, he had just finished designing sets and costumes for a production of *Beauty and the Beast* by the Scottish Ballet when his mother asked him to come home and design a costume for his younger sister, who was slated to be a junior Carnival queen. Minshall obliged, crafting an iridescent hummingbird outfit layered with scales of green, blue, and violet that shimmered in the sunlight. It took twelve people five weeks to make, but at Carnival it was an instant sensation. Decades later, Minshall's work has become so synonymous with Trinidadian Carnival that there he is simply known as mas man.

"Mas is a powerful, communicative expression of the spiritual and physical energy of human beings," Minshall has said. And what he does is harness that natural release of energy and expand it, using oversize elements that amplify the dancers' bodies, often to several times human scale. One of his Carnival queens, fittingly called *Joy to the World*, wore a magnificent set of angelic wings splashed with a watercolor pattern that fanned out from her body like a colorful aura. Another year, the centerpiece of the festival was a character called *Firebird from Paradise*, a man dressed in gold and adorned with enormous red and orange plumes, as if his appendages were throwing fire. As time went on, Minshall invented ingenious mechanisms that turned his costumes into a kind of dynamic puppetry. One of these was a character called the *Merry Monarch,* a giant skeleton over fifteen feet tall, its bones painted with colorful stripes and a spray of wiry, multi-colored hair cascading down its back. What looked at first like a piece of set design was in fact worn by a dancer who stood underneath it, controlling the giant puppet with sticks attached to his feet and wrists. Each of the dancer's movements was echoed at a grander scale by the "super puppet" above him.

Watching the dancers in these stunning creations, I realized that Minshall's designs aren't just about making something big and eye-catching. They're cleverly designed to amplify the natural shape of the joyful body. In a moment of intense joy, our bodies burst open. We throw our arms up in triumph. We jump with legs splayed in jubilation. Our bodies go from small to big as joy courses from the center of our hearts to the ends of our extremities. And this is exactly what Minshall's creations do. Speaking about the hummingbird costume he designed for his sister, he once said, "At first she looked like nothing—just a little blue and turquoise triangle, bobbing along among those grand plumed and glittering chariots, a little tent bobbling along. And then, the hummingbird burst into life, like a sapphire exploding." With wings and feathers, fans and ruffles, Minshall's designs trace radiating lines out from the body like rays emanating from a star.

Radiating shapes like this have long been a part of celebratory attire across cultures. The traditional festive costume of the Waghi people of Papua New Guinea includes an enormous sunlike headpiece made of feathers from four different birds of paradise. In Burkina Faso, the Bobo people wear funeral masks made of long, twisted fibers in bright colors, such as red or purple, that hang the full length of the body. When animated by dance, the fibers create a spectacular, wild spinning motion aimed at driving away ill-tempered spirits. A contemporary example can be found in the pom-poms that cheerleaders wave. These flared adornments catch the eye, drawing the observer's gaze out to the edges of the body to maximize the impact of the spirited cheers. By magnifying the intrinsic gestures of celebration, these costumes and accessories make the joy of the revelers more visible and contagious within the crowd.

Like the pop of a champagne cork, bursting shapes suggest the release of energy under pressure, which mirrors the sudden outpouring of joy that happens during a celebration. So it's not surprising that we often find bursting elements used to create a celebratory atmosphere. Chief among these are fireworks, which historians believe have been used since 200 B.C. in China. The first firecrackers were simply pieces of bamboo tossed into a fire. As the natural air pockets in the bamboo expanded, they gave off a loud pop that people believed could ward off evil spirits. Chinese alchemists added gunpowder, and Italian craftsmen in the 1830s added color, giving us the dazzling flashes and bangs we now associate with holidays like the Fourth of July. The handfuls of rice we use to shower a newly married couple or the confetti we throw up in the air on New Year's Eve are simpler ways of achieving the same effect. Some flowers, such as allium and Queen Anne's lace, have joyful bursting shapes, as do pom-poms and tassels, which can bring a celebratory feeling to both party decorations and everyday interiors.

The expansive quality of the celebration aesthetic reflects the fact that in the throes of revelry we find not only communion but also release: a sense that as joy bursts out of us, it shatters our boundaries and brings our true self into the open. Carnival provides a space in which the strictures of daily life are eased, allowing latent emotions that normally must be kept under wraps to emerge. Like the bursting of a firecracker, this can be a bit volatile. Still, I don't think we realize how necessary the visceral release of a celebration like Carnival is to our well-being. Without it, it's easy to convince ourselves that the responsible, rational, workaday persona we wear most of the time is the sum total of who we are. The regular drumbeat of celebration in primitive life served not only to connect people to one another but also to give them access to a more effusive and instinctual side of themselves. As social media has locked our identities, there's a growing desire for spaces where we can escape the control that defines so much of our existence. The timeless allure of Carnival, and the rising appeal of festivals like Burning Man, are that, in the wild outburst of emotion from the crowd, we find the freedom to be anyone we want.

In this light, Carnival artists like Minshall play an important role in a culture, framing up a space for this ecstatic release of energy. Their work manifests the emotion of the occasion in a tangible way, facilitating a kind of communal catharsis. Perhaps this is why, in the midnineties, Minshall's work caught the eye of the planners of the 1996 Summer Olympic Games in Atlanta, Georgia. If anyone could figure out how to create a joyous celebration for millions of people worldwide, it would be Minshall, and he was tapped to be the artistic director of the opening ceremonies. For this event, he envisioned a set of dynamic sculptures larger than anything he had ever created. They would be like his super-puppets, but instead of being operated by dancing men and women, they would be powered by air. To bring them to life, Minshall turned to an LA-based artist named Doron Gazit, who used a fan-based mechanism to create the dancing figures. The resulting sculptures, which Minshall called *Tall Boys,* stood sixty feet tall and danced ecstatically, their bodies swaying and rolling like the Trinidadian dancers on the streets of Carnival.

The opening ceremonies were a success, and afterward Minshall went back to Trinidad and continued to dream up ever-grander Carnival performances. Meanwhile, Gazit decided to patent the technology for the inflatable sculptures, licensing it out for halftime shows and corporate events. Copycats sprang up, and soon there were inflatable tube men gyrating in the parking lots of strip malls, jiving outside electronics stores, and doing the samba next to farm stands, where they often do double duty as scarecrows.

They may be tacky, but in their tireless dance, they distill the heady exuberance of Carnival and bring it into the most unlikely settings. As they repeat the expansive gestures of celebration again and again, they offer a whimsical reminder that joy can burst out at any time.

SPARKLE AND FLARE

One Fourth of July a few years ago I found myself on a plane taking off from JFK. I've always loved looking out the window on night flights as the plane lifts away from the shimmering city skyline. But that night, as I pressed my nose against the round plastic window, I noticed something even more spectacular: tiny pops of colorful fireworks spreading out over the landscape. At first, I saw just a cluster of them down by the water, where the dark ocean meets the lit-up land. But as the plane rose higher, I could see them everywhere. Each community had its own display, and from the Brooklyn parks to the shore towns of Long Island, the vibrant sparks made the world seem effervescent.

From the moment our ancestors first danced around a fire, cinders flickering in the darkened sky, celebrations have inspired us to light up the night. With fireworks and lanterns, birthday candles and bonfires, festive occasions chase away the shadows and carve out a space for joy within the darkness. It's hard to imagine now, in a world that glows with electric light, how rare and special it once was to see the world lit up at night. But until the advent of gas-lit streetlamps in the early nineteenth century, most cities were completely dark after sunset. Only on special occasions, like the emperor's birthday in China or on holy days in Europe, would medieval people have seen such light.

The dynamic interplay between light and dark remains a defining feature of our celebrations. Though we could flood our parties with lumens if we chose to, invariably such bright and steady light kills the mood. Instead, we find ourselves drawn to lights that glimmer, dance, and, most of all, sparkle. "Sparkle wakes up the eye," said David Rockwell, who had a shimmering curtain made of two hundred thousand Swarovski crystals commissioned for the Oscars, creating a scintillating backdrop for the sparkling jewelry worn by the attendees. Even a little bit of sparkle makes an experience feel instantly more festive, whether in the form of glittering decorations, sparklers lit on a summer evening, or a glass of champagne, also known as sparkling wine.

Yet according to Rockwell, sparkle is on the decline in our lives. "I think there's a very close connection between sparkle and glare, as there is between love and hate," he said. Both glare and sparkle come from shiny, reflective surfaces, but while glare feels harsh and distracting, sparkle is more delicate and alive. "With LEDs and screens there's a tendency for environments to read very flatly," he said. "I think the world has become seamless in a way that has eliminated glare, but it has also eliminated sparkle." He believes that this is a subtle reason that it's hard for digital experiences to feel as celebratory as in-person ones. "Sparkle doesn't exist in this world," he said, gesturing to his phone, "because it's processed through a screen."

How do we recapture sparkle? As I thought about the joy of fireworks, I realized that sparkle is simply light burst open. The pleasure of fireworks is fleeting, but we can create a more durable version of this delight with fixtures that capture the bursting quality of light in static form. For example, the chandeliers at the Metropolitan Opera House in New York feature starbursts of glittering crystals that resemble galaxies seen from a distance. The "sputniks," as they are affectionately known, were inspired in part by a book about the Big Bang. I think these fixtures help explain why it always feels so exciting to go to a performance at the Met, even if, like me, you're not much of an opera buff. Smaller versions of these starburst light fixtures can create a festive feeling in the home. For a more seventies-style sparkle, a mirrored disco ball can scatter light in a festive way.

Reflective materials of all kinds can create sparkle: metallic garlands and ribbon, tinsel and sequins, rhinestones and lamé, and, of course, glitter. "Glitter celebrates," the late actor and writer Carrie Fisher once said in an interview. "It's happy. It makes you look like you're up for a good time." An outspoken advocate for mental health, Fisher was known to wear glitter particularly when she was feeling down, as a way of lifting her spirits. When she signed autographs, she would occasionally throw a pinch of it at her fans. I can attest to glitter's power to create

sputniks

a celebratory feeling. I recently bought a pair of shoes covered in gold glitter. Though I originally intended them for special occasions, I've started wearing them on errands to make ordinary days more festive. I've found that people look at the shoes and smile as if they assume I'm celebrating something. Which, in turn, makes me feel like I am.

THE BALLOON GIRL

Jihan Zencirli never expected anything to come from the balloons. The first one was just a birthday gift for her best friend. She ordered a giant balloon from an Etsy shop and fashioned a large, colorful tassel from scraps of fabric and ribbons she'd saved. She had the balloon filled with helium, attached the tassel, and marched her creation down the street to her friend's party. Measuring three feet in diameter, the balloon floated above her like a festive moon.

"I got there on the early side, about six-thirty," Zencirli recalled, "and the front of the restaurant was full of older diners and families." She laughed as she remembered the bemused faces, the necks craning to get a better look, the smiles and the stares. People were even more amazed when she turned and walked into the restaurant. Inside the space, the large balloon became not a moon but a sun, a focal point around which the activity revolved. She tied it to her friend's chair. "All night, people stopped by and wanted to talk to her and ask her about her balloon," she said. "And it became a part of our evening." The reaction to the balloon made an indelible impression on Zencirli. "It's the first time I experienced what it was like to have something that draws in so much attention," she said. "And I could see people looking at my friend, and at this thing, and it was bringing them so much joy."

After that, Zencirli began carrying balloons on a regular basis. She drove a Volkswagen Beetle that had a trunk perfectly sized to hold a single giant balloon, and every day she'd inflate one and take it with her. "I became this 'balloon girl,' and people in my neighborhood would recognize me," she said. One day a woman who had seen Zencirli with a balloon at a bar tracked her down on the street and begged her to bring her signature balloons to a party she was throwing for her husband's birthday, handing a fistful of cash through the window of her SUV. It was Zencirli's first commission.

Overwhelmed, she rounded up a caravan of seven friends to help her bring all the balloons to the event. It turned out to be a success, and she soon attracted other clients. But in those early days, she still had a full-time job, and making the balloons was a side project. She set up a bare-bones website, Geronimo Balloons, with a PayPal link. There weren't even any photos on the site. Then a prominent Los Angeles blogger wrote a post about the giant balloons, and the next day Zencirli woke up with thirty thousand dollars' worth of orders to fill. "Of balloons!" she said, still incredulous. She hadn't even thought to charge people sales tax.

From there, well, Geronimo Balloons started to blow up. Zencirli refined the design, crafting the tassels out of tissue-paper fringe, sometimes adding sparkly gold or silver elements. The balloons became a favorite of event planners and magazine editors and were often spotted floating over the heads of glowing moms-to-be at baby showers or replacing flowers along the aisles at wedding ceremonies. The price point was high, between fifty and seventy-five dollars per balloon, but each was so enormous and festive that just one could transform a room.

"People are so happy to receive them that I've never actually had a complaint," she said. Eventually Zencirli left her job, moved to LA, and hired a team to keep up with demand. Now, a few years later, giant balloons with big tassels have become commonplace, and Geronimo is kind of like the Kleenex of giant balloons.

I had watched the proliferation of Geronimo Balloons with interest, and a bit of curiosity. A helium balloon is inherently joyful—equal parts playful and transcendent—but making the balloon bigger and adding a flurry of ribbons takes its joy to another level. I began to notice that oversize objects often make an appearance in celebratory contexts. At carnivals, when people win big at Skee-Ball or the ring toss, they receive a giant stuffed animal, often bigger than the person who won it. And in those ceremonies for lotto winners that are sometimes shown on local TV, there is always a giant check to represent the jackpot. A magnum of champagne is more festive than two standard bottles, a stretch limo more celebratory than two regular cars. At Christmas, we bring an entire, full-sized tree into our homes—the bigger, the better. What is it about making something bigger that makes it more festive?

Large-scale elements signal that something different and important is happening in the life of a community. Giant balloons, numbers (for a birthday party), hearts (for Valentine's Day), baby blocks (for a shower), and other big things stand out as different from everyday décor. Oversize food items can also play this role and have the advantage of lending themselves well to sharing. As Julia Child famously said, "A party without cake is just a meeting." A pig roast, a punch bowl, and a champagne or chocolate fountain are other examples of food or drink scaled up to create a focal point for a celebration. The same principle can also apply to dress, particularly for women. Ladies attending the Royal Ascot horse race in London wear enormous hats decorated with feathers and bows. Some men wear top hats as well. If horse races aren't on the agenda, a statement necklace, flower crown, or cocktail ring are other oversize festive touches.

Put simply, big things express big joy. They function as a nucleus for the festivities, a beacon that draws people in. It's easy to underestimate the importance of this. Recently I was reminiscing with a friend, and we realized that one year during our childhoods both of our families had abruptly stopped putting up a Christmas tree. Though we still played carols, hung lights, and opened presents in the years that followed, it never felt as joyous as it had in the years before. Without a focal point, a celebration has no center of gravity. Throughout history, the tangible anchors of celebration—bonfires and feasts, maypoles and parade floats—have had a magnetic power to draw us into physical proximity. They make us forget about our worries and our differences, grounding us in the joy of the moment.

In the past few years, Jihan Zencirli has expanded on the joy of celebration. She cut back her direct and wholesale business, leaving the market for betasseled giant balloons to her imitators, and began creating large-scale balloon installations. For the tenth anniversary of a friend's blog, she covered the façade of a San Francisco building in a flood of multicolored balloons. They tumbled off the roof line like a chromatic bubble bath overflowing the tub, grazing the awning of the produce shop three stories below. To coincide with the New York Pride March in 2017, she created an enormous rainbow balloon wall, featuring more than ten thousand balloons of different sizes and hues. And on the façade of the Hollywood Sunset Free Clinic, a nonprofit healthcare facility in Los Angeles, she did a surprise installation purely for the joy of it, making the building seem as if it were festooned with giant gumballs and gobstoppers.

Zencirli takes commissions from individuals and companies, usually to commemorate significant occasions like openings or anniversaries. But she has one firm rule: she works only in places that are visible to the public—no private homes or gardens—so that people passing by have the chance to experience the joy of her work. This feels like such a novel and generous gesture, yet it reminds me that for so much of human history, celebration was a public affair. From the communal fire to the churches to the streets: a fête for one meant a festival for all. By making a part of each celebration public, Zencirli turns the celebration inside out. It is no longer owned exclusively by the hosts and the lucky few on the invite list. It is there for everyone's delight.

At the heart of celebration is a kind of mathematical paradox: the more we share joy, the more it grows. The implication of this is that we should manage joy in the exact opposite way that we manage money. We should spend it all, at every chance we get. What celebration does, with music and fireworks, giant balloons and glitter, is broadcast our joy far and wide so that others can join in. Because the more generous we are with our joy, the more we have for ourselves.

10.

RENEWAL

March 24, 2012: my thirty-second birthday, and the day the tingling started. At first it was just a bit of pins and needles in the ball of my left foot, as if my leg had fallen asleep. I wiggled my toes and rolled my ankle, and the feeling subsided. But it came back several times over the next few days, sometimes in one foot, sometimes the other. Occasionally I would reach down to feel my foot, and it would be numb. If I had been smart, I would've scheduled an appointment that day to see my doctor, or called my parents, both physicians. Instead, I tried to ignore it and threw myself into work.

Work was a good place to hide. I had a job I loved, and an enthusiastic team happy to stay up until all hours pulling off the most complicated project any of us had ever done. I ate breakfast, lunch, and dinner at my desk most days, or I ate them from plastic containers in airports and rental cars. I responded to clients first thing upon waking in the morning and just before turning out the lights at night. In this way, I was able to hide from the online dating app filled with profiles of men I was sure were going to be just as noncommittal as the last one I had dated. I was able to escape the flood of wedding invitations and baby announcements that filled my mailbox, reminders that my friends were all moving on to "adult life," a place I couldn't seem to find the entrance to myself. And I could avoid the brochures about egg freezing that my gynecologist had handed to me on my last visit, which I couldn't bring myself to look at. But I wasn't able to hide from my body, which insisted on coming with me wherever I went and sending waves of prickles through my extremities several times a day. If the cause was something terrible, I wasn't ready to hear it yet. Still, the overall message was clear: I was in a rut.

We dream of a durable kind of happiness, a state of bliss that, once found, has the constancy of granite. And while there are many things we can do to create a reservoir of joy that helps us amplify the highs and buffer the lows of everyday life, sometimes we have to accept that joy moves through our lives in an unpredictable way. There will always be aspects of life that are out of our control: the demands of our bosses and customers, the moods of our partners and families, the ups and downs of the economy, politics, and the weather. Challenges appear from unexpected sources. The things we wish for don't always arrive on the schedule we set for them. Sometimes even when we get what we'd hoped for, it doesn't make us as happy as we'd imagined. And in these difficult moments, it's easy to feel a bit lost or stuck, that joy has somehow forgotten about us or passed us by.

Which is how I felt six years ago as I shuttled to and from work each day, wishing for a stroke of serendipity that would transform my life into what I'd dreamed it could be. That didn't happen, but something else did. I was asked to lead a workshop in Dublin and saw an opportunity to get away for the weekend. Then just as I'd gotten excited about a new adventure, I learned the workshop was canceled. I'd already spent numerous late-night hours researching inns in the Irish countryside, and that night I came home to find all the websites still open in my browser. I checked my frequent-flier mileage balance and, on a whim, booked the trip myself.

The Northeast was still snug under the gray blanket of winter, but Ireland was fluorescent green, in the throes of an early spring. No surface was uncovered by grass or lichen, no branch left unbowed by a corolla of leaves. Ferns sprang out of tufts of olive-hued moss on tree trunks filmed with algae. Grasses raced skyward, indecorously. Duckweed forgot its place, tracing a lacy path up drains onto driveways, a cheery, swampy carpet. On my first afternoon there, I kept having to rub my eyes. It felt like I had stepped into a dreamy cliché.

Over the next few days, I explored the verdant landscape on lazy walks with Dumpling, the innkeeper's hedonistic terrier, whose low-slung body would disappear into the dandelion-strewn grass and reappear in splashes at the muddy edges of the pond. When I got tired, I curled up in a corner of the library with a pot of strong tea and thick slices of brown bread, the windows a green wallpaper around me. Then back out into the chlorophyll frenzy of emerald and jade, viridian and mint.

As I boarded the flight home, I felt like a different person. I knew I was heading back to the same life I'd left a few days before. I still had tingling feet, a summer full of weddings to attend, and no one to join me. But I was more hopeful than I'd been in a long time. I found myself thinking about all the things my present lack of attachment gave me time to do. I spent entire Saturdays guiltlessly reading magazines in bed, signed up for Caribbean dance classes, and began plotting my next solo vacation. Eventually, I worked up the courage to see my doctor and discovered the tingling was benign—a symptom of anxiety that began to ease almost as soon as the words were out of her mouth.

In the freedom chapter, we saw how natural environments can restore our emotional resources, refilling the reserves that get depleted in everyday life. This was part of the effect I experienced in Ireland, to be sure, yet the feeling was deeper and more profound. It wasn't just restoration, but wholesale renewal. Instead of feeling overwhelmed by the disappointment of my unfulfilled wishes, it was like the slate had been wiped clean, and I was starting fresh right where I was, imperfect but complete.

We find this joy of renewal in many different moments and contexts. Ending an addiction or finding a new faith can provide a sense of renewal, of being reborn into a new life. Near-death experiences can bring renewal, as can the feeling of being given a second chance after a terrible mistake. A common moment of renewal comes from the birth of children or grandchildren, and people often describe the pleasure of rediscovering the world through the naïve eyes of a child, gaining a renewed flush of wonder at well-worn joys. There are also many smaller moments that give us this feeling of newness and potential. A really great haircut can sometimes do it, as can a fresh load of laundry or a hot shower with a loofah. Cleaning can be a path to renewal. One of my favorite days of the year is when a troop of men swinging Tarzan-style from ropes arrives to wash the windows in my apartment building, and I look out to see a crisp world I had forgotten was there.

Just as there are personal moments of renewal, there are also collective ones; springtime in Ireland, with its hyperbolic greenness, was undoubtedly one of them. It made me think of these words from the Persian mystic poet Jalaluddin Rumi:

We began
as a mineral. We emerged into plant life
and into the animal state, and then into being human,

and always we have forgotten our former states,
except in early spring when we slightly recall
being green again.

Spring restores our consciousness of time and, even more so, of possibility. The thawing of the hard earth, the flowing of sap, the bursting open of millions of buds: as the slow land quickens, we feel the energy of new beginnings around us, and our attention turns to the future. We are reminded of what a thrill it is to know that joy is speeding toward us, and to stand awaiting it with open arms.

Finding happiness isn't a matter of creating a perfectly even-keeled experience of the world, where no sadness ever intrudes. Instead it means riding the waves of joy, and trying to find our way back upward when we've been knocked down. In renewal we find a kind of resilience, an ability to bounce back from difficulty by reigniting the optimism and hope that rises within us when we believe that joy will return. What I found in Ireland was a landscape that made me feel new inside. What other landscapes had this effect, I wondered, and could there be qualities that we could import into our surroundings to cultivate moments of renewal in daily life?

FLOWER BLIZZARD

The blossom front moves north through Japan like a pink tide, starting on the island of Okinawa as early as February, sweeping up through the archipelago, and eventually reaching the mountains of Hokkaido sometime in May. Cherry blossom forecasts resemble typical weather maps, but in shades of blush and fuchsia. They depict the country's gradual efflorescence in rosy bands. In each prefecture, meteorologists study the buds on designated "sample trees," offering daily updates on the projected timing of the year's bloom. The first day of blossom season is announced when five or six flowers are open on a sample tree. It lasts at most two weeks.

Like weather reports, blossom forecasts are notoriously unreliable, and it was with trepidation that I landed at Narita Airport late on April 3, nearly a week after Tokyo's predicted peak bloom. On the train ride to the city, I peered out the windows, searching for signs that I wasn't too late, but I saw only a blur of fog from an earlier rainstorm and the glare of the train lights on the glass. Soon I was in Shibuya, winding my way out of the station into the flashing chaos of lights and people. I scanned for trees in the patchwork of buildings and signs, shuffling through the crowd of commuters and club kids. Nothing. It wasn't until I had lugged my suitcase up the stairs to a pedestrian bridge that I caught sight of a small cluster of cherry trees, fluffy like cotton balls, lit up by the brilliance of the LED signs. I ran toward them, the wheels of my suitcase clattering behind me, my face beaming. I wasn't too late after all.

I woke up the next morning to a landscape that seemed to have burst open, like a sofa with the stuffing coming out of it. On the narrow streets along the Meguro River, fringed on both sides by cherry trees, dark branches laden with blossoms swooped out over the water, casting pinkish reflections on the green-brown surface. The blooms were everywhere, light and frothy, sometimes emerging right from the sides of the tree trunks. Pink lanterns hung along the streets, and flutes of pink champagne were served from temporary kiosks on the sidewalk. In the restaurants, cherry blossom petals were crushed into mochi, a sweet rice cake, and infused into iced tea. In the convenience stores, I found pale pink Kit Kats and cherry blossom Pepsi, a liquid with a lurid hue that seemed almost to glow. People strolled around in a daze as petals drifted softly down around them, waving and fluttering. The blue-suited garbagemen were flecked all over with petals. A businessman I passed had a petal stuck right in the center of his forehead.

The opening of the cherry blossoms, or *sakura,* is an occasion almost of madness in Japan. In the brief season of their bloom, a culture known for its quiet reserve opens up and becomes giddy. People throw themselves into the evanescent joy of the season, taking time off from work to gather for *hanami,* the traditional blossom-watching picnics that date back to the eighth century. In Ueno Park, the site of more than a thousand cherry trees, men in suits and women in dresses lay sprawled out on blue and green plastic tarps, gazing up into the canopy. Friends gathered in clusters, laughing and talking, taking turns snapping photos of one another with their faces next to the blossoms. Children reached up to grasp the falling petals. One little girl lay on her back and flailed her arms like she was making a snow angel. During cherry blossom season people drop their usual masks, smiling broadly in the parks and the streets.

Watching Japan plunge headlong into the delight of the sakura was a reminder that while the fluctuations of joy in our lives can be unpredictable, our planet has rhythms of renewal that regularly bring joy back to us. As the earth traces its annual loop around the sun and pirouettes daily on its axis, we co-travelers are subject to a host of natural cycles. We can't feel the earth's movement directly, but we see it in the oscillations of light and color, temperature and texture, that sweep through our surroundings. The blossoming of the trees, the rising of the sun, the flow of the tides: these recurring events remind us of time's circular nature and create an underlying cadence of joy that we can rely on.

The notion of time as cyclical has been an intimate truth for most of human evolution. Our ancestors' connection to the earth made an awareness of its patterns unavoidable. No hunter-gatherer would have failed to notice the changing light of the moon as it moved through its phases, nor missed the opportunity presented by a full moon to pursue nocturnal prey. No early farmer could have afforded to ignore the subtle signs of thaw or the lengthening daylight that heralded the beginning of the growing season. Early civilizations codified these cycles in their calendars, punctuated with seasonal festivals that petitioned deities for favorable conditions and helped to synchronize the activities of a community to ensure a bountiful harvest. This circular concept of time remains prevalent in the religion and philosophy of many indigenous and Eastern cultures. But in the West, our awareness of cycles has been overshadowed by a linear view of time, one that emphasizes beginnings and endings and strives for progress over repetition.

Why did linear time come to dominate the Western way of thinking? Part of the reason is cultural, having to do with the way that Judeo-Christian thought describes the story of humanity not as a wheel but as a distinct trajectory through time. But equally important is that as we have come to see ourselves as separate from nature, we have built structures and systems that distance us from its circular rhythms. Electric light allows us to keep our own schedules, obscuring the phases of the moon and draining the sunrise and sunset of the meaning they once carried. Rather than matching our appetites to the harvests, we match the harvests to our desires. We have big watery strawberries all year round, forgetting that there was once a time when they were available only in June and tasted like sweet red fire. Our buildings heat and cool the air to a consistent temperature regardless of the weather outside. Our sound machines play any birdsong on demand, regardless of where those birds are in their migratory arc. Thus, disconnected from participation in these natural cycles, we have forgotten that time moves in loops as well as lines.

It's not that linear time is bad. Our ability to learn from our mistakes, grow, and innovate derives from our belief that time has a forward thrust and that we can build on history to create a better future. The problem is that an overemphasis on linear time tends to magnify the pain we feel when joy ebbs. If we view the future as a blank, uncertain space, then it's hard to trust that joy will return once it has gone. Each downswing of joy feels like a regression, each nadir like stagnation. But if instead we can rely on the repetition of certain delights at regular intervals, then the wavelike quality of joy becomes more present in our lives. Cycles create a symmetry between past and future that reminds us joy will come back again.

This can be particularly powerful in moments of loss or struggle. When a devastating earthquake and tsunami hit the Tōhoku region of Japan in March of 2011, the survivors found themselves digging out of the wreckage just as the cherry blossoms were beginning to bloom. Workers and residents, masked to protect their bodies from radiation from the damaged Fukushima nuclear reactor, moved somberly among houses that lay upturned and peeled open. Yet amid this ruinous scene, pink blossoms began to open as they always do. In her documentary *The Tsunami and the Cherry Blossom*, Lucy Walker captures the amazement of residents as they discover that the trees, which had only weeks before been submerged in seawater, had survived and begun blooming. "Spring comes when it's time," says a cherry tree master, the owner of a nursery that has been growing trees for sixteen generations. "It makes me keep up with the metronome of my life. The cherry trees lead us."

Cherries are striking in that they flower before any leaves appear. So as the blooms emerged from the bare branches, they seemed to symbolize what might happen to the ravaged towns. In the simple joy of blossoms, people who had lost everything found a measure of hope and resilience.

Whether in hard times or good ones, the benefit of cycles is that they give us something to look forward to, and this anticipation can be a pleasure in its own right. Here's Winnie the Pooh's response in *The House at Pooh Corner* when Christopher Robin asks him about his favorite things to do:

> "Well," said Pooh, "what I like best—," and then he had to stop and think. Because although Eating Honey was a very good thing to do, there was a moment just before you began to eat it which was better than when you were, but he didn't know what it was called.

Sensitive Pooh intuits what scientists are just now discovering. Studies have found that a period of anticipation can significantly enhance the joy that we find in an experience. Researchers believe that this may be because we create detailed mental simulations of future events, so imagining a future joy fills our minds with rich sensations and exciting possibilities. Similarly, even though Friday is a workday, it's usually considered more joyful than Sunday, which for many people brings on a depression known as Sunday blues. On Friday we have the whole weekend ahead of us, while on Sunday, we're already thinking about the week ahead. Cycles create regular moments of anticipation that bring future joy into the present, ensuring we always have something to look forward to.

The Japanese are particularly good at creating moments of anticipation. Instead of having only four seasons to look forward to, they have seventy-two. The ancient Japanese calendar divides the year into a series of microseasons, each only four or five days in length, with names that capture small changes in the surrounding environment. Hibernating Creatures Open Their Doors marks the tail end of winter, followed a bit later by Leaf Insects Turn into Butterflies. In June, the Plums Turn Yellow, and in October the Geese Arrive and the Grasshopper Sings. The names made me think of other seasonal moments that naturally seem to stir feelings of renewal: the whiteout blanket of the first snowfall, the hard drenching of an April rain, the blush of sunrise, and the golden glow of a harvest moon. There is a joy in the first day cold enough to light a fire in the fireplace, the first one warm enough to go outside without a jacket, and the first blinking of fireflies in the summer yard. By building excitement for these subtle transitions, we can invite more cyclical anticipation into our lives.

Finding a closer relationship to the cycles of the earth is often as simple as reconnecting with nature. The farm-to-table and local-food movements bring a greater awareness of growing cycles to the dinner table, offering up the joy of discovering heirloom variants overlooked by the food industry and the delight of learning to anticipate the brief, intense seasons of our favorite produce. The recent proliferation of farmers markets and community-supported agriculture shares (CSAs) has made this joy much more widely accessible. And even mass-produced foods have begun to feature more seasonal ingredients in limited-edition flavors. Of course, gardening naturally creates an awareness of cycles, particularly with perennials that come up on their own each year, alerting us to the changes of the seasons. Indoor plants, too, can have their own cycles. One of my favorite houseplants is a black oxalis, a relative of the shamrock, with purple leaves that open each morning to greet the day and close up in the evening when the sun sets. Seasonal crafts and rituals, such as carving pumpkins or covering the house with lights and decorations for the holidays, can also be a source of this kind of joy.

Yet while seasonal pleasures can be particularly intense, they also have a bittersweet undercurrent. "When I see the cherry blossoms I feel joyful and sad at the same time," a young woman named Aya told me, gazing up wistfully at a tree in full flower. Almost as soon as they open, the delicate blossoms begin to shed their petals. While through a Western lens, it seems this might diminish their joy, for the Japanese it actually heightens it. They have a phrase, *mono no aware*, that is hard to translate into English but loosely means "the gentle sadness of things." It's used to describe a pang of pleasure that exists alongside an awareness of its fleeting nature. It brings a strange consciousness that the intensity of joy we feel is in direct proportion to the loss soon to follow. In the West, we tend to shy away from these fleeting pleasures. I was reminded of something the florist Sarah Ryhanen had said when we met in her studio. "The number one question you get when you have a flower shop is, 'How long is this going to last?'" She shrugged her shoulders, as if she simultaneously understood the impetus for the question and was frustrated by it. "Sometimes the most beautiful experience with a flower is brief—like these garden roses from the field. They are so fragile because they put all their energy into making this intoxicating scent, which means that they don't last more than twenty-four hours on your kitchen table. But those twenty-four hours you have to smell that flower are pretty amazing."

Our efforts to prolong our joy sometimes diminish its intensity, for example, when we choose blooms genetically engineered for hardiness over short-lived varieties bred for scent. But rather than avoid the transient nature of their favorite season, the Japanese lean into it. I was surprised to discover that the vast majority of cherry trees planted in Tokyo and around Japan are from just one species, the Yoshino cherry. By choosing to plant just the one type of tree, the Japanese have created a landscape designed to burst open in one glorious éclat, to herald the arrival of spring not with a steady trickle of different blooms but a single abundant spectacle.

And while the beginning comes all at once, so does the end. The flowers had become more pink over the days I'd been there, a sign that they were getting ready to fall, and when the wind picked up, the petals whipped around in great clouds that the Japanese call *hanafubuki*, which means "flower blizzard." They landed in small piles at the edge of the street, where passing cars swirled them up into mini cyclones, and in the river, which was speckled as if with confetti. People quickened their pace, aware that it was time to get back to normal life. But as they rushed through the petal snow, I  could already see a hint of anticipation for the inevitable joys of blossoms yet to come.

FLOWER POWER

But what about the blossoms themselves? What is it about flowers that inspires such ardor? This question struck me while reading the essay

"How Flowers Changed the World," by science writer Loren Eiseley, which offers a chilling description of the earth before the evolution of flowering plants, a hundred million years ago. "Wherever one might have looked," he writes, "from the poles to the equator, one would have seen only the cold dark monotonous green of a world whose plant life possessed no other color." Can you imagine it? No cherry blossoms lining the Meguro River, no tulip fields striping the Dutch plains. No bluebells on roadsides, no carnations in cellophane sleeves at the market, no peonies in the arms of brides. No dozens of species of roses in the hothouses at the botanical gardens and, for that matter, no botanical gardens. No flowered dresses, or Monet water lilies, or daisies on the wallpaper in Grandma's kitchen.

A flowerless world seems dim, dystopian—not dead, exactly, but not fully alive either. Yet flowers don't fill our bellies, nor do they keep the chill off our backs. And while a few varieties find use as spices or medicines, such as the saffron-producing crocus or skin-soothing calendula, the most common applications for flowers are aesthetic. We use them to scent our bodywash and eau de parfum. We adorn our homes and gardens with them. We give them as gifts and tributes and use them to brighten our celebrations. Such appreciation for flowers dates back at least to the Egyptians, who built large ornamental gardens around their palaces and temples. Flowers figured heavily into their funerary rites and banquets, where guests wore lotus buds in their hair, and hosts draped their wine jars with floral garlands. Ancient Chinese, Aztec, and Roman societies also had flower gardens. The task of populating those gardens with choice specimens often fueled trade and even conquest. In the seventeenth century, the Dutch tulip frenzy highlighted just how mad people can sometimes go for flowers. During one three-year period, a single tulip bulb of a treasured variety could sell for as much as an entire house. Today, it's estimated that people spend fifty-five billion dollars worldwide each year on flowers.

Why, of all the varied products of nature, do we lavish so much attention on the beautiful, useless flower? I had a chance to reflect on this question one early Saturday morning in October, when I paid a visit to the New York flower market. I was throwing a party to celebrate my mother's seventieth birthday and was on a mission to gather blooms for the arrangements. All along the block of Twenty-Eighth Street between Sixth and Seventh Avenues, suppliers lined the sidewalks with their wares: big bunches of roses, slender stems of orchids, and countless other varieties. Fashionable women in long coats gathered armloads of tropical-looking proteas and wintry hellebores, deftly navigating the crowded sidewalks with their paper-wrapped purchases slung over their shoulders.

As I strolled among the different stores, red bucket in hand, I felt a thrill: it was like walking through the garden of a large, well-tended estate, except that I could pick anything I wanted. And I realized that many different aesthetics of joy were on display. The ranunculus caught my eye first, a picture-perfect illustration of energy, their candy-colored pops of brightness arranged in rows of yellow, orange, coral, and hot pink. Harmony, too, was evident in the intricate symmetries of the different blooms. Some flowers contained an abundance of smaller florets, some were round and playful; some had a celebratory burst like a pompom. Some were transcendently light, others iridescent and magical, and still others had surprises inside, like a hidden color that appeared when they reached full bloom. When I had finished gathering, I looked down into the bucket and saw a microcosm of the landscape of joy.

All this would be more than enough to explain our unique affection for flowers. But upon bringing them home and arranging them into centerpieces, I noticed something else. Flowers come in different forms—cups and cones, stars and clusters—but all of them have an expansive quality, harnessing the energy of sunlight and water to open outward and show their insides to the world. With their broadening shapes and unfurling petals, flowers have a dynamic energy that suggests emergence and becoming. We find an implicit understanding of this in the way we use the word "blossoming" to describe someone coming into her own or "late bloomer" to denote a person who has taken longer than usual to reach his potential. The word "flourish" derives from the same root as "flower." Flowers signify a kind of uncontainable verve, a life force that can't help but find its way out.

The connection between flowers and flourishing isn't just metaphorical. For our foraging ancestors, flowers offered an important piece of information about the landscape: they gave clues to the future locations of edible fruits and seeds, several weeks or months ahead of time. Flowers were like coming attractions for food, and early humans who were smart enough to notice them would have been able to plan their return so as to harvest the ripened fruit before birds or other rivals could devour it. Over time, an appreciation for flowers may have provided enough of a survival advantage that it became an intrinsic human attribute, so universal that indifference to flowers is a common sign of depression. In a world where we pick our fruits from the produce aisle rather than the vine, we have lost the conscious connection between flowers and food. But our delight in flowers bears traces of an anachronistic anticipation, a cue to expect future joy.

Cut flowers can seem like an extravagance, and I know many people who love them but struggle to justify the expense. But the effect of even a single bloom on a space can be dramatic. Think of the way the small bud vase that used to be built into the dashboard of the Volkswagen Beetle changed the whole feeling of the car's interior. Flowers bring an element of nature's dynamism into the more static context of the man-made world. Our couch cushions don't change color with the seasons. Our rugs don't burst into bloom. Our lamps don't wane and wax like the moon. While the static nature of the objects around us engenders comfort and predictability, it also drains away our connection to the vibrancy of the earth. It's the opposite of the fervid growth of Ireland and the blossoming profusion of the sakura. And at moments when our lives feel a bit stuck, our inanimate surroundings can quietly aggravate the problem.

Flowers, light and ebullient, have an energy that shatters this stasis. And curiously, the effect holds even when the flowers aren't real. Stand in front of a Georgia O'Keeffe canvas of poppies or orchids and you feel the same delicate power as when you hold a blossom in your hand. Nearly every era of design has taken advantage of this fact and used floral elements in décor, whether embroidered, carved, painted, or sculpted. I happen to love paper flowers, which have been making a comeback lately and have roots in the craft traditions of Mexico, China, and Victorian England. They are fun and inexpensive to make and, unlike most artificial flowers, can be easily recycled when they start to look tattered. Floral motifs are also some of the most common patterns for fabrics and wallpapers, and there are few limits on the ways that floral designs can be incorporated into everyday spaces.

Another approach uses the shape of flowers in a more refined way. For example, the *Swan Chair* by the Danish designer Arne Jacobsen and many pieces by the French designer Pierre Paulin have flared forms like a corolla of petals, subtly mimicking the expanding shape of a flower blossoming. While floral motifs can sometimes seem over-the-top, these chairs look restrained enough that they often find use in offices, bringing a joyful, blooming quality to places that can have a sedate feeling. One of my favorite flowerlike designs is the *Cabbage Chair* by the Japanese design team Nendo. The chair arrives as a cylinder of rolled-up sheets of paper, which the owner peels back and folds down, blossoming the chair into shape. Other decorative objects can have a blossoming quality. For example, many pendant lights have a flowerlike shape, as do the big feathered circles of the Cameroonian juju hats that have become popular as wall decorations in recent years. Fashion, too, offers examples of floral shapes used to create a sense of energetic lightness. Circle skirts, peplums, and bell sleeves are especially popular in spring fashion, where they mirror the blooming forms in the landscape.

Floral elements create a kind of eternal spring in our surroundings. Yet there's a paradox here. Flowers suggest transformation, but wallpaper blossoms and flowerlike chairs don't actually change at all. If the source of a flower's joy lies in its dynamic quality, why doesn't freezing it in time destroy its appeal? Even in static form, the blooming shapes of flowers suggest a momentum toward a more abundant world. Painted blossoms don't substitute for our engagement in the cycles of the world around us, but they do help to create a hopeful feeling, interjecting reminders of spring into joy's winters.

OBVIOUS CURVES

Are flowers and blossoming shapes the only way to bring the joy of renewal indoors? I thought back to my trip to Ireland. There weren't many flowers blooming at the time, yet the landscape brimmed with a sense of potential. Surely this was due in large part to the abundance of the color green. But was that the only reason? Or was there something else that made that vernal terrain so enlivening?

An answer to this question came to me by way of an unlikely object: a gravy boat, photographed in black and white, pinned with a red thumbtack over my studio mate's desk. Every time I passed by, I found myself stopping to look at it. This was during my first year of design school, and although I didn't know yet that this object was a design classic, I could tell that it was special. For a few minutes every day I stared at it and tried to understand why. It wasn't like any gravy boat I'd ever seen. It looked like the ends of a long leaf had been curled up to meet each other, creating a rounded hammock for the sauce inside. At the top, the two ends met and tipped gently away from each other, yielding a shape like a pair of pursed lips. It was a voluptuous form, but cast in creamy white ceramic, it felt unfussy and modern. More than anything, the gravy boat struck me because it felt almost alive, as if it were still growing.

This was how I first learned about Eva Zeisel, an icon of midcentury modern design. Zeisel was born in 1906 to an upper-middle-class family in Hungary. As a child, she spent time in the large, ranging garden that surrounded her Budapest home, sometimes sleeping outside with her pet dog on warm nights. It was in this garden that she found her first creative impulses. She used the gardener's cottage as a workshop to make rounded pots in the traditional Hungarian folk style; they had a black surface from being fired in the underground kiln that she built herself. Though it wasn't considered appropriate for women of her social status to train as artisans, at the age of seventeen she flouted convention and apprenticed with one of the last master potters in the guild system. She gained experience designing for mass production in

Germany and then in Russia, but her life took a sudden dark turn when, at the age of twenty-nine, she was arrested and falsely accused of plotting to assassinate Joseph Stalin. After nearly fifteen months in prison, much of it in solitary confinement, she was released and deported to Vienna, and not long after made her way to New York.

Zeisel quickly attained fame in the United States for designing tableware that married lush forms with the practical needs of day-to-day living. She became the first woman designer ever to have a solo show at the Museum of Modern Art, and by the middle of the twentieth century she was a household name. At the time of her death in 2011 at the age of 105, she was still creating new pieces, and many of her designs are considered collector's items. Her works have an irresistible, touchable quality. As one reviewer commented in 1946, "Their clear-cut, rhythmic silhouettes are not only good to look at, but have a pulling power that draws the fingers to touch and lift them." I confess that when Zeisel's daughter Jean Richards invited me into her mother's studio at her upstate refuge in Rockland County, I stood paralyzed, caught between the desire to touch everything and the fear that I might break something. Fortunately, Richards didn't seem to notice and passed me a steady stream of teapots and mugs and sugar bowls to cradle. "She meant all her designs to be touched," she said emphatically. I felt a frisson of delight, as if I were holding pieces of music in my hands.

For help in understanding what made Zeisel's work so joyful, I turned to Olivia Barry, who worked as her assistant for the last twelve years of her life. She had been the one who took the aging designer's rough sketches and drafted them, refining the forms to Zeisel's precise standards and getting them ready for production. Over the course of her time working with Zeisel, Barry began to notice something strange: all of the curves in Zeisel's sketches matched a set of templates known as French curves. French curves are a kind of stencil with a curlicue shape used by designers to trace smooth arcs when drafting a design. Think of the edge of an urn or a wineglass seen in profile: getting that curve to bend in just the right spots and not be lumpy or bumpy requires more than just a steady hand. To draw the right shape, designers usually have to piece together a curve from sections of different French curves, but with Zeisel's designs, Barry always seemed to find one template that fit exactly. "One day I said to her, 'Eva, this is funny. There's always a French curve that fits your drawing.'" Zeisel had replied, "Darling, it's because we do very obvious curves."

What did Zeisel mean by "obvious curves," I asked. She thought for a second, then ventured, "I think she meant that they're the most satisfying to look at. Maybe they're from nature, and maybe they're connected to mathematical equations somehow." She shrugged. "The obvious ones are the best."

Yet in the context of design at the time, Zeisel's curves were far from obvious. In fact, that she chose to use curves at all was an unconventional decision. This was the 1940s and 1950s, the height of modernism, which devoted itself to straight lines and right angles and had a near-allergic aversion to organic forms. While Zeisel embraced the clean contours and practical sensibility favored by modernists, she bristled at their restrictive palette of shapes, which she felt resulted in design that was cold and soulless. "The program of the modern movement made it impossible to express feelings," she said. "Following its principles, the designs of the last century have lost emotional appeal. The design process has become sensible instead of sensitive." Modernists wouldn't have refuted these charges. They aspired to a rationalist mode of design free of sentimental flourishes, and for them, right angles exemplified precision and purity. But for Zeisel, who believed that design should be lively, varied, and evocative, curves were indispensable.

But not just any type of curve. In chapter 5, we saw that curves can have a bubbly, playful quality. This kind of curve, which you find on a beach ball or a chubby baby, is what designers call a neutral curve, because the rate of curvature doesn't change over the length of the curve. Zeisel used these playful curves in her work (and in fact was famously inspired by babies' bottoms). But the majority of her pieces exhibit more elongated, sensuous lines. In particular, Zeisel viewed one type of curve as the most essential and expressive: the compound curve, or S curve.

Zeisel's studio was a heaven of S curves, from the nested trio of ceramic bells that hung from a wooden bracket on the wall to the swooping handles of the pitchers and coffeepots to the graceful profile of that gravy boat. And as I looked at all these curves, I realized that Olivia Barry had been right about the connection to nature. S curves are ubiquitous among living things, particularly plants. On the edge of an oak leaf, the contour of a pear, or the new shoot of a young vine, we find sinuous curves that suggest growth, burgeoning, and transformation. Zeisel herself acknowledged the connection to growth in her work, saying of the *Museum* series that she had designed the pieces to look "as if they were growing up from the table." S curves alert us to the fact that a landscape is alive and ever changing. This is part of what makes spring so thrilling (in Ireland, or anywhere else). The flat, bare land comes alive with curves, and we get the feeling that if we come back in a few days, the whole scene will look different. By using these curves, Zeisel's work pulls the dynamic qualities of the natural world into the man-made one, infusing a sense of potential into everyday objects.

Organic forms bring the fluidity of the living world back into our space. Obviously plants and flowers can do this, but so can more abstract forms that incorporate S curves into their shapes. Things formed on a wheel or a lathe, such as hand-thrown pottery and turned wooden table legs, often have curvy profiles. So do objects made by bending metal, wood, or wire. Ruffles and scallops add an S-curvy edge to clothing and other textiles. As with flowers, it doesn't take a large dose of these elements to bring a sense of freshness into a space. Even subtle accents like the curve of a chairback or the arc of a handle can make the difference between whether something feels inert or alive.

Particularly important, in Zeisel's view, are the edges or ends of an object. In her book *On Design*, she uses the Chrysler Building as an example and reflects on what it would feel like if a flat roof replaced its elegant pointed spire. "When shapes culminate in lively upper contours, like parts of the whole, objects feel like growing things — seashells, pods, or flowers," she said. On the other hand, "buildings or inkwells or vases or pitchers which look as though they were cut off haphazardly seem incomplete, unfinished, unsatisfactory." Organic forms taper, flare, or coil at the ends. A flat edge suggests a sudden event, possibly a traumatic one. When I brought this up with Olivia Barry, she turned spontaneously to the planter next to the table where we were sitting, which held a large tuft of ornamental grass. "Look at these grass ends," she said. "They're just so beautiful, and they curl in the right way." She broke off a few and laid them out on the table, separating them with her fingertips. "Oh, like this!" she exclaimed, pointing to a pair of delicate crescents. "They're just curves, but they're perfect." Looking at the grass tips reminded me that the end of a stem is usually where the hormones that drive cell division are located in a plant. Flattening out the top of a form, like cutting off a stem, removes the dynamic force and makes an object look more static. The difference is that plants always seem to find a way to keep growing, sending up new shoots out of the wound. But man-made objects, once cut off, stay that way indefinitely.

Now that Zeisel had opened my eyes to the power of a simple line to suggest vitality, I began to notice other aesthetics that signified dynamism and change. The spiral, for example, is also deeply associated with growth. Darwin observed that as plants grow, their tips move in spiral oscillations with a circular or elliptical shape. In 80 percent of plants, the leaves grow in a spiral pattern, too. Some mollusks, such as the nautilus, grow in a spiral shape, as do ram's horns and the cochlea of the inner ear. Spirals (and helixes, the technical term for a spiral that moves in three dimensions as opposed to two) can be found in the coil of a fern frond, the petals of artichokes, the fruitlets of a pineapple, and the bracts of a pinecone. Many of these spirals exhibit a rate of expansion that correlates with the Fibonacci sequence, a mathematically significant group of numbers in which each is the sum of the preceding two (0, 1, 1, 2, 3, 5, 8, 13, 21, 34, 55). Dividing successive Fibonacci numbers yields a ratio known as the golden mean (approximately 1.61803), which some historians believe was used by the ancient Egyptians in the design of the Pyramids at Giza and by the ancient Greeks in the Parthenon. Though these uses of the golden mean are hotly debated, the ratio and the spirals it relates to have been a subject of fascination for at least two thousand years. Whether in the form of a spiral staircase, a coil pot, or a braided rug, spirals bring a powerful kind of dynamism into a space. An extraordinary spiral detail appears on the ceiling of Antoni Gaudí's Casa Batlló in Barcelona, with sculpted ridges resembling a whirlpool. But perhaps the most famous spiral in architecture is the corkscrew-like Guggenheim Museum building on Fifth Avenue in Manhattan. Its architect, Frank Lloyd Wright, has described it as "a curving wave that never breaks," capturing the essence of upsurging energy that lies at the heart of the renewal aesthetic.

A RENEWAL OF JOY

I never fail to feel joy when I see a little flower poking through a crack in the sidewalk, blithely asserting itself among the solid rectangles of the modern city. Though it stands alone in a place where it obviously doesn't belong, it bears no self-consciousness and seems unbothered by the obstacles presented by the site in which it happened to sprout. It does its best to harvest the rays of sunlight, capture the rains, and smile open its petals to the sky. If it can avoid being trampled, it might last long enough to scatter a few seeds across the concrete, and with luck and a good breeze, a few might find cracks of their own in which to settle. Next year perhaps it will have the company of sons and daughters, and a small start at a meadow will have begun.

It was some variation on this process that transformed the High Line, which we saw in chapter 3, from a disused railroad into a secret garden. Originally built for freight trains to reach the factories and warehouses along New York's west side, the High Line was in operation until 1980. By the nineties, the structure had become so derelict that local residents were lobbying for its demolition. As landscape architect James Corner

tells it, "Most people had only ever seen the underside of the High Line, and it was just big hulking steel, rusting and dripping and dark and dank. Nobody knew that the topside had this beautiful self-sown carpet of green." Whether blown by winds or excreted by passing birds, seeds landed in the rotting wood of the railroad ties and took root. "There were vines up there and grasses and perennial flowers and weird shrubs," said Corner. "It was just magical. You couldn't help but be impressed by nature's resiliency, in terms of being able to just body forth this amazing playground of life in a bereft landscape." Inspired by this self-created Eden, a foundation formed with the purpose of turning it into an urban park, and architects from around the world were invited to submit ideas for its design. Many designers treated the site as a blank canvas, a site like any other to develop. But for Corner, who was enchanted by the renewal that had already begun, it seemed the right thing to do was as little as possible. Though many subtle changes were made to enable safe access, create a system of planting beds and water collection, and increase the biodiversity of the vegetation, the High Line feels like a space still in the process of revival, a continuation of what nature began for itself.

Given only the most basic elements and time, nature will reclaim any space in which humans have lost interest, filling it up with a luxurious assembly of flora and fauna. In the Cambodian jungle near Angkor Wat, the twelfth-century temples of Beng Mealea and Ta Prohm stand in the shadows of trees whose roots engulf the carefully laid stones like a web. In the wasteland left by the meltdown of the Chernobyl reactor in 1986, still considered unsafe for human habitation, a weedy landscape plays host to species like wolves and lynx. Out of ends, renewal creates beginnings. Out of destruction, creation. This aesthetic reminds us that nothing is irredeemable in this world, nothing so ruined that it is ever beyond hope.

In renewal, we find perhaps the clearest expression of a truth that underlies all of the aesthetics in this book: that the drive toward joy is synonymous with the drive toward life. From that first revelation of the ancestral link between bright color and ripeness to the simplicity of the S curve, this correlation has held true. Joy evolved for the express purpose of helping to steer us toward conditions that would encourage us to flourish. It is our inner guide to the things that animate, stimulate, and sustain us. Put more simply, joy is what makes life worth living.

And yet for some reason, we have decided that it is superfluous — the icing on the cake, rather than an integral part of the cake itself. We sort our lives neatly into buckets of *needs* and *wants,* and even though joy's origins lie in highlighting what is essential for our survival, it has come to signify the ultimate luxury, an extra we allow ourselves only if all our needs are met. The problem is that without joy, we may be surviving, but we are not thriving. If we rarely laugh or play, if we never have glimpses of magic or flashes of transcendence or bursts of celebration, then no matter how well fed and comfortable we are, we are not truly alive.

Once we accepted the notion that joy is inessential, it became easy for it to slip out of the center of our lives. Work became about endless gains in productivity, rather than the joy of craft or creation. School became a push for achievement, rather than an exploration or an adventure. Systematically, joy was squeezed out of the places where we spend most of our days. And the same thing happened to our physical environment. Buildings presented themselves as canvases for the display of status or ideology or brand identity, rather than spaces for the cultivation of joy. As joy moved to the edges of our world, to playgrounds and beaches, nature preserves and candy stores, the rest of the world was left to languish.

The notion of environmental renewal is now a well-accepted one. While debate exists about just how to repair the damage we have done to fragile ecosystems with our sprawling development and ravenous appetite for natural resources, there is broad consensus that such renewal is necessary for us to survive and flourish on this planet. What we need now is a similar revitalization of the man-made world, a humanistic renewal to parallel the naturalistic one already under way. We need to bring joy back into the heart of our lives. We need to bring our world back to life.

The beauty of renewal is that it has its own momentum, propelled by the relentless ambition of life to endure and propagate. Life multiplies, and so does joy. The infectious quality of joy makes its dispersion as efficient as the most prolific weed. Even the smallest efforts—a painted mural, a knit cozy around a parking meter, a single flower—can be the beginning of an upward spiral that changes a community, a neighborhood, a life. To fix the world is a tall order, but to renew it is not nearly so daunting. The lesson of renewal is that from small seeds big things grow. And though I never would have suspected it eight years ago when I started writing this book, it's not far-fetched to believe that from the seeds of our own joy, a whole world can be reborn.

JOYFUL TOOLKIT

"Each of us is an artist," the Irish philosopher John O'Donohue once said, because "everyone is involved, whether they like it or not, in the construction of their world." In this book, we've seen how people from a wide range of different backgrounds are doing just this. With paint and markers, yarn and flowers, they are constructing a more joyful world. Now it's your turn.

This chapter is designed to help you take the ideas in this book and translate them into your own life. Whether you want to give your life a full joy makeover, tackle a specific project (like redesigning a room or throwing a party), or simply sprinkle a bit more joy here and there, these exercises will help you figure out how to bring more joy into your world.

You may want to photocopy the worksheets provided so that you can reuse them. (You can also download them from the "Resources" section of aestheticsofjoy.com.) In working with these tools, I've found that people's answers tend to change over time, depending on what's happening in their lives and what they need at a particular moment.

There's no set process, so feel free to customize these exercises to suit your needs, and have fun with them!

STEP 1: FIND YOUR JOY

The exercises in this section are designed to help you reflect on what joy means to you and see which aesthetics of joy you naturally gravitate toward.

Joy Journal

As you go about your daily life this week, keep a Joy Journal. Use it to take note of any time you feel a sense of joy. Pay attention to moments when you smile or laugh, when you're tempted to say "Yay!" or "Wow," or even just when you become aware of a subtle, pleasant feeling. You can also include any joyful memories that come to mind. For each moment, write down:

- Where you are.
- Whom you are with.
- What you are doing.
- What sights, sounds, aromas, textures, or flavors are associated with your joy.

At the end of the week, look for patterns. You can note your patterns in the Joyfinding worksheet on page 302.

Joyfinding

The goal of this exercise is to help you identify the different sources of joy in your life and to understand a bit more about why they bring you joy. Use your Joy Journal to help you fill it out. A brief example is on the next page, but feel free to use as much space as you need.

Once you've completed the worksheet, tally up the aesthetics of joy you've listed in the right-hand column. Which ones come up to the top? It's okay if you don't see a clear pattern—it just means you have *lots* of different aesthetics that bring you joy!

N O T E : As you do this exercise, you may find examples of things that bring you joy *in the moment* but have a negative long-term influence on your joy. For example, "eating cookies" is an activity that brings me joy, but if I did it all the time, it would actually make me feel less joyful. Other examples might include drinking alcohol, watching TV, smoking, shopping, spending time with an ex, and so on. I recommend you note these things on your worksheet with a minus (-) sign next to the ones you'd like to do in moderation, and an *X* next to the ones you'd like to avoid completely. Understanding which aesthetics these behaviors are tied to may help you find more constructive alternatives that feel good to you.

JOYFINDING: WORKSHEET

PLACES

Places can be near or far, from your life now or a time in your past.

Where do I feel most joyful?	What is joyful about these places?	What aesthetics define these places?

PEOPLE

These can be people you know now or once knew or famous people you admire.

Who are the most joyful people I know?	What is joyful about these people?	What aesthetics do these people embody?

THINGS

You can include objects you once owned but no longer have.

What are the most joyful objects in my house?	What is joyful about these things?	What aesthetics do these things exhibit?

ACTIVITIES

These can be things you do now or things you used to do.

What activities bring me the most joy?	What is joyful about these activities?	What aesthetics are present in these activities?

JOYFINDING: EXAMPLE

PLACES

Places can be near or far, from your life now or a time in your past.

Where do I feel most joyful?	What is joyful about these places?	What aesthetics define these places?
HAWAII	SUNSHINE, WARMTH, TROPICAL	ENERGY, FREEDOM
BROOKLYN BRIDGE PARK MEADOW	WILD NATURE, WATCHING BIRDS	FREEDOM, RENEWAL
CAFÉ ACROSS THE STREET	WALLPAPER, POPS OF COLOR	ABUNDANCE, ENERGY
KATIE'S HOUSE	PLANTS AND OPEN SPACE	FREEDOM

PEOPLE

These can be people you know now or once knew or famous people you admire.

Who are the most joyful people I know?	What is joyful about these people?	What aesthetics do these people embody?
ALBERT	ACTIVE INNER CHILD	PLAY
JEAN	PASSIONATE ABOUT NATURE	FREEDOM, ENERGY
SHELLY	ALWAYS UP TO SOMETHING DIFFERENT	SURPRISE
IRIS APFEL	SURROUNDS HERSELF WITH VIBRANCY	ABUNDANCE, ENERGY

THINGS

You can include objects you once owned but no longer have.

What are the most joyful objects in my house?	What is joyful about these things?	What aesthetics do these things exhibit?
SPECKLED MUGS	PATTERN AND TEXTURE	ABUNDANCE
YELLOW CHAIRS	YELLOW!	ENERGY
MELONS POSTER	BRIGHT AND CHEERY	ENERGY
COLOR-CODED BOOKS	VIBRANT YET ORGANIZED	ENERGY, HARMONY
GLITTER SHOES	MAKES AN OUTFIT FEEL LIKE A PARTY	CELEBRATION
POM-POM NECKLACE	SILLY AND UNEXPECTED	PLAY, SURPRISE

ACTIVITIES

These can be things you do now or things you used to do.

What activities bring me the most joy?	What is joyful about these activities?	What aesthetics are present in these activities?
SINGING	THE MELODIES AND RHYTHMS	HARMONY
BEING IN THE WATER (SWIMMING, KAYAKING, DIVING)	I FEEL BUOYANT AND FREE	FREEDOM, TRANSCENDENCE
TRAVELING	NEW SENSATIONS	ABUNDANCE
PAINTING	ALL THE COLORS!	ENERGY

Killjoys

This exercise is similar to the last one, though a little less fun. Still, it can be helpful to identify the things that sap your joy.

PLACES	
Where do I feel least joyful?	What about these places kills my joy?

THINGS	
What are the least joyful objects in my house?	What about these things kills my joy?

ACTIVITIES	
What activities bring me the least joy?	What about these activities kills my joy?

More or Less

Look over your Joyfinding worksheet and list below all that you'd like more of in your life. Then scan your Killjoys worksheet, and list all you'd like less of. You don't need to break your list into categories (unless you want to)—this should be more like a catchall to help you see at a glance what might bring more joy into your life.

MORE	LESS
—	—
—	—
—	—
—	—
—	—

MORE OR LESS: EXAMPLE

MORE	LESS
—POPS OF COLOR	—GRAY
—SINGING AND MUSIC	—DARK WOOD FURNITURE
—SPARKLE	—CLUTTER
—TROPICAL VIBES	—TV (BOTH THE OBJECT AND THE ACTIVITY)
—SUNSHINE AND WARM LIGHT	—BLACK-AND-WHITE ARTWORK
—NATURE	—TOO-DIM LIGHTING

A good time to pull out your More or Less worksheet is whenever you're making changes in your life: moving to a new apartment or new city, looking for a new job, buying new clothes. These are all times to remind yourself of what brings you joy and how you can keep it at the center of your life. You can also fill in this worksheet with a roommate or partner to find overlaps in your joy priorities, which you can use as anchors for designing your shared space.

Bonus exercise: Make a moodboard or Pinterest board of the More side of your worksheet to have a visual reference of the things that bring you joy.

Bonus exercise: Make lists of Places to Go, People to See, and Activities to Try that you can keep handy for when you're planning a trip or just have some free time.

STEP 2: MAKE YOUR JOY

By now you should have a handle on some of the things and aesthetics that bring you joy. But how do you actually apply that knowledge? This section contains exercises to help you move from inspiration to action, creating more joy in your daily life.

For this next section, it helps if you have a specific "project" in mind. A project could be:

- A physical space (redesigning a bedroom, renovating a house, sprucing up an office cubicle)
- An object (designing a poster or a website, choosing a gift, or making a craft project, such as a quilt)
- A collection of objects (updating a wardrobe, creating a gallery wall, putting together a special outfit)
- An occasion (planning a wedding, corporate gathering, or even a dinner party)
- An intangible experience (planning a vacation or choosing an exercise regimen)

Aesthetics Finder

If you already know what aesthetics you want to focus on, feel free to go straight to the Joyful Project worksheet on page 308. Otherwise, use this tool to figure out which aesthetics will help you create the kind of joy you want for your project. If your project is about redesigning something that already exists, start with Fix, below. If your project is about creating something entirely new, skip to Feel, next page.

Fix

Which words describe how this place or thing feels to you now? Circle the words that describe the feelings you want to change with this project. Then look below for the aesthetics that match the words you've chosen. Try to focus on two or three aesthetics when deciding what changes to make.

LACKLUSTER	BARE	CONFINING	UNSTABLE	SOMBER
DREARY	STARK	STIFF	DISORGANIZED	REPRESSED
DRAINING	BLAND	ARTIFICIAL	CHAOTIC	SEVERE
COLD	SPARTAN	RESTRICTIVE	OVERWHELMING	STRESSFUL
ENERGY	*ABUNDANCE*	*FREEDOM*	*HARMONY*	*PLAY*
BORING	HEAVY	ORDINARY	ISOLATING	STATIC
MONOTONOUS	GLOOMY	PLAIN	LONELY	LIFELESS
PREDICTABLE	CUMBERSOME	BANAL	DULL	STUCK
OVERSIMPLIFIED	DENSE	BASIC	MUTED	PLODDING
SURPRISE	*TRANSCENDENCE*	*MAGIC*	*CELEBRATION*	*RENEWAL*

Feel

How do you want the place, thing, or event you're creating to feel? Circle the words that best describe how it will feel when your project is complete. Then look below for the aesthetics that match each set of words. Focus on two or three aesthetics as inspiration for your joyful project.

VIBRANT	STIMULATING	LOOSE	BALANCED	SPONTANEOUS
ENLIVENING	SUMPTUOUS	UNRESTRAINED	GROUNDING	FUN
INVIGORATING	MULTIFACETED	SPACIOUS	PEACEFUL	SILLY
EXUBERANT	LUSH	VERDANT	RHYTHMIC	CREATIVE
ENERGY	*ABUNDANCE*	*FREEDOM*	*HARMONY*	*PLAY*
BOLD	LIGHT	ETHEREAL	VIVACIOUS	DYNAMIC
QUIRKY	ELEVATING	WONDROUS	COMMUNAL	SENSUOUS
UNEXPECTED	AIRY	INTRIGUING	DAZZLING	NURTURING
WHIMSICAL	AWE INSPIRING	ENCHANTING	EFFERVESCENT	ALIVE
SURPRISE	*TRANSCENDENCE*	*MAGIC*	*CELEBRATION*	*RENEWAL*

Joyful Project Worksheet

This worksheet guides you through a series of steps for turning your aesthetic inspiration into reality.

STEP 1: KEY ELEMENTS

Choose up to three aesthetics to use as inspiration for your project. Using the Joyful Palette on pages 13–17 as a reference, list the elements you want to include for each of your main aesthetics. You will probably find it useful to look at the "Signature Elements" section first, and then review any specific sections relevant to your project (e.g. "Décor and Ambience" for a physical space, "Activities and Experiences" for an event, etc.).

STEP 2: SUPPORTING ELEMENTS

Add any joyful elements from other aesthetics that you know you want to include in your project. This is also a good space to note elements that are already a part of the space or thing you're creating (for example, if your space has high ceilings or built-in mirrors, you could note that here).

STEP 3: COMBINATIONS

This is the fun part! Looking at the joyful elements you have listed, how can you combine elements to create unique joyful gestures? The goal is to have a list of four to six specific ideas that combine aspects of different aesthetics in ways that bring *you* joy. See the examples on the following pages for inspiration.

STEP 4: SUMMARY

Once you have your combinations, you should begin to see a theme emerge. Write down your theme and a brief description of one or two sentences. You can use this to help others understand your vision for the project and as a reminder for yourself as you work to bring your project to life.

STEP 5: PLAN

Now it's time to make a plan to execute your project. Under "Add," make a list of things you'll need to make, borrow, or buy. Under "Change," you can list existing things you might need to rearrange, repaint, or otherwise adjust to make them work with your new design. Under "Remove," list things you want to sell, donate, or discard.

JOYFUL PROJECT:			
STEP 1: **KEY** **ELEMENTS**	*Aesthetic 1* — — — — —	*Aesthetic 2* — — — — —	*Aesthetic 3* — — — — —
STEP 2: **SUPPORTING** **ELEMENTS**	— — — — —		
STEP 3: **COMBINATIONS**	_____ + _____ = _____ _____ + _____ = _____ _____ + _____ = _____ _____ + _____ = _____ _____ + _____ = _____		
STEP 4: **SUMMARY**	*Theme*		
	Description		
STEP 5: **PLAN**	*Add* — — — — —	*Change* — — — — —	*Remove* — — — — —

JOYFUL PROJECT WORKSHEET: PLACE EXAMPLE

JOYFUL PROJECT: REDESIGN LIVING ROOM			
STEP 1: **KEY** **ELEMENTS**	*Abundance* —Wallpaper —Layered textures —Artisan textiles —Lots of art	*Freedom* —Nature motifs —Houseplants —Open space —Indoor swing	*Harmony* —Lines of symmetry —Mirrors —Groups of similar objects —Strong patterns
STEP 2: **SUPPORTING** **ELEMENTS**	—Round coffee table (Play) —Pops of color (Energy) —Bright, warm lighting (Energy)		
STEP 3: **COMBINATIONS**	Wallpaper + nature motifs = jungle wallpaper Lots of art + groups of similar objects = gallery wall Houseplants + lines of symmetry + mirrors = potted plants framing a large mirror to create two axes of symmetry Strong patterns + artisan textiles = patterned throw pillows Pop of color + indoor swing = swing chair painted red to contrast with wallpaper		
STEP 4: **SUMMARY**	*Theme* Joy in the Jungle A jungle-inspired room that balances wildness with a subtle sense of harmony, using strong symmetries to ground an abundance of natural patterns and textures		
STEP 5: **PLAN**	*Add* —Throw pillows —Houseplants —Jungle wallpaper —Indoor swing	*Change* —Re-cover white sofa —Gather art for gallery wall —Move big mirror —Repurpose two round accent tables as new coffee table	*Remove* —Oversize square coffee table —Beige armchair

PROJECT WORKSHEET: EVENT EXAMPLE

JOYFUL PROJECT: JANIE'S FIFTIETH BIRTHDAY PARTY			
STEP 1: **KEY** **ELEMENTS**	*Transcendence* —Elevation —Things that draw the eye upward —Light, sky-like colors and gradients —Lightweight materials	*Celebration* —Sparkle —Twinkling lights —Intimate setting —Oversize elements —Bursting shapes —Music and dancing	
STEP 2: **SUPPORTING** **ELEMENTS**	—Natural textures (Freedom) —Round accents (Play) —Mysterious lights (Magic)		
STEP 3: **COMBINATIONS**	Elevation + intimate setting = treehouse party! Things that draw the eye upward + mysterious lights = lanterns hung from branches Things that draw the eye upward + sparkle + dancing = disco ball Oversize elements + lightweight materials = tiered cake with marshmallow frosting		
STEP 4: **SUMMARY**	*Theme* Transcendent Treehouse Disco		
	A treehouse disco party for fifteen close friends that captures Janie's love of dancing and nature, designed to make her feel like she's floating on air on her big day		
STEP 5: **PLAN**	*Add* —Lanterns —Cake —Disco ball	*Change* —Move furniture in the treehouse to make space for dancing	*Remove* —n/a

JOYFUL PALETTE

"How wonderful it is that nobody need wait a single moment before starting to improve the world," wrote Anne Frank. To create something is an inherently optimistic act, and to create joy especially so. By putting joy into the world around you, you're expressing the hope that tomorrow can be better than today, and the belief that it is worth trying to make it so. You have the knowledge, the tools, and a growing community of joymakers to support you. What happens next is up to you.

Use these pages as a reference when bringing the aesthetics of joy to life in the world around you.

	ENERGY	ABUNDANCE
LOOK AND FEEL	Vibrant Colorful Warm Bright	Maximal Layered Varied Textured Kaleidoscopic
SIGNATURE ELEMENTS	Saturated colors Neon and fluorescent pigments Yellow Sunlight Vibrant, dynamic lighting	Rainbows Multicolor Polka dots or stripes Confetti Layered patterns and textures
DÉCOR AND AMBIENCE	Add small pops of bright color and Day-Glo accents Install full-spectrum bulbs (for workspaces) or warm light bulbs (for homes) Paint walls white or light colors Repaint and reupholster old furniture Paint a colorful mural, or buy a removable one Accent with neon signs or other decorative lighting	Use patterned or textured fabrics, wallpaper, and tiles Source artisan textiles, e.g., suzanis, kantha, Moroccan rugs, mudcloth, kilims, frazadas, etc. Layer multiple patterns in a space Use multicolor or rainbow-color palettes Display lots of art or decorative objects Add confetti-like textures by painting or using a material like terrazzo
ARCHITECTURAL FEATURES	Windows that let in ample sunlight Light fixtures that create varied levels of light throughout a space	Lots of decorative trim and moldings
FASHION	Colorful clothing and accessories, such as coats, workout wear, umbrellas, rain boots, scarves, and shoes	Layered accessories and jewelry Mix-and-match prints Striped and polka-dot accents
PLACES	Tropical locales Art museums and galleries	Flea markets and antiques shops Grand hotels Candy stores and buffets
ACTIVITIES AND EXPERIENCES	Run a color run or play paintball Go on a street-art walk	Take a field trip to a place that activates the senses: a perfume bar, spice shop, or market
THINGS TO AVOID	Grey, beige, and other dull hues Dim or too-flat lighting	Minimalist décor

FREEDOM	HARMONY	PLAY
Natural Open Expansive Wild Unrestrained	Orderly Symmetrical Patterned Balanced Flowing	Round Curvy Cute
Open space (negative space) Prospect and refuge Greenery Nature motifs and textures	Patterns (repeating or geometric) Bilateral, radial, or fractal symmetry Repetition Rhythm	Circles and spheres Bubbly shapes Squiggles, loops, and waves Polka dots
Downsize overly large furniture Install indoor swings and slides Add houseplants Display natural objects such as shells, stones, or pinecones Decorate with wildflowers and foliage (fresh or dried) Incorporate nature imagery and textures (plant and animal) Use a diffuser to add scents from essential oils Play birdsong or other natural sounds Plant perennials and grasses in gardens Hang a bird feeder	Group similar objects together Create or emphasize lines of symmetry Use mirrors to enhance symmetry Arrange objects in grids Coordinate colors to bridge spaces Use matching hangers, magnets, or pushpins to unify a display Accent with patterns Hang mobiles Display collections Color-code books Declutter, especially the entryway	Choose circular and spherical furnishings, rugs, and lighting Look for furniture with rounded corners Keep balls, balloons, and Hula-Hoops handy for spontaneous play Decorate with cutensils and other objects with cute attributes Accent with pom-poms Use googly eyes to add whimsy
Open floor plans (remove walls if renovating) Picture windows Glass doors that open to the outside	Strongly symmetrical floor plans Well-placed windows, doors, and trim that enhance perception of symmetry	Floor plans with circuits Arches and vaulted or domed ceilings Porthole windows
Flowing, loose-fitting clothing Natural fabrics	Patterned fabrics Symmetrical silhouettes	Bubble skirts Polka-dot fabrics Pom-poms as accessories or trim
Meadows, beaches, and other open natural spaces National parks and wildlife refuges	Traditional buildings (e.g., churches or temples), which tend to exhibit more symmetry	Amusement parks, fairs, and playgrounds Curvy buildings
Walk around in bare feet Go for a walk (especially in nature) Hike, camp, or kayak Exercise outdoors Learn to forage for wild foods	Attend a dance performance or class Ride a bike, go ice- or roller-skating, surf, or do another balance-testing activity	Keep a ball near your desk or in your car for spontaneous play Do activities with curved motions, e.g., yoga, swimming, Hula-Hooping, hula dancing Spend time playing with kids or pets
Artificial materials and textures (e.g., plastic, concrete) Oversize furniture	Disorganized or disordered spaces Clutter	Sharp corners or angles

	SURPRISE	TRANSCENDENCE
LOOK AND FEEL	Bold Incongruous Eye-catching Imperfect	Light (not heavy) Elevated Airy Buoyant
SIGNATURE ELEMENTS	Contrast Incongruous bursts of joy Hide-and-reveal Playing with proportion and scale	Elevation Upward gestures Light, sky-like colors and gradients Lightweight objects and materials
DÉCOR AND AMBIENCE	Tuck bright color or pattern into out-of-the-way spaces (inside drawers or closets) Add contrasting elements, such as tiles or dishes in a different color Make imperfect patterns, such as potato-print polka dots Choose furnishings that play with scale or proportion Choose decorative objects with quirky, offbeat designs Fix broken objects with colorful tape or glue Hide notes or objects for loved ones to find	Paint ceilings and walls in light colors to make rooms seem taller Paint spaces blue or use gradients to create a sky-like feeling Use hanging light fixtures and other decorative objects to draw the eyes upward Keep hanging décor lightweight Choose lightweight, leggy furniture over heavy pieces Decorate with lightweight, translucent materials Accent with inflatable furniture or objects, such as pool floats or balloons
ARCHITECTURAL FEATURES	Mobile homes Secret nooks or other hidden spaces	Elevated sites Lofts, landings, and lookouts with wraparound windows High ceilings Skylights and clerestory windows
FASHION	Clothes with colorful linings Whimsical undergarments or socks Hide souvenirs in pockets	Light, airy fabrics and silhouettes
PLACES	Dollar stores and vintage stores City streets (walkable neighborhoods)	Treehouses and towers Balconies, roofs, and hills Inflatable structures
ACTIVITIES AND EXPERIENCES	Plan a trip or excursion for a friend or family member without telling them the destination Throw a surprise party Go for a walk in a (safe) city without choosing a specific destination, just following what looks interesting to you Put a joyful, temporary installation up in your neighborhood without telling anyone who did it	Walk upstairs to get an elevated view or look out the window if you're on a high floor Take time to gaze up at the clouds or the stars Choose a window seat when flying Go hot-air ballooning, paragliding, skiing, or mountain climbing Jump on a trampoline
THINGS TO AVOID	Startling or otherwise unpleasant surprises	Heavy furniture or architectural elements Underground spaces

MAGIC	CELEBRATION	RENEWAL
Luminous Ethereal Elusive Prismatic	Sparkling Convivial Effervescent Embracing	Nurturing Dynamic Seasonal Alive
Optical illusions Iridescence Mysterious lights and movements Translucent color Defiance of natural laws	Sparkle and glitter Shimmering light Bursting shapes Oversize objects Music and dance	Flowers Expanding shapes S curves and spirals Seasonal elements
Hang a prism in a sunny window Suspend decorative objects from fishing line to make them appear to levitate Choose paints and fabrics made of iridescent materials, e.g., mother of pearl, mica, etc. Install op art mural or wallpaper Use mirrors to play with reflections Select light fixtures with faceted sheaths or those made of dichroic glass Place a pinwheel, wind sock, or wind chimes in the garden Replace a downspout with a rain chain	Create an intimate setting with lighting or furniture that brings people together Arrange seating so that people can see one another Anchor a celebration with an oversize focal point, such as a giant balloon, large cake, bonfire, or Christmas tree Play strong, rhythmic music that invites singing, clapping, and dancing Use small points of light—candles, torches, or string lights—to create a twinkling effect Add sparkle with metallic accents, glitter, or tinsel Decorate with bursting shapes, such as tassels and pom-poms Hang a disco ball	Place vases of cut flowers in rooms Plant flowering trees and shrubs or ones with vibrant seasonal displays Choose wallpaper, art, and textiles with floral motifs Select furnishings and accents with expanding, blossoming shapes, such as flower-shaped chairs or pendant lights or feathered juju hats Look for objects with S curve or spiral shapes and flared or curved edges Choose spiral accents, such as braided rugs and coil pots Decorate for the holidays and seasons
Sites with unconventional weather patterns: wind, fog, geothermal features	Intimate spaces that aren't too large or exposed	Spiral staircases Curved walls or nooks
Op art–style prints Iridescent or holographic materials and fabrics	Sparkly materials (e.g., sequins or lamé) and glittery accents Bursting shapes, such as radiating collars Matching or themed clothes or accessories	Curved silhouettes, such as peplums, circle skirts, and big rounded collars Ruffled or scalloped accents
Wild places with invisible forces, e.g., Puerto Rico's bioluminescent bays, Yellowstone's geysers, etc.	City Hall Local festivals Holiday store windows	Botanical gardens
Look for rainbows in water glasses and puddles Catch fireflies in summer Eat wintergreen Life Savers and watch them spark in the dark Watch a magic show or learn card tricks to dazzle your friends Fly a kite or go sailing or windsurfing Make time to look at meteor showers or eclipses	Break open a piñata or use sparklers or firecrackers Attend a concert, do karaoke, or go out dancing Seek out opportunities to sing and dance in groups: choirs, dance lessons, dance-based workout classes Wear festive clothes while doing errands Throw a party just because	Watch the sunrise or sunset or look at the full moon Plan a calendar of seasonal pleasures Eat at farm-to-table restaurants or join a CSA Plant a garden or visit a botanical garden Press flowers or fall leaves to put on display
Magic that feels spooky or creepy	Spaces that are too big or too bright	Static, cutoff forms

ACKNOWLEDGMENTS

This book has been many years in the making, and along the way I've been lucky to find collaborators who not only have enhanced it beyond measure but also have brought a great deal of joy into my life. From the beginning, my agent, Richard Pine, has been an unflagging champion of the cause of joy, pairing a lighthearted spirit with a serious dedication to bringing new ideas into the world. Richard saw the book that was in my heart, sometimes even more clearly than I did, and helped me get it out onto the page. I'm grateful to him and to everyone at Ink-Well, particularly Eliza Rothstein, Lyndsey Blessing, and William Callahan.

Likewise, my editor, the incomparable Tracy Behar, has shown her passion for this project at every step along the way. Tracy performed a kind of magic with this book, infusing each page with an energy that makes the words feel more lucid and vibrant. I couldn't imagine a better partner in bringing a book to life. Everyone I've met at Little, Brown has brought warmth, insight, and a generous spirit to our work together. I'm deeply grateful to Reagan Arthur for her belief in this project and her enthusiasm for it and to many others at Little, Brown, including Peggy Freudenthal, Mario Pulice, Carrie Neill, Ian Straus, Lauren Harms, Susan Betz, and Jessica Chun, who have helped to shape this book and share it with the world.

Fred Blumlein, my adviser at Pratt, shepherded this project though its earliest stages with bighearted exuberance. Ashlea Sommer, Kiley Reid, and Ian Shapira gave insightful comments on my early drafts, brainstormed ideas with me, and offered moral support. Daniel Stancato reviewed the manuscript with a fine-toothed comb and gave invaluable feedback on its scientific foundations. Ginevra Drinka provided diligent research and sourcing. Gabriele Wilson designed the perfect cover for this book, and Deb Wood graced its pages with elegance and whimsy. Katie Levy and Mike McVicar designed a beautiful brand to go along with it. And this book would not be what it is without mentorship, encouragement, and feedback from Anne Kreamer, Kurt Andersen, Dacher Keltner, Allan Chochinov, Tina Roth Eisenberg, Virginia Postrel, Rob Walker, and Adam Grant.

IDEO has enthusiastically supported this project since its early days. Thanks to Fred Dust, Tom Eich, Paul Bennett, Whitney Mortimer, Debbe Stern, Tim Brown, David and Tom Kelley, Jane Fulton Suri, Mitch Sinclair, Dan DeRuntz, Clark Scheffy, Michael Hendrix, Brendan Boyle, Mike Peng, Anna Moore Silverstein, Annette Ferrara, Erika Lee, Warit Tulyathorn, Karin Soukup, Alex Gallafent, Jason Baker, Ben Swire, and Mollie West Duffy, who stand out among the many IDEOers who have generously contributed to this work.

It's impossible to find words to express my appreciation for the brilliant and generous people who gave their time and opened the doors to their studios and homes to be featured in this book. Thank you for your stories, your ingenuity, and your joy. In addition, many people went out of their way to share knowledge, make connections, or host me in places near and far, including Olivia Barry, Brent Brolin, Gabriele Chiave, Robert Conte, James Corner, Melanie DeMore, Sylvie DiChristo, Andrew Evans, Bobby George, Twig George, Maggie Hartnick, Jean-Pascal Hesse, Jonas Hjorth, Sofie Juul Hjorth, Momoyo Homma, Matthew Hutson, Margaret Jankowsky, Gayatri Keskar, Takeyoshi Matsuda, Emmanuelle Moureaux, Mary Ann Pettway, Jenny-Sayre Ramberg, Jean Richards, Simone Roodnat, Sarah Ryhanen, Clark Scheffy, Anne Scholder, Ruth Lande Shuman, Fujiko Suda, Justina van Bakel, Ghislaine Viñas, Beth Viner, Marjolein Wintjes, and Jihan Zencirli.

Of course, none of this would have been possible without my family and friends. I'm grateful to my parents, Michael and Jill, for fanning the flames of my curiosity about the world, for their unconditional and abundant love, and their unwavering belief in me. And to Cathy for her loving encouragement and many insightful conversations over the years. The seeds of this book can be found in childhood influences from Nana and Grandpa, who filled my summer days with craft projects, road trips, and other joyful pursuits; Jean, who nurtured my love of writing and nature; and Lola, who was the glue that kept it all together. In addition, I'm grateful to friends and family who were gentle and patient with me during the long, quiet months of putting words to paper, and liberal with their love and encouragement throughout.

Most of all, thank you to Albert, my great love and the light of my life. I'm grateful to you for understanding the depth of my commitment to this project and for supporting my determination to see it through. This experience reminded me how fortunate I am to have found a partner who never does anything halfway. Albert gave me the sharpest critique and the most buoyant pep talks, the deepest belly laughs and the tightest hugs, and made even the hardest days a joy. Everything that I make in this world is better for the fact that you love me, and you let me love you.

Last, I'm indebted to the readers of my blog, *The Aesthetics of Joy.* Since 2009, you've shared with me your inspiration and ideas, your celebratory moments and your simple delights. Thank you for all the joy you bring into the world.

NOTES

INTRODUCTION

5: **People with sunny workspaces:** M. Boubekri et al. (2014). "Impact of Windows and Daylight Exposure on Overall Health and Sleep Quality of Office Workers: A Case-Control Pilot Study." *Journal of Clinical Sleep Medicine* 10(6): 603–11. R. S. Zadch et al. (2014). "The Impact of Windows and Daylight on Acute-Care Nurses' Physiological, Psychological, and Behavioral Health. *HERD: Health Environments Research & Design Journal* 7(4): 35–61.

5: **Flowers improve:** J. Haviland-Jones et al. (2005). "An Environmental Approach to Positive Emotion: Flowers. *Evolutionary Psychology* 3(1).

1. ENERGY

14: **"The city was dead":** Architecture Foundation (2009). *Architecture + Art: Edi Rama and Anri Sala*, video file. Retrieved from https://vimeo.com/8254763

15: **Jump up and down:** B. Campos et al. (2013). "What Is Shared, What Is Different? Core Relational Themes and Expressive Displays of Eight Positive Emotions." *Cognition and Emotion* 27(1): 37–52.

16: **While the symbolic meanings:** F. M. Adams and C. E. Osgood (1973). "A Cross-Cultural Study of the Affective Meanings of Color." *Journal of Cross-Cultural Psychology* 4, 135–56.

17: **Preschool children's drawings:** C. J. Boyatzis and R. Varghese (1994). "Children's Emotional Associations with Colors." *Journal of Genetic Psychology* 155(1): 77–85.

17: **The strip showing the colors:** O. O'Brien (2006). "Emotionally Vague: A Research Project About Emotion, Sensation and Feeling." Retrieved from http://emotionallyvague.com

17: **The Dieri tribe:** I. McBryde (1987). "Goods from Another Country: Exchange Networks and the People of the Lake Eyre Basin." In D. J. Mulvaney and J. P. White, eds., *Australians to 1788*. Sydney: Fairfax, Syme and Weldon.

17: **The ancient Romans:** V. Finlay (2003). *Color: A Natural History of the Palette*. New York: Random House.

17: **"Man's highly developed color sense":** A. Huxley (1952). *The Doors of Perception*. New York: Harper Collins.

18: **Yet our eyes are adept:** F. A. Geldard (1972). *The Human Senses*, 2nd ed. New York: John Wiley and Sons.

18: **Sugar-rich ripe fruits:** D. Osorio and M. Vorobyev (1996). "Colour Vision as an Adaptation to Frugivory in Primates." *Proceedings of the Royal Society: Biological Sciences* 263(1370).

18: **Research suggests that color vision:** Y. Gilad et al. (2004). "Loss of Olfactory Receptor Genes Coincides with the Acquisition of Full Trichromatic Vision in Primates." *PLOS Biology* 2(1): e5.

19: **Predicted nourishment:** To this point, neuroscientists have observed that in mammals projections from both retinal and olfactory bulbs tend to converge in areas of the brain involved in the experience of emotion, such as the orbitofrontal cortex. See D. Öngür and J. L. Price (2000). "The Organization of Networks Within the Orbital and Medial Prefrontal Cortex of Rats, Monkeys and Humans." *Cerebral Cortex* 10(3): 206–19.

19: **"Color is life":** J. Itten and F. Birren (1970). *The Elements of Color*, trans. E. van Hagen. New York: John Wiley and Sons.

20: **"A trash city":** Supporting Edi Rama, Comments (2004). "Edi Rama, Mayor of Tirana," The 2004 Project, World Mayor. Retrieved from http://www .worldmayor.com/worldmayor_2004/comments_rama.html

20: **"In five years":** E. Rama (May 2012). *Take Back Your City with Paint*. Retrieved from https://www.ted.com/talks/edi_rama_take_back_your_city_with_paint

20: **"In the beginning":** Architecture Foundation, *Architecture + Art: Edi Rama and Anri Sala*.

20: **"Even a blind person":** Supporting Edi Rama.

21: **Edi Rama acknowledges:** Architecture Foundation, *Architecture + Art: Edi Rama and Anri Sala*.

22: **"The old factory":** F. Léger (1943). "On Monumentality and Color." In G. Siegfried, *Architecture, You and Me: The Diary of a Development*. Cambridge, MA: Harvard University Press.

23: Comprehensive research: R. Küller et al. (2006). "The Impact of Light and Colour on Psychological Mood: A Cross-Cultural Study of Indoor Work Environments." *Ergonomics* 49(14): 1496–1507.

23: The drab tones: P. Barrett et al. (2013). "A Holistic, Multi-Level Analysis Identifying the Impact of Classroom Design on Pupils' Learning." *Building and Environment* 59, 678–89.

27: Educated people: J. R. Stilgoe (1999). *Outside Lies Magic: Regaining History and Awareness in Everyday Places.* New York: Bloomsbury.

29: "I want to make spaces": G. Malin (Feb. 8, 2016). "Inspiration Spotlight: Ellen Bennett." Retrieved from https://www.graymalin.com/lifestyle/inspiration-spotlight-ellen-bennett/

29: "Savage nations": J. W. Goethe (1840). *Goethe's Theory of Colours,* trans. C. L. Eastlake. London: John Murray.

33: "A luminous arc": O. Sacks (1998). *The Island of the Colorblind.* New York: Vintage.

34: We rely on sunlight: M. N. Mead (2008). "Benefits of Sunlight: A Bright Spot for Human Health." *Environmental Health Perspectives* 116(4). R. J. Wurtman (1968). "Biological Implications of Artificial Illumination." *Illuminating Engineering* 63(10): 523–29. X. Yu et al. (2013). "TH17 Cell Differentiation Is Regulated by the Circadian Clock." *Science* 342(6159): 727–30.

34: "People use open space": C. Alexander et al. (1977). *A Pattern Language: Towns, Buildings, Construction.* Oxford: Oxford University Press.

35: Employees who sit near windows: L. Heschong et al. (2003). "Windows and Offices: A Study of Office Worker Performance and the Indoor Environment." California Energy Commission. Boubekri et al. "Impact of Windows and Daylight Exposure." 603–11.

35: Study of elementary schools: L. Heschong et al. (1999). "Daylighting in Schools: An Investigation into the Relationship Between Daylighting and Human Performance." Summary for the Pacific Gas and Electric Company on behalf of the California Board for Energy Efficiency Third Party Program.

35: Hospital patients: A. Joseph (2006). "The Impact of Light on Outcomes in Healthcare Settings." Concord, CA: Center for Health Design.

35: Light therapy: R. N. Golden et al. (2005). "The Efficacy of Light Therapy in the Treatment of Mood Disorders: A Review and Meta-Analysis of the Evidence." *American Journal of Psychiatry* 162(4): 656–62.

35: Among Alzheimer's patients: R. F. Riemersma-Van Der Lek et al. (2008). "Effect of Bright Light and Melatonin on Cognitive and Noncognitive Function in Elderly Residents of Group Care Facilities: A Randomized Controlled Trial." *JAMA* 299(22): 2642–55.

35: **Light is not as lucrative:** Golden et al., "Efficacy of Light Therapy."

36: **"Put the pale withering plant":** F. Nightingale (1980). *Notes on Nursing: What It Is, and What It Is Not.* New York: Appleton.

37: **People generally prefer:** J. A. Veitch (2001). "Psychological Processes Influencing Lighting Quality." *Journal of the Illuminating Engineering Society* 30(1): 124–40.

38: **The brightest pigments:** H. Rossotti (1983). *Colour: Why the World Isn't Grey.* Princeton, NJ: Princeton University Press.

39: **Fluorescent colors:** Ibid.

2. ABUNDANCE

45: **People consistently choose:** J. D. Balling and J. H. Falk (1982). "Development of Visual Preference for Natural Environments." *Environment and Behavior* 14(1): 5–28; J. H. Falk and J. D. Balling. 2010. "Evolutionary Influence on Human Landscape Preference." *Environment and Behavior* 42(4): 479–93.

45: **Biodiverse parks:** R. A. Fuller et al. (2007). "Psychological Benefits of Greenspace Increase with Biodiversity." *Biology Letters* 3(4): 390–94.

51: **"a place where":** S. Tsuji (2014). "Reversible Destiny Loft in Action: A Tentative Report from a Resident." In L. Lambert, ed., *The Funambulist Pamphlets: Arakawa + Madeline Gins,* vol. 8. Brooklyn: Punctum Books.

51: **Monkeys and cats:** G. Wallenstein (2008). *The Pleasure Instinct: Why We Crave Adventure, Chocolate, Pheromones, and Music.* Hoboken, NJ: John Wiley and Sons.

51: **Mice will spend:** H. Van Praag, G. Kempermann, and F. H. Gage (2000). "Neural Consequences of Environmental Enrichment." *Nature Reviews Neuroscience* 1(3): 191–98.

52: **"pleasure instinct":** Wallenstein, *Pleasure Instinct.*

53: **Adult brains:** Ibid.

53: **Studies of touch:** T. Field (2014). "Massage Therapy Research Review." *Complementary Therapies in Clinical Practice* 20(4): 224–29.

53: **Sensory deprivation tanks:** J. Turkewitz (2015). "Climb In, Tune In: A Renaissance for Sensory Deprivation Tanks." Retrieved from http://www.nytimes.com/2015/10/18/us/climb-in-tune-in-a-renaissance-for-sensory-deprivation-tanks.html

53: **As few as fifteen minutes:** O. J. Mason and F. Brady (2009). "The Psychotomimetic Effects of Short-Term Sensory Deprivation." *Journal of Nervous and Mental Disease* 197(10): 783–85.

53: **Participants left alone:** T. D. Wilson et al. (2014). "Just Think: The Challenges of the Disengaged Mind." *Science* 345(6192): 75–77.

54: **Sessions of Snoezelen therapy:** J. A. Staal et al. (2007). "The Effects of Snoezelen (Multi-Sensory Behavior Therapy) and Psychiatric Care on Agitation, Apathy, and Activities of Daily Living in Dementia Patients on a Short Term Geriatric Psychiatric Inpatient Unit." *International Journal of Psychiatry in Medicine* 37(4): 357–70. C. Gómez et al. (2016). "Characterization of EEG Patterns in Brain-Injured Subjects and Controls After a Snoezelen Intervention." *Computer Methods and Programs in Biomedicine* 136, 1–9. G. A. Hotz et al. (2006). "Snoezelen: A Controlled Multi-Sensory Stimulation Therapy for Children Recovering from Severe Brain Injury." *Brain Injury* 20(8): 879–88.

54: **Long-term-care facilities:** B. Cross (May 23, 2016). "Kicking the Antipsychotic Drug Habit at Long-Term Care Homes." Retrieved from http://windsorstar.com/news/local-news/kicking-the-antipsychotic-drug -habit-at-long-term-care-homes

56: **Evil characters:** B. Critton et al. (2010). *Evil People in Modernist Homes in Popular Films.* New Haven, CT: Number One.

57: **"They missed their old":** C. Montgomery (2013). *Happy City: Transforming Our Lives Through Urban Design.* New York: Farrar, Straus and Giroux.

67: **"Scarlett O'Hara–drops–acid":** M. Owens (2001). "Going for Baroque." Retrieved from http://www.nytimes.com/2001/08/12/magazine/style-going -for-baroque.html

68: **"What is being done":** C. Varney (2012). *In the Pink: Dorothy Draper, America's Most Fabulous Decorator.* New York: Pointed Leaf Press.

69: **"The Drab Age is over":** Ibid.

70: **"The Kaffir, the Persian":** A. Loos and A. Opel (1998). *Ornament and Crime: Selected Essays.* Riverside, CA: Ariadne Press.

71: **Displays of abundance:** D. Dutton (2009). *The Art Instinct: Beauty, Pleasure, and Human Evolution.* New York: Bloomsbury.

72: **Not just the length:** Ackerman cited in A. W. Schaef (1990). *Meditations for Women Who Do Too Much.* San Francisco: Harper Collins.

72: **"Too much":** S. Louvish (2007). *Mae West: It Ain't No Sin.* New York: Macmillan.

3. FREEDOM

76: ***Most Wanted* paintings:** For more, see Dutton, *Art Instinct*. E. Dissanayake (1998). "Komar and Melamid Discover Pleistocene Taste." *Philosophy and Literature* 22(2): 486–96. V. Komar and A. Melamid (March 14, 1994). "Painting by Numbers: The Search for a People's Art," interview. *The Nation*, 334–48.

76: **Aesthetic imperialism:** Dutton, *Art Instinct.*

77: **Appears in real-life contexts:** P. H. Kahn (1997). "Developmental Psychology and the Biophilia Hypothesis: Children's Affiliation with Nature." *Developmental Review* 17(1): 1–61.

77: **In Central Park alone:** R. Rosenzweig and E. Blackmar (1992). *The Park and the People: A History of Central Park.* Ithaca, NY: Cornell University Press. N. Rich (Sept. 2016). "When Parks Were Radical." Retrieved from http://www.theatlantic.com/magazine/archive/2016/09/better-than-nature/492716/

77: **There's some debate:** For more on the role of the savanna in hominid evolution, see S. Tucci and J. M. Akey (2016). "Population Genetics: A Map of Human Wanderlust." *Nature* 538(7624): 179–80.

77: **The savanna had distinct advantages:** Dutton, *Art Instinct.*

78: **Internal Eden:** G. H. Orians and J. H. Heerwagen (1992). "Environmental Aesthetics." In J. H. Barkow, L. Cosmides, and J. Tooby, eds., *The Adapted Mind: Evolutionary Psychology and the Generation of Culture.* New York: Oxford University Press. J. Appleton (1986). *The Experience of Landscape.* Chichester, UK: John Wiley and Sons.

78: **Savanna-like landscape:** Balling and Falk, "Development of Visual Preference." Falk and Balling, "Evolutionary Influence." R. S. Ulrich (1983). "Aesthetic and Affective Response to Natural Environment." In I. Altman and J. Wohlwill, eds., *Human Behavior and Environment, Vol 6: Behavior and Natural Environment.* New York: Plenum, 85–125.

78: **Cross-cultural preference:** Orians and Heerwagen, "Environmental Aesthetics."

78: **People will pay more:** E. O. Wilson (1984). *Biophilia: The Human Bond with Other Species.* Cambridge, MA: Harvard University Press.

78: **Patients recovering:** R. Ulrich (1984). View Through a Window May Influence Recovery from Surgery. *Science* 224(4647): 224–25.

79: **Students' attention:** D. Li and W. C. Sullivan (2016). "Impact of Views to School Landscapes on Recovery from Stress and Mental Fatigue." *Landscape and Urban Planning* 148, 149–58.

79: **"Micro-restorative effect":** R. Kaplan (1993). "The Role of Nature in the Context of the Workplace." *Landscape and Urban Planning* 26(1–4): 193–201. R. Kaplan (2001). "The Nature of the View from Home: Psychological Benefits." *Environment and Behavior* 33(4): 507–42.

80: **"It's pretty straightforward":** K. Bowman (Feb. 25, 2015). "Furniture Free Freak?" Retrieved from https://nutritiousmovement.com/furniture-free-freak

82: **A love of wild sensations:** S. R. Kellert and E. O. Wilson, eds. (1995). *The Biophilia Hypothesis.* Washington, DC: Island Press.

82: **Access to nature:** R. S. Ulrich (2002). "Health Benefits of Gardens in Hospitals." Paper Presented at Plants for People: International Exhibition Floriade, Haarlemmermeer, Netherlands. P. James et al. (2016). "Exposure to Greenness and Mortality in a Nationwide Prospective Cohort Study of Women." *Environmental Health Perspectives* 124(9). D. S. Grigsby-Toussaint et al. (2015). "Sleep Insufficiency and the Natural Environment: Results from the US Behavioral Risk Factor Surveillance System Survey." *Preventive Medicine* 78, 78–84.

83: **People living in greener areas:** A. E. Van den Berg et al. (2010). "Green Space as a Buffer Between Stressful Life Events and Health." *Social Science and Medicine* 70(8): 1203–210. M. P. White et al. (2013). "Would You Be Happier Living in a Greener Urban Area? A Fixed-Effects Analysis of Panel Data." *Psychological Science* 24(6): 920–28. K. M. Beyer et al. (2014). "Exposure to Neighborhood Green Space and Mental Health: Evidence from the Survey of the Health of Wisconsin." *International Journal of Environmental Research and Public Health* 11(3): 3453–472. I. Alcock et al. (2014). "Longitudinal Effects on Mental Health of Moving to Greener and Less Green Urban Areas." *Environmental Science and Technology* 48(2): 1247–255.

83: **Subgenual prefrontal cortex:** G. N. Bratman et al. (2015). "Nature Experience Reduces Rumination and Subgenual Prefrontal Cortex Activation." *Proceedings of the National Academy of Sciences* 112(28): 8567–572.

84: **Our cities are designed:** J. B. Jackson and E. H. Zube, eds. (1970). *Landscapes: Selected Writings of J. B. Jackson.* Amherst: University of Massachusetts Press.

84: **Buildings with more surrounding greenery:** F. E. Kuo and W. C. Sullivan (2001). "Environment and Crime in the Inner City: Does Vegetation Reduce Crime?" *Environment and Behavior* 33(3): 343–67.

84: **Displayed fewer aggressive tendencies:** P. H. Hasbach (2016). "Nature Imagery in Prisons Project: The Impact on Staff and Inmates in Solitary Confinement." Paper presented at the American Psychological Association 124th Annual Convention, Denver.

85: **Frequency of hostile outbursts:** For a review, see F. E. Kuo and W. C. Sullivan (2001). "Aggression and Violence in the Inner City: Effects of Environment via Mental Fatigue." *Environment and Behavior* 33(4): 543–71.

88: **Windowless room:** V. I. Lohr et al. (1996). "Interior Plants May Improve Worker Productivity and Reduce Stress in a Windowless Environment." *Journal of Environmental Horticulture* 14, 97–100. N. Weinstein, A. K. Przybylski, and R. M. Ryan (2009). "Can Nature Make Us More Caring?

Effects of Immersion in Nature on Intrinsic Aspirations and Generosity."
Personality and Social Psychology Bulletin 35(10): 1315–329.

88: **The color green:** S. Lichtenfeld et al. (2012). "Fertile Green: Green Facilitates
Creative Performance." *Personality and Social Psychology Bulletin* 38(6): 784–97.
S. Studente, N. Seppala, and N. Sadowska (2016). "Facilitating Creative
Thinking in the Classroom: Investigating the Effects of Plants and the Colour
Green on Visual and Verbal Creativity." *Thinking Skills and Creativity* 19, 1–8.

90: **Recordings of natural sounds:** V. Saadatmand et al. (2015). "Effects of
Natural Sounds on Pain: A Randomized Controlled Trial with Patients
Receiving Mechanical Ventilation Support." *Pain Management Nursing* 16(4):
483–92. D. Winterman (May 8, 2013). "The Surprising Uses for Birdsong."
Retrieved from http://www.bbc.com/news/magazine-22298779

90: **Natural killer (NK) cells:** Q. Li et al. (2008). "A Forest Bathing Trip
Increases Human Natural Killer Activity and Expression of Anti-Cancer
Proteins in Female Subjects." *Journal of Biological Regulators and Homeostatic
Agents* 22(1): 45–55. Q. Li et al. (2008). "Visiting a Forest, but Not a City,
Increases Human Natural Killer Activity and Expression of Anti-Cancer
Proteins." *International Journal of Immunopathology and Pharmacology* 21(1):
117–27.

90: **Infuse hotel rooms:** Q. Li et al. (2009). "Effect of Phytoncide from Trees on
Human Natural Killer Cell Function." *International Journal of
Immunopathology and Pharmacology* 22(4): 951–59.

91: **Wilder places:** S. L. Koole and A. E. Berg (2005). "Lost in the Wilderness:
Terror Management, Action Orientation, and Nature Evaluation." *Journal of
Personality and Social Psychology* 88(6): 1014–28.

91: **Work as few as fifteen hours:** J. M. Keynes (1932). "Economic Possibilities for
Our Grandchildren." In *Essays in Persuasion*. New York: Harcourt Brace.

91: **A third of the workforce:** American Time Use Survey (Dec. 20, 2016).
Retrieved from https://www.bls.gov/tus/charts/

91: **One in ten Americans:** Mobile Consumer Habits Study (2013). Retrieved
Nov. 30, 2016, from http://pages.jumio.com/rs/jumio/images/Jumio—Mobile
Consumer Habits Study-2.pdf

92: **"The seeds of instinct":** H. D. Thoreau (June 1862). "Walking." Retrieved
from https://www.theatlantic.com/magazine/archive/1862/06/walking/
304674/

93: **"A wild autumn tablecloth":** J. C. George (1982). *Journey Inward*. New York:
E. P. Dutton.

101: **"The great thinning":** M. McCarthy (2015). *The Moth Snowstorm: Nature and
Joy*. New York: New York Review Books.

102: **Shifting baseline syndrome:** G. Monbiot (2014). *Feral: Rewilding the Land, Sea, and Human Life.* Chicago: University of Chicago Press.

4. HARMONY

105: **"Four bottles of nucleotides":** K. Kelly (2010). *What Technology Wants.* New York: Penguin.
105: **Telltale sign of life:** S. Pinker (2009). *How the Mind Works.* New York: W. W. Norton. V. S. Ramachandran and W. Hirstein (1999). "The Science of Art: A Neurological Theory of Aesthetic Experience." *Journal of Consciousness Studies* 6(6–7): 15–41.
106: **Symmetrical forms:** C. W. Tyler (1995). "Empirical Aspects of Symmetry Perception." *Spatial Vision* 9(1): 1–8.
106: **Disorderly environments:** C. E. Ross and J. Mirowsky (2009). "Neighborhood Disorder, Subjective Alienation, and Distress." *Journal of Health and Social Behavior* 50(1): 49–64.
107: **Studies done in the Netherlands:** K. Keizer, S. Lindenberg, and L. Steg (2008). "The Spreading of Disorder." *Science* 322(5908): 1681–85.
108: **More likely to cheat:** H. P. Kotabe, O. Kardan, and M. G. Berman (2016). "The Order of Disorder: Deconstructing Visual Disorder and Its Effect on Rule-Breaking." *Journal of Experimental Psychology: General* 145(12): 1713.
109: **"Aha!" sensation:** Ramachandran and Hirstein, "Science of Art."
109: **"Don't sprinkle your collection":** Varney, *In the Pink.*
110: **Degree of complexity:** Ulrich, "Aesthetic and Affective Response."
112: **People prefer sitting:** Alexander et al., *Pattern Language.*
112: **"The eye prefers symmetry":** C. Darwin (1888). *The Descent of Man, and Selection in Relation to Sex,* vol. 1. London: John Murray.
112: **Scientific consensus:** A. Pecchinenda et al. (2014). "The Pleasantness of Visual Symmetry: Always, Never or Sometimes." *PLOS ONE* 9(3).
112: **Recognize symmetrical forms:** A. Wilson and A. Chatterjee (2005). "The Assessment of Preference for Balance: Introducing a New Test." *Empirical Studies of the Arts* 23(2): 165–80. M. S. Treder (2010). "Behind the Looking-Glass: A Review on Human Symmetry Perception." *Symmetry* 2(3): 1510–43.
112: **"Pleasure," "paradise," and "heaven":** A. D. J. Makin, A. Pecchinenda, and M. Bertamini (2012). "Implicit Affective Evaluation of Visual Symmetry." *Emotion* 12(5): 1021–30. M. Bertamini, A. Makin, and G. Rampone (2013). "Implicit Association of Symmetry with Positive Valence, High Arousal and Simplicity." *I-Perception* 4(5): 317–27.

113: **Zygomaticus major:** A. D. Makin et al. "Symmetry Perception and Affective Responses: A Combined EEG/EMG Study." *Neuropsychologia* 50(14): 3250–61.

113: **Symmetrical faces:** T. K. Shackelford and R. J. Larsen (1997). "Facial Asymmetry as an Indicator of Psychological, Emotional, and Physiological Distress." *Journal of Personality and Social Psychology* 72(2): 456.

113: **Studies of reproductive health:** D. Buss (1994). *The Evolution of Desire: Strategies of Human Mating.* New York: Basic Books. See also Wallenstein, *Pleasure Instinct.*

113: **Studies of infants:** G. K. Humphrey and D. E. Humphrey (1989). "The Role of Structure in Infant Visual Pattern Perception." *Canadian Journal of Psychology/Revue Canadienne de Psychologie* 43(2): 165–82.

114: **Navajo weavings:** S. J. Tisdale, ed. (2011). *Spider Woman's Gift: Nineteenth-Century Diné Textiles,* 1st ed. Albuquerque, NM: Museum of New Mexico Press.

114: **Classic abstract patterns:** R. A. Cárdenas and L. J. Harris (2006). "Symmetrical Decorations Enhance the Attractiveness of Faces and Abstract Designs." *Evolution and Human Behavior* 27(1): 1–18.

115: **Salient axis of symmetry:** Treder, "Behind the Looking-Glass."

116: **Table with a centerpiece:** Alexander et al., *Pattern Language.*

118: **Babies are comforted:** Wallenstein, *Pleasure Instinct.*

118: **The earliest instruments:** S. Johnson (2016). *Wonderland: How Play Made the Modern World.* New York: Macmillan. B. S. Akshaya (May 26, 2012). "Earliest Musical Instrument Discovered." Retrieved from http://www.ibtimes.co.uk/earliest-musical-instrument-discovered-345647

118: **These intervals sound pleasant:** E. G. Schellenberg and S. E. Trehub (1996). "Natural Musical Intervals: Evidence from Infant Listeners." *Psychological Science* 7(5): 272–77.

119: **Music reduces stress:** M. V. Thoma et al. (2013). "The Effect of Music on the Human Stress Response." *PLOS One* 8(8).

119: **Coloring in a structured pattern:** N. A. Curry and T. Kasser (2005). "Can Coloring Mandalas Reduce Anxiety?" *Art Therapy* 22(2): 81–85.

120: **Patternicity:** M. Shermer (2008). "Patternicity: Finding Meaningful Patterns in Meaningless Noise." *Scientific American* 299(5).

120: **"Fractals":** B. B. Mandelbrot (1983). *The Fractal Geometry of Nature.* New York: W. H. Freeman.

121: **Jackson Pollock's swirls:** R. P. Taylor et al. (2011). "Perceptual and Physiological Responses to Jackson Pollock's Fractals." *Frontiers in Human Neuroscience* 5. A. J. Bies et al. (2016). "Aesthetic Responses to Exact Fractals Driven by Physical Complexity." *Frontiers in Human Neuroscience* 10.

121: **Hindu temples:** I. M. Rian et al. (2007). "Fractal Geometry as the Synthesis of Hindu Cosmology in Kandariya Mahadev Temple, Khajuraho." *Building and Environment* 42(12): 4093–107.

121: **Entire villages in Africa:** R. Eglash (June 2007). *The Fractals at the Heart of African Designs.* Retrieved from https://www.ted.com/talks/ron_eglash_on _african_fractals

131: **Gee's Bend women:** J. Beardsley et al. (2002). *The Quilts of Gee's Bend.* Atlanta, GA: Tinwood Books.

132: **"Get-togethers":** Ibid.

5. PLAY

134: **Archaeologists have found:** S. Crawford (2009). "The Archaeology of Play Things: Theorising a Toy Stage in the 'Biography' of Objects." *Childhood in the Past* 2(1): 55–70.

135: **Playful behavior:** S. Zielinski (Feb. 20, 2015). "Five Surprising Animals That Play." Retrieved from https://www.sciencenews.org/blog/wild-things/five -surprising-animals-play. L. Sharpe (May 17, 2011). "So You Think You Know Why Animals Play…" Retrieved from https://blogs.scientificamerican.com/ guest-blog/so-you-think-you-know-why-animals-play/

135: **"Play face":** S. Chevalier-Skolnikoff (1974). "The Primate Play Face: A Possible Key to the Determinants and Evolution of Play." In E. Norbeck, ed., *The Anthropological Study of Human Play.* Rice University Studies, vol. 60, 9–29. J. H. Fowler and N. A. Christakis (2008). "Dynamic Spread of Happiness in a Large Social Network: Longitudinal Analysis over 20 Years in the Framingham Heart Study." *BMJ* 337, a2338.

135: **The only known activity:** K. L. Graham and G. M. Burghardt (2010). "Current Perspectives on the Biological Study of Play: Signs of Progress." *Quarterly Review of Biology* 85(4): 393–418.

136: **"Violent offenders":** S. Brown (2009). "Discovering the Importance of Play Through Personal Histories and Brain Images: An Interview with Stuart L. Brown." *American Journal of Play* 1(4): 399–412.

138: **"We still have that child":** E. DeGeneres, J. Gallen, and B. DeRonde (2000). *Ellen DeGeneres, the Beginning,* HBO Home Video.

141: **"It shouldn't surprise us":** G. Thelia, director (2015). *Bounce: How the Ball Taught the World to Play,* motion picture. USA.

141: **Curved forms:** L. Palumbo, N. Ruta, and M. Bertamini (2015). "Comparing Angular and Curved Shapes in Terms of Implicit Associations and Approach/ Avoidance Responses." *PLOS One* 10(10): e0140043.

141: **Right amygdala:** M. Bar and M. Neta (2007). "Visual Elements of Subjective Preference Modulate Amygdala Activation." *Neuropsychologia* 45(10): 2191–200.

142: **Rounded leaves:** C. McCandless (2011). *Feng Shui That Makes Sense: Easy Ways to Create a Home That Feels as Good as It Looks.* Minneapolis: Two Harbors Press.

145: **"Plants don't have eyes":** "Indoor Gardening Tips from a Man Who's Very Scared of Plants," TV series episode (2008). *Saturday Night Live.* New York: NBC. Retrieved from http://www.nbc.com/saturday-night-live/video/googly -eyes-gardener/n12229?snl=1

146: **Baby schema:** M. L. Kringelbach (2009). *The Pleasure Center: Trust Your Animal Instincts.* New York: Oxford University Press.

146: **A rhesus monkey's brain:** D. Barrett (2010). *Supernormal Stimuli: How Primal Urges Overran Their Evolutionary Purpose.* New York: W. W. Norton.

147: **Infant features are detected:** M. L. Kringelbach et al. (2016). "On Cuteness: Unlocking the Parental Brain and Beyond." *Trends in Cognitive Sciences* 20(7): 545–58.

147: **The attraction to infant features:** Kringelbach et al., "On Cuteness." C. E. Parsons et al. (2011). "The Motivational Salience of Infant Faces Is Similar for Men and Women." *PLOS One* 6(5): e20632.

147: **Increases social engagement:** G. D. Sherman and J. Haidt (2011). "Cuteness and Disgust: The Humanizing and Dehumanizing Effects of Emotion." *Emotion Review* 3(3): 245–51.

148: **Peak shift effect:** Ramachandran and Hirstein, " Science of Art."

148: **Animals are susceptible:** Barrett, *Supernormal Stimuli.*

148: **Zygomaticus major:** L. Miesler, H. Leder, and A. Herrmann (2011). "Isn't It Cute: An Evolutionary Perspective of Baby-Schema Effects in Visual Product Designs." *International Journal of Design* 5(3).

149: **Intense concentration:** H. Nittono et al. (2012). "The Power of Kawaii: Viewing Cute Images Promotes a Careful Behavior and Narrows Attentional Focus." *PLOS One* 7(9): e46362.

150: **"Today, I visited":** M. Butler (June 27, 2016). "Elie Wiesel Visits Disneyland." Retrieved from http://www.tabletmag.com/jewish-arts-and-culture/206125/ elie-wiesel-visits-disneyland

153: **Participants who moved fluidly:** M. L. Slepian and N. Ambady (2012). "Fluid Movement and Creativity." *Journal of Experimental Psychology: General* 141(4): 625–29.

153: **Curved movements decreased rigidity:** M. L. Slepian et al. (2014). "Fluid Movement and Fluid Social Cognition Bodily Movement Influences Essentialist Thought." *Personality and Social Psychology Bulletin* 40(1): 111–20.

154: **Banned the use of curves:** R. Booth (Dec. 31, 2012). "Michael Gove Faces Rebellion over No-Curves Schools Plan." Retrieved from https://www

.theguardian.com/education/2012/dec/31/michael-gove-rebellion-no-curves -schools

155: **The curved shape:** D. Budds (Aug. 26, 2016). "The School an Entire Town Designed: Rebuilding Sandy Hook Elementary." Retrieved from https:// www.fastcodesign.com/3062562/the-school-an-entire-town-designed -rebuilding-sandy-hook-elementary

156: **"We have a circular field":** A. Marashian (spring/summer 2008). "For Antti Lovag Architecture Is a Form of Play—Spontaneous, Joyful, Full of Surprise." *AnOther Man*, 302–7.

156: **"I don't know":** Ibid.

160: **"I love this house":** J. Hesse and L. Breydel (2012). *The Palais Bulles of Pierre Cardin*. Paris: Assouline.

160: *Jouers* **and** *aventuriers***:** Marashian, " For Antti Lovag."

160: **"Everything in the universe":** Hesse and Breydel, *Palais Bulles*.

161: **"It is the body":** Ibid.

161: **"Current opinion always holds":** R. Barthes (1977). "La Couleur/Colour." In *Roland Barthes by Roland Barthes*, trans. Richard Howard. New York: Hill and Wang.

6. SURPRISE

167: **These physiological changes:** D. Huron (2007). *Sweet Anticipation: Music and the Psychology of Expectation*. Cambridge: Massachusetts Institute of Technology Press.

167: **Upward spirals:** B. L. Fredrickson and T. Joiner (2002). "Positive Emotions Trigger Upward Spirals Toward Emotional Well-Being." *Psychological Science* 13(2): 172–75. H. A. Wadlinger and D. M. Isaacowitz (2006). "Positive Mood Broadens Visual Attention to Positive Stimuli." *Motivation and Emotion* 30(1): 87–99.

167: **Study of Olympic athletes:** A. P. Mcgraw, B. A. Mellers, and P. E. Tetlock (2005). "Expectations and Emotions of Olympic Athletes." *Journal of Experimental Social Psychology* 41(4): 438–46. B. A. Mellers et al. (1997). "Decision Affect Theory: Emotional Reactions to the Outcomes of Risky Options." *Psychological Science* 8(6): 423–29.

169: **"All I wanted":** M. Sayeg (Nov. 2015). *How Yarn Bombing Grew into a Worldwide Movement*. Retrieved from https://www.ted.com/talks/magda _sayeg_how_yarn_bombing_grew_into_a_worldwide_movement

169: **People stopped their cars:** M. Wollan (May 18, 2011). "Graffiti's Cozy, Feminine Side." Retrieved from http://www.nytimes.com/2011/05/19/fashion/ creating-graffiti-with-yarn.html

170: **Infants are able to detect:** S. A. Adler and J. Orprecio (2006). "The Eyes Have It: Visual Pop-Out in Infants and Adults." *Developmental Science* 9(2): 189–206. S. A. Adler and P. Gallego (2014). "Search Asymmetry and Eye Movements in Infants and Adults." *Attention, Perception, and Psychophysics* 76(6): 1590–608.

172: **"Attention is the beginning":** M. Oliver (2016). *Upstream: Selected Essays.* New York: Penguin.

173: **A plausible origin story:** B. Gopnik (March 3, 2009). "'Golden Seams: The Japanese Art of Mending Ceramics' at Freer." Retrieved from http://www .washingtonpost.com/wp-dyn/content/article/2009/03/02/AR2009030202723 .html

176: **Annie Dillard:** A. Dillard (2013). *Pilgrim at Tinker Creek.* New York: Harper Perennial Modern Classics.

181: **"The home should be":** L. Corbusier (ca. 1920). Letter to Henry Frugè. Pessac, France.

186: **Need for accommodation:** D. Keltner and J. Haidt (2003). "Approaching Awe, a Moral, Spiritual, and Aesthetic Emotion." *Cognition and Emotion* 17(2): 297–314.

186: **Mind-set becomes more fluid:** M. Mikulincer, P. Kedem, and D. Paz (1990). "Anxiety and Categorization—1. The Structure and Boundaries of Mental Categories." *Personality and Individual Differences* 11, 805–14. K. J. Johnson and B. L. Fredrickson (2005). "'We All Look the Same to Me': Positive Emotions Eliminate the Own-Race Bias in Face Recognition." *Psychological Science* 16(11): 875–81. G. Rowe, J. B. Hirsh, and A. K. Anderson (2007). "Positive Affect Increases the Breadth of Attentional Selection." *Proceedings of the National Academy of Sciences, USA* 104, 383–88. A. M. Isen and K. A. Daubman (1984). "The Influence of Affect on Categorization." *Journal of Personality and Social Psychology* 47, 1206–17. C. A. Estrada, A. M. Isen, and M. J. Young (1997). "Positive Affect Facilitates Integration of Information and Decreases Anchoring in Reasoning Among Physicians." *Organizational Behavior and Human Decision Processes* 72(1): 117–35.

187: **These prosthetics:** J. Mroz (Feb. 6, 2015). "Hand of a Superhero: 3-D Printing Prosthetic Hands That Are Anything but Ordinary." Retrieved from https:// www.nytimes.com/2015/02/17/science/hand-of-a-superhero.html. J. Newman (Jan. 24, 2017). "The Girl Behind the Sparkle-Shooting Prosthetic Arm Is Just Getting Started." Retrieved from https://www.fastcompany.com/3067354/ the-girl-behind-the-sparkle-shooting-prosthetic-arm-is-just-getting-sta

188: **Hedonic adaptation:** E. Diener, R. E. Lucas, and C. N. Scollon (2006). "Beyond the Hedonic Treadmill: Revising the Adaptation Theory of Well-Being." *American Psychologist* 61(4): 305.

7. TRANSCENDENCE

192: **People recognize positive words:** B. P. Meier and M. D. Robinson (2004). "Why the Sunny Side Is Up: Associations Between Affect and Vertical Position." *Psychological Science* 15(4): 243–47.

192: **Study done in the 1920s:** A. T. Poffenberger and B. E. Barrows (1924). "The Feeling Value of Lines." *Journal of Applied Psychology* 8(2): 187.

192: **Upward movements:** D. Casasanto and K. Dijkstra (2010). "Motor Action and Emotional Memory." *Cognition* 115(1): 179–85.

193: **Starts with our own bodies:** G. Lakoff and M. Johnson (2011). *Metaphors We Live By.* Chicago: University of Chicago Press.

193: **"A man in this state":** C. Darwin (2009). *The Expression of the Emotions in Man and Animals,* ed. J. Cain and S. Messenger. London: Penguin (original work published 1872), 195.

194: **"The idea that a body":** Quoted in R. P. Hallion (2003). *Taking Flight: Inventing the Aerial Age from Antiquity Through the First World War.* Oxford: Oxford University Press.

194: **"Nothing can compare":** Ibid.

196: **The Ferris wheel debuted:** J. Brox (2010). *Brilliant: The Evolution of Artificial Light.* Boston: Mariner Books. J. Malanowski (June 2015). "The Brief History of the Ferris Wheel." Retrieved from http://www.smithsonianmag.com/history/history-ferris-wheel-180955300

196: **Expensive real estate:** Dutton, *Art Instinct.*

199: **Sleeping platforms:** H. J. Birx, ed. (2010). *21st Century Anthropology: A Reference Handbook.* Thousand Oaks, CA: SAGE Publications. J. Welsh (Apr. 16, 2012). "Apes' Simple Nests Are Feats of Engineering." Retrieved from http://www.livescience.com/19708-primates-build-sleeping-nests.html

199: **A long history:** P. Henderson and A. Mornement (2005). *Treehouses,* 1st ed. London: Frances Lincoln.

201: **Gaining elevation:** M. L. Slepian, E. J. Masicampo, and N. Ambady (2015). "Cognition from on High and down Low: Verticality and Construal Level." *Journal of Personality and Social Psychology* 108(1): 1–17. K. Fujita et al. (2006). "Construal Levels and Self-Control." *Journal of Personality and Social Psychology* 90, 351–67. R. S. Friedman et al. (2003). "Attentional Priming Effects on Creativity." *Creativity Research Journal* 15(2–3): 277–86.

202: **Ellen Bennett:** A. Sims (Feb. 15, 2016). "Inside Hedley and Bennett's Factory-Playground, Whimsy Reigns." Retrieved from https://food52.com/blog/15918-inside-hedley-bennett-s-factory-playground-whimsy-reigns

204: **Stress on our necks:** A. Cuddy (Dec. 12, 2015). "Your iPhone Is Ruining Your Posture—and Your Mood." Retrieved from https://www.nytimes.com/2015/12/13/opinion/sunday/your-iphone-is-ruining-your-posture-and-your-mood.html

204: **Daydreaming engages:** K. Christoff et al. (2009). "Experience Sampling During fMRI Reveals Default Network and Executive System Contributions to Mind Wandering." *Proceedings of the National Academy of Sciences* 106(21): 8719–24. R. E. Beaty et al. (2015). "Default and Executive Network Coupling Supports Creative Idea Production." *Scientific Reports* 5, 10964.

206: **Research conducted in China:** X. Zhao, X. He, and W. Zhang (2016). "A Heavy Heart: The Association Between Weight and Emotional Words." *Frontiers in Psychology, 7.*

206: **Inflatable structures:** M. Dessauce (1999). *The Inflatable Moment: Pneumatics and Protest in '68.* Princeton, NJ: Princeton Architectural Press. P. Sisson (Jan. 21, 2016). "More Than Hot Air: The Lasting Impact of Inflatable Architecture." Retrieved from http://www.curbed.com/2016/1/21/10844774/inflatable-architecture-geodesic-dome-design-legacy

208: **Emotion called awe:** Keltner and Haidt, "Approaching Awe."

209: **The small self:** Y. Bai et al. (2017). "Awe, the Diminished Self, and Collective Engagement: Universals and Cultural Variations in the Small Self." *Journal of Personality and Social Psychology* 113(2): 185–209. M. N. Shiota, D. Keltner, and A. Mossman (2007). "The Nature of Awe: Elicitors, Appraisals, and Effects on Self-Concept." *Cognition and Emotion* 21(5): 944–63. M. Rudd, K. D. Vohs, and J. Aaker (2012). "Awe Expands People's Perception of Time, Alters Decision Making, and Enhances Well-Being." *Psychological Science* 23(10): 1130–36.

209: **"State of valuelessness":** A. H. Maslow (1970). *Religions, Values, and Peak-Experiences.* New York: Penguin Compass.

211: **Light-colored ceilings:** D. Oberfeld, H. Hecht, and M. Gamer (2010). "Surface Lightness Influences Perceived Room Height." *Quarterly Journal of Experimental Psychology* 63(10): 1999–2011.

214: **Wheeler's "infinity rooms":** R. Kennedy (Jan. 15, 2012). "Into the Heart of Lightness." Retrieved from http://www.nytimes.com/2012/01/15/arts/design/doug-wheeler-builds-infinity-environment-at-david-zwirner.html

214: **The tradition:** I. L. Neubauer. (Nov. 23, 2016). "Chefchaouen: The Electric Beauty of Morocco's Incredible Blue City." Retrieved from http://www.cnn.com/2015/08/03/travel/morocco-blue-city-chefchaouen/

215: **"I put up my thumb":** R. Hanbury-Tenison (2010). *The Oxford Book of Exploration.* Oxford: Oxford University Press.

215: **While orbiting the moon:** *"Earthrise,* William Anders, NASA, 1968." *100 Photographs: The Most Influential Images of All Time* (n.d.). Retrieved from http://100photos.time.com/photos/nasa-earthrise-apollo-8

8. MAGIC

218: **Astronomical events:** C. Cajochen et al. (2013). "Evidence That the Lunar Cycle Influences Human Sleep." *Current Biology* 23(15): 1485–88.

219: **Financial markets:** G. M. Lepori. (2009). "Dark Omens in the Sky: Do Superstitious Beliefs Affect Investment Decisions?" Unpublished manuscript, Copenhagen Business School, Department of Finance, Copenhagen, Denmark.

219: **Quality of purpose:** P. Kesebir and T. Pyszczynski (2014). "Meaning as a Buffer for Existential Anxiety." In A. Batthyany and P. Russo-Netzer, eds., *Meaning in Positive and Existential Psychology.* New York: Springer, 53–64.

219: **"Meant to be":** K. I. Pargament, H. G. Koenig, and L. M. Perez (2000). "The Many Methods of Religious Coping: Development and Initial Validation of the RCOPE." *Journal of Clinical Psychology* 56(4): 519.

219: **People who believe in magic:** M. Hutson (2012). *The Seven Laws of Magical Thinking: How Irrational Beliefs Keep Us Happy, Healthy, and Sane.* New York: Hudson Street Press.

220: **Survey conducted in Iceland:** T. Gunnell (2007). "Modern Legends in Iceland Survey." Unpublished manuscript, University of Iceland, Reykjavik. Figures are a weighted average across the 2006 and 2007 portions of the sample. The 58 percent figure includes people who responded "certain," "probable," and "possible."

223: **Group of boulders:** N. Inalsingh, director (2006). *Huldufólk 102,* motion picture. Iceland.

226: **Haloclines:** M. Kaplan (2015). *Science of the Magical: From the Holy Grail to Love Potions to Superpowers.* New York: Scribner.

226: **A fifteen-thousand-year-old grave:** A. W. Crosby (2006). *Children of the Sun: A History of Humanity's Unappeasable Appetite for Energy.* New York: W. W. Norton.

227: **Medieval people:** K. Thomas (1971). *Religion and the Decline of Magic.* London: Penguin.

229: **"The first fall of snow":** J. B. Priestley (1968). *Essays of Five Decades.* New York: Little, Brown.

233: **The secret of life:** O. Wilde (2014). *A Woman of No Importance.* Urbana, IL: Project Gutenberg. Retrieved from https://www.gutenberg.org/files/854/854-h/854-h.htm

235: **Descartes:** R. Descartes (2010). *The Passions of the Soul,* ed. J. Bennett. Retrieved from http://www.earlymoderntexts.com/assets/pdfs/descartes 1649part2.pdf

236: Architect Kazuyo Sejima: J. Bristol (March 23, 2016). "SANAA's Kazuyo Sejima Has Plans to Design a Reflective Japanese Express Train." Retrieved from http://www.architecturaldigest.com/story/sanaas-kazuyo-sejima-design -reflective-japanese-express-train

237: Work of demons: Hallion, *Taking Flight.*

241: Mother-daughter pair: L. Stinson (Apr. 25, 2016). "This Tricky Crosswalk Stops Drivers with an Optical Illusion." Retrieved from https://www.wired .com/2016/04/crosswalk-tricks-drivers-optical-illusion/

241: The Maya used paints: D. Hansford (Feb. 7, 2008). "Ancient Maya Used 'Glitter' Paint to Make Temple Gleam." Retrieved from http://news .nationalgeographic.com/news/2008/02/080207-maya-temple.html

241: Some ancient Egyptians: Kaplan, *Science of the Magical.*

243: Fueling innovation: Thomas, *Religion and the Decline of Magic.*

243: Nikola Tesla: M. Seifer (2016). *Wizard: The Life and Times of Nikola Tesla: Biography of a Genius.* New York: Citadel.

244: "The universe is full": E. Phillpotts (1918). *A Shadow Passes.* London: C. Palmer and Hayward.

9. CELEBRATION

246: When elephants are reunited: *Unforgettable Elephants: Elephant Emotions.* (Oct. 14, 2008). Retrieved from http://www.pbs.org/wnet/nature/ unforgettable-elephants-elephant-emotions/5886/

246: Wolves are also known: S. A. Johnson and A. Aamodt (1987). *Wolf Pack: Tracking Wolves in the Wild.* Minneapolis: First Avenue Editions.

247: Typical chimpanzee celebration: F. De Waal (1996). *Good Natured: The Origins of Right and Wrong in Humans and Other Animals.* Cambridge, MA: Harvard University Press.

247: Celebrating positive events with others: S. L. Gable et al. 2012. "Safely Testing the Alarm: Close Others' Responses to Personal Positive Events." *Journal of Personality and Social Psychology* 103(6): 963–81.

247: People who regularly celebrate: S. L. Gable et al. 2004. "What Do You Do When Things Go Right? The Intrapersonal and Interpersonal Benefits of Sharing Positive Events." *Journal of Personality and Social Psychology* 87(2): 228–45.

248: More likely to laugh: R. R. Provine (2001). *Laughter: A Scientific Investigation.* New York: Penguin.

248: "Grief takes care of itself": M. Twain (1983). *Mark Twain: Selected Writings of an American Skeptic.* Amherst, NY: Prometheus Books.

250: **Emotions are naturally contagious:** E. Hatfield, J. T. Cacioppo, and R. L. Rapson (1993). "Emotional Contagion." *Current Directions in Psychological Science* 2(3): 96–99.

251: **Shared identity:** F. Neville and S. Reicher (2011). "The Experience of Collective Participation: Shared Identity, Relatedness and Emotionality." *Contemporary Social Science* 6(3): 377–96. D. Novelli, J. Drury, and S. Reicher (2010). "Come Together: Two Studies Concerning the Impact of Group Relations on Personal Space." *British Journal of Social Psychology* 49(2): 223–36.

253: **"Music washes away":** B. Auerbach (1867). *On the Heights*, trans. F. E. Bunnett. Leipzig: Bernhard Tauchnitz.

253: **Music activates:** J. A. Grahn and M. Brett (2007). "Rhythm and Beat Perception in Motor Areas of the Brain." *Journal of Cognitive Neuroscience* 19(5): 893–906.

253: **Study sponsored by Apple:** "Music Makes It Home." (Feb. 9, 2016). Retrieved from http://musicmakesithome.com

254: **Guitarists playing a short melody:** U. Lindenberger et al. (2009). "Brains Swinging in Concert: Cortical Phase Synchronization While Playing Guitar." *BMC Neuroscience* 10(1): 22.

254: **Studies of choir singers:** B. Vickhoff et al. (2013). "Music Structure Determines Heart Rate Variability of Singers." *Frontiers in Psychology* 4, 334.

254: **Synchrony:** S. S. Wiltermuth and C. Heath (2009). "Synchrony and Cooperation." *Psychological Science* 20(1): 1–5. P. Valdesolo and D. Desteno (2011). "Synchrony and the Social Tuning of Compassion." *Emotion* 11(2): 262–66.

254: **When participants rocked:** P. Valdesolo, J. Ouyang, and D. Desteno (2010). "The Rhythm of Joint Action: Synchrony Promotes Cooperative Ability." *Journal of Experimental Social Psychology*, 46(4): 693–95.

254: **"Collective effervescence":** D. Páez et al. (2015). "Psychosocial Effects of Perceived Emotional Synchrony in Collective Gatherings." *Journal of Personality and Social Psychology* 108(5): 711–29.

254: **"Keeping together in time":** W. H. McNeill (1995). *Keeping Together in Time: Dance and Drill in Human History.* Cambridge, MA: Harvard University Press.

255: **Cave drawings:** I. Reznikoff (2006). "The Evidence of the Use of Sound Resonance from Palaeolithic to Medieval Times." In C. Scarre and G. Lawson, eds., *Archaeoacoustics*, 77–84. Cambridge: University of Cambridge. K. Than (July 2, 2008). "Stone Age Caves May Have Been Concert Halls." Retrieved from http://news.nationalgeographic.com/news/2008/07/080702 -cave-paintings.html

255: **Depictions of dancing figures:** Y. Garfinkel (2003). *Dancing at the Dawn of Agriculture.* Austin: University of Texas Press.

256: **The Neolithic dance craze:** Ibid.

258: **Early medieval festivals:** B. Ehrenreich (2006). *Dancing the Streets: A History of Collective Joy.* New York: Metropolitan Books.

259: **"Mas is a powerful":** D. Narine, director (2010). *Mas Man Peter Minshall,* motion picture. USA.

260: **Our bodies:** E. A. Crane and M. M. Gross (2013). "Effort-Shape Characteristics of Emotion-Related Body Movement." *Journal of Nonverbal Behavior* 37(2): 91–105.

260: **"At first she looked":** P. Ganase (autumn 1992). "Lord of the Dance: Peter Minshall." Retrieved from http://caribbean-beat.com/issue-3/lord-dance -peter-minshall

260: **Costume of the Waghi:** E. Dissanayake (1995). *Homo Aestheticus: Where Art Comes From and Why.* Seattle: University of Washington Press.

260: **The Bobo people:** C. Beckwith and A. Fisher (1994). "Spinning Bobo Funeral Masks—Carol Beckwith and Angela Fisher." Retrieved from https://www .google.com/culturalinstitute/beta/u/0/asset/spinning-bobo-funeral-masks/ uAFnj_SfRnNbVw

261: **The first firecrackers:** A. Stempian (July 1, 2015). "The Evolution of Fireworks." Retrieved from https://ssec.si.edu/stemvisions-blog/evolution -fireworks

262: **Minshall's work:** S. Greenspan, producer (Dec. 2, 2014). *Inflatable Men,* podcast. Retrieved from http://99percentinvisible.org/episode/inflatable -men/. S. Dean (Oct. 20, 2014). "Biography of an Inflatable Tube Guy." Retrieved from https://medium.com/re-form/biography-of-an-inflatable -tube-guy-c3e8d4f04a63

264: **Only on special occasions:** Brox, *Brilliant.*

265: **"Sputniks":** J. Barron (July 18, 2008). "Bright Lights of the Met Opera Lobby Are Put Out for Repair." Retrieved from http://www.nytimes.com/2008/ 07/18/nyregion/18chandelier.html

265: **"Glitter celebrates":** C. Fisher (Dec./Jan. 2015/2016). Interview by M. Rochlin. *More,* 49.

10. RENEWAL

274: **We began / As a mineral.** J. A. Rūmī (2004). *The Essential Rumi,* trans. C. Barks. New York: HarperCollins.

278: **Early civilizations:** Garfinkel, 2003.

278: **Judeo-Christian thought:** M. Eliade (1987). *The Sacred and the Profane: The Nature of Religion.* Orlando, FL: Harcourt.

279: **"Spring comes":** L. Walker, director (2011). *The Tsunami and the Cherry Blossom*, motion picture. USA.

280: **"Well," said Pooh:** A. A. Milne (2009). *The House at Pooh Corner*, illus. E. H. Shepard. New York: Penguin.

280: **Period of anticipation:** J. Nawijn et al. (2010). "Vacationers Happier, but Most Not Happier After a Holiday." *Applied Research in Quality of Life* 5(1): 35–47. H. H. Chun, K. Diehl, and D. J. MacInnis (2017). "Savoring an Upcoming Experience Affects Ongoing and Remembered Consumption Enjoyment." *Journal of Marketing* 81(3): 96–110.

281: **Ancient Japanese calendar:** Heibonsha Limited (2013). 72 Seasons (version 1.1.0), mobile application software. Retrieved from http://itunes.apple.com

284: **"Wherever one might have looked":** L. Eiseley (1946). *The Immense Journey*. New York: Random House.

284: **Such appreciation:** E. C. Semple (1929). "Ancient Mediterranean Pleasure Gardens." *Geographical Review* 19(3): 420.

284: **The task of populating:** J. M. Bigelow (2000). "Ancient Egyptian Gardens." *Ostracon* 2(1): 1.

284: **Dutch tulip frenzy:** S. L. Buchmann (2016). *The Reason for Flowers: Their History, Culture, Biology, and How They Change Our Lives.* New York: Scribner.

285: **Fifty-five billion dollars:** C. Van Rijkswick (2016). *World Floriculture Map 2016.* Retrieved from https://research.rabobank.com/far/en/sectors/regional-food-agri/world_floriculture_map_2016.html

287: **Paper flowers:** A. Azzarito (Aug. 17, 2017). "Paper Flowers: The Global, Ancient Roots of a Contemporary Maker Fixation." Retrieved from https://www.architecturaldigest.com/story/paper-flowers-the-global-ancient-roots-of-a-contemporary-maker-fixation

289: **As a child:** P. Kirkham, P. Moore, and P. Wolfframm (2013). *Eva Zeisel: Life, Design, and Beauty.* San Francisco: Chronicle Books.

289: **She gained experience:** Ibid.

290: **Clear-cut, rhythmic silhouettes:** E. Sheppard (Apr. 17, 1956). "China Service Is Displayed in Modern Shapes." *New York Herald Tribune.* Retrieved from https://www.nypl.org/collections/articles-databases/new-york-tribune-1841-1922

291: **The modern movement:** E. Zeisel (2011). *On Design: The Magic Language of Things.* New York: Overlook Duckworth.

292: **"As if they were growing":** Sheppard, "China Service Is Displayed in Modern Shapes."

293: **"When shapes culminate":** Zeisel, *On Design.*

294: **Darwin observed:** D. Chamovitz (2012). *What a Plant Knows: A Field Guide to the Senses.* New York: Scientific American/Farrar, Straus and Giroux.

294: **Grow in a spiral pattern:** P. Ball (2011). *Shapes.* Oxford: Oxford University Press.

294: **Used by the ancient Egyptians:** R. Lawlor (1994). *Homage to Pythagoras: Rediscovering Sacred Science,* ed. C. Bamford. Hudson, NY: Lindisfarne Press.

295: **"A curving wave":** P. Goldberger (May 25, 2009). "Spiraling Upward: Celebrating Fifty Years of Frank Lloyd Wright's Guggenheim." Retrieved from https://www.newyorker.com/magazine/2009/05/25/spiralling-upward

JOYFUL TOOLKIT

299: **"Each of us":** J. O'Donohue (Aug. 6, 2015). "John O'Donohue: The Inner Landscape of Beauty," interview by K. Tippett, *On Being with Krista Tippett.* Retrieved from https://onbeing.org/programs/john-odonohue-the-inner -landscape-of-beauty

INDEX

ABOUT THE AUTHOR

Ingrid Fetell Lee is a designer and the founder of the blog *The Aesthetics of Joy*. She has been featured as an expert on design and joy by outlets such as the *New York Times, Wired,* PRI's *Studio 360,* CBC's *Spark,* and *Fast Company,* and her 2018 TED talk received a standing ovation. Lee was formerly design director at global innovation firm IDEO and was a founding faculty member in the Products of Design program at the School of Visual Arts in New York City. She holds a master's in industrial design from Pratt Institute and a bachelor's in English and creative writing from Princeton University.